# MEMO TO JFK

# Memo to
# JFK

## FROM NBC NEWS

*National Broadcasting Company, inc.*

FOUNDED 1838

GPPS

G. P. PUTNAM'S SONS     NEW YORK

© 1961

by National Broadcasting Company Inc.

Library of Congress Catalog

Card Number: 61-15082

# Contents

FOREWORD *by Robert E. Kintner*     7

1. COMMUNICATIONS:
   *Path to Freedom*     13
   WILLIAM R. MCANDREW

2. BRITAIN:
   *"The Logical Base"*     26
   JOSEPH C. HARSCH

3. FRANCE:
   *"Valuable if Troublesome Ally"*     56
   EDWIN NEWMAN

4. GERMANY:
   *"Story of Contradictions"*     85
   JOHN RICH

5. ITALY:
   *"Two Countries"*     114
   IRVING R. LEVINE

6. RUSSIA:
   *"Real Peace Is Impossible"*     146
   JOHN CHANCELLOR

7. AFRO-ASIA:
   *"Freedom, Fragmentation and Ferment"*     168
   WELLES HANGEN

8. JAPAN:
   *"Switzerland of Asia"*     194
   CECIL BROWN

**9.** SOUTHEAST ASIA:
*"The Massive Issue ... Red China"* 238
JAMES ROBINSON

**10.** LATIN AMERICA:
*"Presidents and Dictators"* 260
WILSON HALL

**11.** WASHINGTON:
*"No Reason for Despair"* 292
SANDER VANOCUR

# Foreword

Back in the twenties, prophecies of doom and destruction were common among groups of harmless though fanatic eccentrics. From time to time the shepherd of one of these flocks would announce the exact date and hour of the approaching end of the world. These apocalyptic revelations always seemed titillating enough to command some newspaper space.

On one of these occasions, *The New York Times* assigned the late Meyer Berger, one of its best reporters, to cover the vigil of a flock that had gathered in the countryside to await the predicted Doomsday. In covering important stories like a major election or a big trial, it is good newspaper practice in the interest of speed to prepare different lead paragraphs to cover every possible outcome. With his fine sense of whimsy, Berger filed two alternate leads; his readers saw one of them the following morning. The one they did not see read: "The world ended at 4:31 A.M. today."

In those days it was possible to chuckle over that story without a chilling afterthought. Today we live in the oppressive knowledge that the world really has the power of Doomsday in its own hands. The threat of global suicide grows as more nations acquire the capacity to detonate nuclear weapons. We are entering a period in which we may well look back upon the nuclear stalemate of the cold war as an era of uncommon stability.

Dramatic and overwhelming as the issue of survival must be, it is only one of a whole complex of problems related to

it—the problems of exploding population and awakened nationalism, the spread of Communism and the scourges of
hunger and disease. Even at home the United States is beset
by serious problems. It is faced with the realities of slums,
hard-core unemployment, delinquency, racial tensions, educational shortcomings and the sapping of natural resources.
Fortunately, these domestic ailments do not doom the species.
They do, however, bear upon the abilities of the nation to
endure. The foreign problems, on the other hand, may easily
affect the survival of the world.

Yet the situation is not nearly as gloomy as the bizarre
prophecies of the twenties. One reason is man's ability to
communicate swiftly, clearly and eloquently on a mass scale.
Mankind's saving grace may be that our technological capacity for mass communication has kept pace with our mas-
tery of the means of mass destruction. Today the entire
nation can see and hear its leaders instantly in times of emergency—and, more to the point, it can gain, more effectively
than ever before, the information and insight that will help
us as a nation to head off emergencies and to meet them when
they come. Tomorrow, with the advent of satellites as relay
stations in space, the power of communications will be even
greater as a global force.

In the final analysis, however, our highly advanced techniques of communication can be no better than the men who
use them. Thus the potential of these modern facilities and
the crucial need for information and understanding combine
to impose the heaviest responsibility ever thrust upon journalism. To meet its share of that responsibility, the National
Broadcasting Company determined to build and maintain a
skilled corps of experienced journalists to gather, report and
interpret the events of our time throughout the world.

In all, more than 600 men and women work at the job of
making NBC News a news-gathering organization second to
none. They work as cameramen, technicians, editors, engi-

neers and executives as well as on-the-scene correspondents. Thanks to their teamwork, dozens of millions of Americans are as close to the world's news centers as to their television and radio sets. In the forefront of the team are the seasoned correspondents who head our news bureaus in various parts of the world, supervising the coverage of wide areas and themselves handling the most significant stories.

Because each of these men in his own way is so canny an observer of the people and places he covers and the challenges that these present to the United States under President John F. Kennedy, we have asked the leading foreign correspondents of the NBC News staff to focus upon the issues and problems of their particular area from the standpoint of the Administration now entrusted with our country's destiny.

No two of these correspondents are alike any more than any two individuals are alike. Each has his own method of observing the scene and his own style of recounting what he learns. The various chapters differ as much as the problems of the areas covered by the contributing correspondents, and as much as the separate personalities of the men. Yet taken as a whole, the book pulls together a comprehensive pattern of fact and analysis that helps to make sense of our tangled foreign relations in a crucial period of history.

The contributors come to their assignments with a wealth of professional experience. William R. McAndrew, the NBC Executive Vice-President who runs the News Department, has more than fifteen years of managerial news experience, most of it worldwide in scope. Joseph C. Harsch, senior among our European correspondents, is one of the country's most highly regarded diplomatic reporters and knows Britain as well as his native United States. Edwin Newman, now working in New York, took over the Paris bureau after service in London, Cairo and Rome. John Rich, currently covering France, brought to coverage of a divided Germany firsthand knowledge of divided countries obtained from his reporting of the Korean conflict. Irving R. Levine came to Rome after a tour in Russia in which he made a distinguished reputation as a discerning reporter. John Chancellor had an advance look at his Soviet assignment from a vantage point in Vienna and also saw service in Western Europe, Africa and Asia before going to Moscow. Welles Hangen studied the African and Asian people from many different bases, including Cairo, Johannesburg, Ankara, Beirut, Amman, Leopoldville and Damascus. Cecil Brown, whose first book dealt with the lands from Suez to Singapore, is an old hand at the Far East and its problems. James Robinson taught in China before editing newspapers in Southeast Asia, where he joined NBC News. Wilson Hall watched the Nasser dictatorship in action before covering the dictators of Latin America. Sander Vanocur followed the fortunes of President Kennedy from preconvention forays into the White House. The inevitable role behind the scenes—in this instance, co-ordinating and editing these contributions from all parts of the world—was filled by Arthur Hepner of NBC News in New York.

The result of this team effort, in my judgment, is a useful and illuminating guidebook through an international maze in which to tread carelessly is to court disaster. And while it is couched, not too presumptuously, we hope, as a "Memo to JFK," it is also our hope that it will be read with interest and profit by his constituents as well.

—ROBERT E. KINTNER

# MEMO TO JFK

# 1.

## COMMUNICATIONS:

## *Path to Freedom*

ON June 18, 1959, several men and women huddled around television sets in the RCA Building in New York's Radio City. As they sipped their midmorning coffee, a jet transport plane sped across the North Atlantic; its position at that moment was approximately midway between London Airport and the Canadian coastline. The jet had left England two hours earlier ferrying its principal passengers, Queen Elizabeth II and the Duke of Edinburgh, to a visit of Canada and parts of the United States.

Television cameras of the British Broadcasting Corporation had reported the Royal Couple's departure from Buckingham Palace and the cheering crowds along the Mall. They also had recorded the farewells at the Airport and the ascent of the Royal plane to the skies. According to plan, the jet was to put down in the Western Hemisphere five hours later.

Yet while the plane was still aloft, only halfway to its first destination, television viewers in the United States and Canada watched the London take-off. Faster than jet travel, Europe that morning had been linked for the first time by motion picture with the North American continent. Films of events in England were shown on this side of the Atlantic, as the plane that would have carried them was still in mid-journey flight.

The group sipping coffee in New York consisted of journalists invited to witness an historic accomplishment in intercontinental communication. They were observing the first demonstration of cablefilm, a process developed by the BBC and seen in the U. S. through the National Broadcasting Company. This shortened distances by precious hours. As motion pictures traveled by cable beneath the surface of the ocean in the form of electrical impulses, the journalists saw what happened abroad almost as fast as it took place. Europe's experiences thus could now be viewed in America within two hours of their occurrences.

The world's dimensions had shrunk once more. What the telephone and telegraph had started a century before was nearly complete. Radio and the transoceanic cable had provided instantaneous communication between any two places. Then huge piston airplanes flew motion picture film over the oceans within a day. The jets narrowed the day to hours; space-age rockets and missiles, not to mention the eventual bouncing of radio and television signals off a satellite or another planet, could whittle minutes into seconds. In terms of transport and intelligence the world grew so small that there was no place to hide any longer. A shot fired at Concord Bridge in the nineteen sixties might be seen and heard around the world as fast as the speed of sound and light.

There can be little doubt that the world we live in is far more complicated, technologically, scientifically and politically, than the world of our forefathers. Nevertheless, it is a far less complicated world in many respects. We talk to each other more easily and readily; we see each other's images on screens more quickly. The lines of political problems emerge sharper and clearer; the issues dividing nation from nation are more distinguishable; and the obstacles to knowing about them have been shorn away. An uprising at a remote outpost is common knowledge almost before the smoke rises. The pronouncement of an official in Washington, London, Moscow or Peiping circulates throughout the world even as the echo of his voice fades. Whether we like the notion or not, we are now all part of a single world so far as what may happen or be said.

In a sense, the improvements in facilities for finding out about one another and telling about it have stripped the world of its protective covering. Everything lies virtually bare to the public eye. Little may be concealed from the other fellow or the other nation as the newest techniques for gathering information and spreading it convert the globe into an enormous, transparent goldfish bowl. This has special reference to the military and scientific tests that some governments may wish to conduct unbeknownst to others. The secrecy vanishes with the highly sensitive instruments capable of ferreting out the most carefully guarded experiments and the devices for making them known everywhere. The world soon becomes privy to any secret design, no matter how ingenious the effort to camouflage it.

What applies to military and scientific matters pertains more so to diplomatic maneuvering. Because of the vigil of newsmen and their techniques for circulating the word, it is much more difficult to make deals in the dark or negotiate under the table any more. This is all to the good. For things that happen in any part of the world often bear heavily on the rest of it, especially at a stage in history in which the balance hangs so delicately between peace and violence.

Actually the world is most fortunate to have at its command such highly developed tools for collecting and dispensing important pieces of information. As we know, because of the division into free and Communist societies, the world is subject to many stresses and strains emerging out of the continuance of cold war. Tensions build up. Nerves are tested. Tempers flare and tendencies toward trigger-happiness appear. If these are allowed to go unchecked and uncontrolled, they could court disaster in varying degrees. Therefore, the more we are aware of these surgings, the more we can know about the objectives and pressures behind them, the slighter the risk of the cold war turning hot and exploding.

Information of any kind, so long as it is reliable, becomes invaluable. It may save a life or many lives. We need to know everything we can about our neighbors and friends, and as much as possible about the people who oppose us and our form of society.

It is not unreasonable to conclude that a bit of random information may have saved the life of a young American under arrest in Cuba. The youth was said to have entered the country illegally for the purpose of assassinating Fidel Castro. He was placed in La Cabaña Fortress, a prison across the bay from Havana, and held without formal charges.

The NBC News Correspondent in Havana at that time went to the fortress prison to interview the prisoner. There had been no news reports of a trial or conviction. Yet the grapevine spread the word that the youth was to face a Castro firing squad the following dawn.

Our correspondent quickly relayed the story to his editors in New York. The rumor had not been substantiated in Havana, but La Cabaña's grapevine had a reputation for accuracy. As the report was broadcast to the American people, the editors alerted the NBC News Bureau in Washington that covers the State Department, and the NBC News Bureau in Chicago, home of the boy's attorney. In Washington, the

State Department's attention was drawn to the situation; through Chicago, the boy's mother and her attorney were notified. Although it was Sunday morning, all entered a life-saving operation immediately.

Phone calls were made to Havana. Cables were sent. Before long, an official of the United States Embassy was at the youth's side in the prison. Cuban officials said nothing. There were no hints of their intentions. Nevertheless, the Embassy official remained close to the prisoner and the rumors of the firing squad began to abate. Finally, the youth was released from La Cabaña and expelled from Cuba.

Nobody can claim for certain that the news report from an alert correspondent saved this lad's life. But it would be hard to deny that fast communication of an offhand piece of information got him safely out of a hostile environment and a very tight spot.

This was only a minor thread in the broader fabric of the whole cold war. It did, however, illustrate the relationship of useful information to the capacity to act effectively. In a larger context, the knowledge of how Nikita Khrushchev would behave in any specific instance could make dealing with him at least more predictable and enable those who must coexist or perish with him to plan their survival programs with greater prospects for success.

The American people had several chances in recent years to watch the Soviet leader close up in action. There was the impromptu kitchen debate in the summer of 1959 with Vice-President Nixon at the United States Trade Exposition in Moscow. It was a rude, bragging Khrushchev that Americans observed; a stubborn, cocksure man whose one theme was "we can do anything you can do, better!" Reluctantly he had to admit that the United States was ahead of the Soviet Union at least in color television. But the main impression he left on the American mind, the impression on which free world

negotiators and statesmen would have to base their business
with him, was Khrushchev's adamant refusal to accommodate.

The next sight of him was as a truculent, angry guest who
ranted and threatened to go home unless his hosts paid him
greater homage and showed more cordiality. He considered
himself insulted at a luncheon given in his honor in Los
Angeles during his visit to the United States in the fall of
1959. He disliked the remarks of the luncheon chairman,
Spyros Skouras, a Greek-born American who had become
one of his adopted homeland's major motion picture mag-
nates; and he resented the security arrangements suggested
by his own agents that prevented him from visiting Disney-
land. Khrushchev growled and snorted, and threatened not to
play any further unless the rules were changed to suit his
requirements.

On the same trip, Americans saw a jovial Khrushchev as he
talked with President Eisenhower at Camp David; a benign
one as he tramped over the farm of a friendly Iowa host,
Roswell Garst; and a clowning one at the Soviet Trade Fair
in New York. The mercurial character of the Soviet Chairman was apparent to anyone who had watched his travels
across the country.

A bluff, rampaging Khrushchev turned up at Paris for the
1960 Summit meeting that he had initiated and then scuttled.
Rarely had worse manners been demonstrated by a major
international leader. He refused to see President Eisenhower,
acted like a man possessed and resolutely declined to carry
out the purpose for which he had come to France, to meet
with Presidents Eisenhower and de Gaulle and Prime Minister
Macmillan. Instead he denounced the United States and its
chief executive for the U-2 overflight and staged a circus
performance, more befitting a jilted prima donna than a
responsible statesman, for the benefit of his coterie, his supporters and the newsmen who were there.

Finally there was his appearance at the fifteenth session of the United Nations General Assembly in New York in September, 1960. Khrushchev banged the table, beat his shoe on his desk, shouted interruptions during Prime Minister Macmillan's address, embraced Fidel Castro as a long-lost political brother and continued to berate Mr. Eisenhower. In unscheduled street interviews, he assailed non-Communist newsmen, their employers, the American people and their leaders. His antics gave the leaders of the free world a clear picture of the character of the man they had to contend with. His opponents may not have liked what they saw, but at least there it was; information and the machinery for distributing it had exposed the nature of the adversary. This was preferable to approaching him unprepared and disarmed, or to grappling with uncertainty.

But in the world as it lined up in the early nineteen sixties, knowledge of Nikita Khrushchev's personality, although valuable indeed, might be less helpful than knowledge of the new states being created in the heart of Africa or of the problems of the people in many of the world's less advanced areas. At the United Nations General Assembly, seventeen new states were admitted to membership in September, 1960. Which way would these lean: East or West? In Latin America, where people yearned for something better than dictatorships and empty stomachs, a new voice was heard: Did Fidel Castro offer a bona fide improvement of their lot? In the Middle East, was Gamal Abdel Nasser the answer to the poverty of the Arabs? In Algeria, was there an equitable solution to satisfy both the French and the Nationalists?

All these questions and similar others deeply concern the United States, and the free world. On their answers hang the weights that can pull the balance to either the world that is free or the world dominated by the Soviet Union. The answers, to be the right ones, must be based on accurate information. Since it is the aim of the United States to keep the world

free through a strengthening of the forces of freedom, its
citizens must be sure of obtaining the intelligence necessary
to the pursuit of this objective.

Modern communication makes the job of informing the
public so much the easier. But gathering the news is not
enough. Perhaps the most significant trend in recent years has
been the growing recognition that journalists must interpret
the meaning of the information which they gather in this
swift-moving world. Determining and presenting the meaning of events cannot be done without exercise of judgment.
But this judgment has to be conscientiously fair-minded and
detached; to be useful it must avoid the grinding of axes and
the special pleading of partisanship.

The Administration, of course, receives its steady flow of
intelligence from its regular ambassadorial and consular
sources. The journalist provides a check that at times may
prove highly valuable in weighing the validity of official communications. In a sense, the newsman is an unofficial ambassador to the country in which he serves.

Not too long ago American foreign correspondents and
their counterparts from other countries concentrated on
diplomatic matters alone. That has changed. Now their attention has broadened to take in all the facets of life in the
countries to which they are assigned. Without ignoring the
problems of government and diplomacy, they have become
increasingly preoccupied with people and the social, economic
and political forces they set in motion. As a result, the more
we learn of events and people at all levels of a foreign society,
the more we want to know.

Because there is such a sharp cleavage in the political design
of the world and since the United States is one of the two
pillars of power in the ideological contest, its people need to
be well briefed on what is happening everywhere in order to
rally behind their leaders as they endeavor to help their side

prevail. The people need reliable information from both sides of the line separating East from West. They need comprehensive, responsible information from the new and uncommitted states. They want, and have, to know who is our ally, who is not, who may be wooed and who may not. Above all, they want to know the best way to go about winning over the teetering and the doubtful, and the chances for converting some of the opponents.

In the same way that the press associations and the principal newspapers maintain listening and reporting posts in the capitals of the world, the broadcast news organizations station large staffs in key places. NBC News, with a total of 693 full and part-time correspondents and cameramen, has the most comprehensive news operation of all. Its foreign-based representatives total 338 spread through more than 70 countries.

Those foreign correspondents who are full-time members of the staff function as regional reporters. Each covers a wide area and is fully familiar with all the problems of the parts of the world that constitute his beat. Each is an experienced observer, skilled and trained in the art of digging out the significant news and presenting it in a clear, cogent style that places every new development in the context of what has gone before and what has happened elsewhere.

The regions to which these correspondents are assigned are all major squares on the cold war checkerboard. They include England, France, Germany, the Mediterranean, Africa, the Soviet Union, Japan, South Asia and Latin America. The newsmen assigned to these places are intimately acquainted beforehand with the politics, the social and economic problems and the mores which they are likely to encounter. They are also sensitive to the hopes and objectives of the peoples in these lands. On the basis of special knowledge and firsthand experience, each of these correspondents knows what his region seeks from the United States and what it is prepared to contribute to the preservation of peace.

Many of the correspondents also have had their tastes of inconvenience, discomfort and hardship. Most have reported wars or revolutions. Their memories at times recall the pathos of a tragic episode that they witnessed. At other times, they remember the ludicrous.

John Chancellor will not forget for some time the travail of settling his family into its Moscow apartment. "The Russians may be doing better than we are in outer space," he wrote, "but in people space they are far behind." Chancellor's Moscow abode is located on the ninth floor of a large building not far from the Moskva River. After a lengthy wait he was assigned to three rooms, each twelve by twelve, a small hall, a kitchen and a bath. There were five in the household including two small children.

The Chancellors drew up elaborate plans to use all the space in the most efficient manner conceivable. "Two children in diapers means a washer and dryer; the difficulties of shopping in Russian grocery stores means a deep freeze is necessary—the stockpiling of canned goods shipped in from Denmark means the hall will look like a supermarket," Chancellor said. "We have plans to redo the electrical wiring and stuff the loose window frames with cotton to keep out the cold. We hope that one day the elevator will be fixed so it stops at our floor."

By Western standards, the Chancellors are somewhat crowded. By Russian standards they are living in luxury. Were Russians to occupy their "multiple occupancy" quarters, one family would live in the nursery, a second in the bedroom and a third in the living room. All would share the kitchen and bath and the chances are good that another family would occupy the hall.

The inconveniences experienced by John Rich in the Congo after the Belgians granted independence were not as aggravating, perhaps, but had their own kind of irksomeness. In the first days of the confusion which followed creation of a Congolese republic, broadcast facilities were not available to correspondents in Leopoldville. To get out their stories, both broadcast and non-broadcast newsmen had to travel across the Congo River by ferry twice daily to use facilities in Brazzaville in the former French Congo.

"The complicating factor," Rich said, "was that the ferry was closed much of the time. Because of the currents and the danger of being swept over the rapids all service across the river, in fear of a breakdown at night, stops at 6 P.M. Besides navigational hazards, the ferry was also shut down from time to time at the whim of confused Leopoldville authorities.

"One day I arrived back from Brazzaville to find the Leopoldville ferry landing swarming with Congolese gendarmes. A colonel informed me that I couldn't come ashore. Then a Sûreté man accused me of violating immigration regulations by intimidating immigration officials at the beach; the ferry landing was known to taxi drivers as Le Beach. I hadn't intimidated anyone, merely had come through, shown my pass, and been waved on. Fortunately there was also a patrol of UN soldiers from Ghana at Le Beach at the time. They verified my story. After a few tense moments of waiting on the boat, unable to step ashore, the word was passed that all could disembark."

Such are the frustrations that sometimes stand in the way of a correspondent's doing his duty of gathering the news and reporting it. It is just as frustrating to the people who depend on him for their information. By and large, however, the roadblocks are minor in comparison with the opportunities to perform a useful public service.

In the chapters that form the rest of this book, a number of NBC News staff members pull together the strands of their experiences observing the international scene and informing the people about them over a period of years. The point of departure in most cases is the end of the Second World War. Each chapter is intended to serve as a briefing guide to the current situation in the arena of the world that the correspondent has been covering. The chapters include the post-war developments that have set the stage for the present drama and indicate the developments likely to occur. The final chapter, by a member of the Washington bureau, which covers the White House, attempts to analyze the plans of the Kennedy Administration to cope with these worldwide situations.

The main point in all this is to lay out the problems that each of the world's principal regions poses to the Kennedy Administration so that the reader understands the background behind the positions the President takes and the things that he must do. Each account is the product of the correspondent's own personal observation and knowledge. All of them are frank and forthright. They note where United States policy or practice has been good and where it has gone astray. There has been no attempt to cover up or excuse diplomatic action not in the best interests of American objectives, just as there has been no hesitation to suggest how the Administration can fortify the position of the free forces in the cold war.

This is by design a book of background and proposal. It is the work of men trained to report and evaluate. To extract the issues that make the difference between a free society and a slave one, and to re-emphasize the directions to be followed by the Kennedy Administration to keep the world alive and free—that is the purpose of this book.

—WILLIAM R. McANDREW

WILLIAM R. McANDREW is executive vice-president, NBC News. A veteran at the news game, his first exposure came while a student at Catholic University in Washington, D.C., his birthplace. After classes and during vacations, he served as a part-time correspondent for the Washington *Herald*. His full-time news career began in 1935; following graduation from Catholic University he joined the staff of the United Press in Washington. Two years later, he moved to the NBC News staff in the capital. Except for brief terms as executive editor of *Broadcasting* Magazine, director of information of the Board of Economic Warfare, and editorial work for the American Broadcasting Company, he has been associated with NBC News. His various posts up the ladder to head of the worldwide NBC News organization have included: director of the Washington newsroom; manager of WRC and WRC–TV, the NBC stations in Washington; manager of news and special events for the NBC radio and television networks; director of NBC News; vice-president, NBC News; and, finally, his present position. As head of a staff of 693 newsmen and cameramen, he runs the world's most comprehensive news organization, giving it the leadership that has put NBC News into the forefront of all news agencies. Under his supervision, NBC News has become the newsgathering source most government officials rely on for their information and the worldwide data they need to carry on their daily responsibilities in an effective manner.

# 2.

## BRITAIN:

## *"The Logical Base"*

A S a college boy doing the usual summer tour to Europe
I did not bother to include Britain in my itinerary,
on the assumption that it would be too much like home to be
interesting, and not particularly important.

Ever since, I have been getting to Britain as often as
possible because it is so different both from home and from
every other country in the world, and because somehow it
does not cease to be important.

Just why Britain does not cease to be important is the core
of John Kennedy's British problem. It sounds much easier
to resolve than many of his other problems and, happily for
him, in many ways it is. History would indicate that it can
also be extremely complicated.

With Germany, he has to worry about what men and what
policies will fill the vacuum which some day (one presumes)
will open where Konrad Adenauer now stands.

With France, he has to wonder whether anything will replace the towering figure of Charles de Gaulle; and whether France, if released from her travail in Algeria, will put her energies at the service of the alliance; and what is the future of the tenacious, if presently small, Communist movement in France.

Such problems do not arise with Britain. There, no single man is indispensable, nor is the fortune of any one British political party of vital moment to the future of the United States, the alliance or of Britain herself. Her political stability, her Westernness, and her sanity are not in question. Her relations with us always are.

They are in question because America has never yet been able to see Britain for what she really is. The view has been distorted by "1776 and all that," the "Victorian Empire," a preference for equating Britain with "colonialism," a clinging suspicion that she entangles us in her "power politics" and an inability to make up our minds whether she is good or bad, asset or liability. Lately it has been further distorted by an inclination to regard her as "Socialist" and hence of dubious respectability as well as of questionable reliability.

We have always viewed Britain through lenses of varying colors. Her view of us is also distorted.

As good a friend of Britain as Franklin Delano Roosevelt was troubled by British astigmatism inherited from his clipper ship forebears. He was determined to liquidate her Empire. Admiral of the Fleet Ernest J. King frankly and loudly "hated the Limeys"—a point of view which did not make for the easiest relations with his British colleagues on the Combined Joint Chiefs of Staff during World War II. Generals Eisenhower and Bradley, in their war memoirs, confess that a major reason for their decision to halt on the Elbe instead of reaching for Berlin, Prague and Vienna was a deep suspicion of all British purposes.

A case can be made that this suspicion of the British

caused our war leaders to miss their chance to end the war in
Europe in the autumn of 1944 and their subsequent chance
to save East Germany and Czechoslovakia from Communism.

Not the least of our mutual difficulties is that we still think
of them in terms of a bad George III, whom they regard as the
least unattractive member of the Hanoverian dynasty.

In subconscious retaliation they persist in seeing us as "the
greatest and most powerful fulfillment of Western imperialism" (London *Sunday Observer*, April 23, 1961), not as the
high-minded nation dedicated to the principles of international fairness, justice and peace which we prefer as the portrait of ourselves.

The problem of appraising the weight of the British in
world affairs and of adjusting to that weight and of handling
it, and them, to best mutual advantage is tricky, difficult and
both potentially rewarding and potentially dangerous. John
Foster Dulles misjudged and mishandled the British. They
went to Suez. Not all the pieces from that explosion have been
picked up yet. It could happen again. The British are predictable and one thing that can be predicted about them is
that they forget the odds when they think that their vital
interests are in danger, or are being neglected by even their
best friends.

The British have been forgetting the odds for some six
hundred years. In that respect, they have not changed. Touch
the spinal nerve of their instinct for survival and there will be
trouble. Treat them with respect and consideration and there
is no steadier or more reliable ally. But let there be no
mistake about one thing—Anglo-American "good" relations
were not ordained by the Deity. They take tending.

The above, however, is the conclusion of the thesis. Let us
go back and start with the details.

As of this writing, John F. Kennedy is the relatively new
President of the United States and Harold Macmillan is the

much less new Prime Minister of Great Britain. The two men had a pleasant, easy and profitable exchange of views in Washington. It followed after an emergency invitation to Key West arising out of the Laos crisis. Mr. Macmillan had responded at once to the call, and at once offered the support which at the moment was much needed and much appreciated. Where do we go from there?

Mr. Kennedy might or might not prefer to see Harold Macmillan at Number 10 Downing Street. He is a useful and helpful vehicle for Anglo-American relations and collaboration. He is not indispensable. Behind him in his Cabinet are a half dozen able possible successors, each one of whom would with equal loyalty support the alliance.

If by some sudden turn of political fortunes the Labour Party should replace the Conservatives at Westminster, there is Hugh Gaitskell, just as loyal to the alliance.

Should Labour be torn apart by its internecine feuds of the moment and should its left wing improbably capture Transport House (official headquarters of the Party) one of two things would happen. Either the new masters at Transport House would slough off their obsolete Socialism and their emotional unilateralism, or the Party would disappear, to be replaced by some new and responsible political combination to be put together out of the wreckage.

There is nothing mercurial or unpredictable about Britain. Oliver Cromwell was the last man who could dominate, tower above, and rule his fellow countrymen. He has been gone for some three hundred years.

New ideas do not suddenly sweep through the British people. True, they can be roused from their daily preoccupation with living; from their football pools, their disreputable and beloved popular press, their passion for not sending their horses to French butchers, their splendid theatre, their teeming cultural life and their "melancholy Edwardian pubs."

They can be roused from these things. But, it takes a clear and evident threat to Britain's survival to rouse them.

There are always a few tens of thousands who will march from anywhere to anywhere to "ban the bomb," "ban capital punishment," "ban blood sports," "restore flogging" or "keep flogging banned." As individuals they are individualists. As individuals, they sustain a score of radical journals any one of which, in America, would automatically double the appropriation for the House Un-American Activities Committee. But the editor of any one of these would count himself triumphantly successful if he could be sure of a steady circulation of ten thousand copies. While the thousands march, the millions jam the highways to swarm under dank clouds over danker seaside resorts.

It is a cliché and a truism, but also true, that the British people are steady. They require one thing of their Government: that it safeguard adequately the welfare and the survival of the nation. So long as it does that, they are content to leave the details to "Whitehall."

Every American is told that he should take a more active part in his Government. So Americans attend current events classes, and study political platforms, and dissect "foreign policy." The British are possessed of no such passion for "participation." It is impossible to explain to a British parent the need or reason for a "Parent Teacher Association." The idea, if vaguely grasped, is regarded as an intolerable reflection on the teacher. A current events class would also be deemed an intrusion on the business of "Whitehall."

The distinction between "Whitehall" and "Westminster" is important to an appreciation of why Britain is "steady" and why Mr. Kennedy's British problem is different from his problems with other allies. Physically, Whitehall is a street which leads into Parliament Square, and Westminster is a borough of the city of London. But the two words, as used in British public life, mean a great deal more than that.

"Whitehall" means the battalions of bowler-hatted, umbrella-carrying, highly educated, superbly trained, anonymous "civil servants" who staff the ministries of British government, whose tenure of office is untouched by election results and whose opinions are unmoved by political winds and tides.

"Westminster" means Parliament, which in turn means the House of Commons, which in turn means the politicians who when out of office indulge briskly in party and personal opinion, but who when in office are firmly if suavely and inconspicuously domesticated by the civil service. No rule book tells how it is done. Constitutionally, it does not happen. In fact, "Whitehall" is the most efficient grinder down of demagogues in history. Britain does not fear the demagogue, with reason. "Whitehall" manages the politicians with that same aloof, sure touch the police employ toward Aldermaston marchers. They march congenially along beside, chat with them, are deferential to them, and bundle them off to the station if there is any infraction of the rules.

In theory Michael Foot, the darling and John the Baptist of the Labour left, could become Prime Minister of Great Britain. In practice, he can never hope to be more than a political gadfly. The Tory right has its gadflies, too. By that subtle, unseen process which sorts out politicians in Britain, such men are sorted out. And "Whitehall" has its unseen hand in the process. This is "the establishment" at work. "The establishment" includes the leaders of the Opposition Party as well as the Government Party. Trade union leaders frequently "belong."

Tories in London could never understand Washington's concern over the possibility that "Nye" Bevan might someday have become Foreign Minister of Britain. "Nye" used to love saying the most hair-raising things. He was also a member in good standing of "the establishment." Had he become Foreign Minister, the Tories would have heckled him happily in the House by day, and slept serenely at night. They knew that "Nye" was as "sound" as Harold Macmillan. Some of them thought he was sounder. He was a welcome guest at "The Palace," which is also part of "the establishment."

Britain is governed not by men, but by institutions. The institutions are stable. The institutions grind carefully and usually very well. They are concerned with one thing and one thing only—the survival of a very ancient kingdom which has longer and more than any other country in history exercised influence well above the level justified by its provable strength and its visible assets.

This margin between strength and influence is a manifestation, not a cause, of the phenomenon of British "differentness." That Britain is "different" is beyond question. The difference rouses in others interest, respect, admiration, affection, irritation, and resentment. No other people profess entirely to understand the British. All are puzzled by them. The French and Germans are particularly puzzled. The Irish, also different, passionately refuse to be ruled by them but insist on dying with them voluntarily in all their wars. Their former colonies are eager to break from their tutelage, but cling to them after the break.

The actual size of their home territory (a third that of Texas or the Ukraine), their numbers (under fifty million), the razor edge on which their economy is balanced (they must export to feed themselves), and the narrow reserve under their currency (it equals the capital of the Ford Foundation) are all rational reasons for equating them with the Italians, or just possibly with the French. These are not reasons for equating them with the United States, Russia, China or India.

These are reasons why repeatedly since the 1914–1918 war others have assumed that the British "no longer count." Adolf Hitler built that assumption into his plans for world power. There were other mistakes built into his planning. The fact is that his plans failed.

The greatest and still inadequately explained mystery of World War II is probably related to the above. It is that while Hitler underestimated and repeatedly miscalculated the British, he also pulled his punches against Britain when conceivably he might have destroyed her. He did not push the pursuit of the British army to Dunkerque, but held his forces back, and was late and never wholehearted in his organization of the projected cross-channel invasion. One possible explanation is that he could not quite bring himself to the task of destroying Britain. In the early stages of the war he intended and even expected to use Britain as a partner in his long-term postwar projects.

There may have been a similar dualism in Russia's attitude toward Britain at the time of Suez. It is reasonably established that the threat to bomb Britain was a carefully labeled bluff. There has always been a touch of respect mingled with the contempt and hostility in the Russian attitude toward Britain. The fact that Karl Marx is buried in London is scarcely sufficient explanation for the respect.

A more plausible explanation is suggested by a remark made to me shortly before Suez by an editor of *Pravda*. "Please believe me," he said. "We do not want to drive the British from the Middle East. We would rather have them there than you Americans." My own assumption is that the Russians regarded the British as the lesser, and hence preferable, evil. In this sense Britain's shortage of tangible resources and physical strength is one of her intangible assets. To her enemies at any given period in history she has usually seemed to be at least the lesser evil.

Mr. Kennedy inherited with his Presidency a similar calculation about the British. It could be contended that the French-German combination in the "common market" would provide a stronger fulcrum than Britain for America's European and alliance policies in Europe. But would it be as safe and reliable a fulcrum? Suppose that someday Germany, under a less "Europeanized" leader than Konrad Adenauer, might decide to pull the alliance into a campaign for the recapture of the "lost territories"? Britain has no irredentist ambitions.

And besides, it is disconcerting to start building plans on a French-German base and suddenly discover that French generals once again have revolted against the government in Paris. Britain is physically weaker than France, but her generals are as good overseas, and domesticated at home.

The Russians do not regard an Anglo-American combination as being a vital threat to them, but rather accept it as a normal feature of the landscape. They might well regard a German-American combination as being a vital threat to them.

Before anyone accepts the proposition that "Britain is finished," one should weigh a number of factors beyond those already mentioned.

One is that there is nothing novel about it. It dates back, in fact, to the battlefield of Crécy. We, who tend to think of her in terms of her Victorian Empire, "Rule Britannia," "Pomp and Circumstance" and "Make Thee Mightier Yet," would do well to remind ourselves that there is nothing unusual about the gap between visible British resources and British achievement. The British were outnumbered four to one at Crécy—and that was in 1346. They were physically outclassed by Philip II (the Armada), Louis XIV (Blenheim), Napoleon (Trafalgar and Waterloo), the Kaiser and Hitler. Britain survived. The empires against which she fought have all receded.

The memory of the Victorian Empire is deceptive. Many tend to think of Britain's normal stature in terms of that Empire and to assume that since it is now liquidated the final end has come. The Empire was outwardly impressive while it lasted. From the inside at the time it seemed as tenuous and artificial as do Harold Macmillan's current efforts to make "The Commonwealth" sound and look like a substitute. The British themselves never took the Empire as seriously as did outsiders. They recognized Disraeli's conversion of the Widow of Windsor into Empress of India as a shady trick of domestic political stage dressing for the benefit of the Tory Party. And besides, it only happened in 1877. Britain has been a force and influence in history since William the Norman landed at Hastings. The date was 1066.

Popular mythology about the industrial revolution compounds the deception. We tend to assume that Britain did invent the industrial revolution and did throughout the Victorian age not only dominate the world in power, but also led it in technical advance. A few facts both about power and the technical record are useful adjustments to perspective.

The finest ships in Nelson's line at Trafalgar had been captured from the French, and the best cannon as well. Fewer than 10,000 native British islanders fought at Waterloo in an allied army of over 100,000. (The rest were Dutch, Belgian, Hanoverian and Prussian.) The banking center of the world at the height of the Victorian Empire was not London, it was Paris. And if a British family in those days wanted the best possible education for a son, whether technical or classical, he was sent to a French or German, not to a British, university.

The short-lived French Empire of Napoleon III was well ahead of Britain in technical knowledge, engineering, the art of banking, capital resources, and modern weapons. Ben Franklin first mastered electricity in Philadelphia.

Britain's greatest period of technical achievement coincided not with the Victorian Empire, but with the gloomy years of the thirties of this century when visible power was draining away, her people were bitterly divided and she had been forced off the gold standard, America had retreated into isolationism, and the ominous figure of Adolf Hitler was casting a deepening shadow over what was left of Western civilization. In those days Britain invented radio and television and was ahead of all others in radar. During the war years came the proximity fuse, the jet engine and the most important preliminary work on the nuclear bomb. These years also saw penicillin emerge from British research laboratories.

Subsequently she failed to match her fuselage designing with the jet engine. The original Comet was not only an engineering but also a commercial tragedy. Had the skin of the Comet been up to the jet engine, the airlines of the world would today be using British, not American, craft. And she suffered another jolting disappointment when "Zeeta" failed to unlock the hydrogen atom as the fuel of the future.

Subsequently she had to abandon the race to space. The conversion of scientific research into applied technology was a process too expensive for her limited resources. The fact remains that "little" Britain has done a disproportionate amount of the original scientific work in these many areas and has scored more than her normal share of successes. On a per capita basis, her achievements are remarkable.

She derives, however, more from necessity than from pride or power. She cannot afford a status symbol. While Americans and Russians race for outer space, Britain specializes in vertical take-off planes and "hovercraft." Her explorations have usually been done by private individuals and groups. The adventurous spirit which can climb Mt. Everest is not enough by itself to put the Union Jack on the moon. In new weapons, she abandons Blue Streak and specializes in undersea detection.

It is also an adjustment of perspective to note that the British Empire, unlike others, did not begin with armies and ships of war, but with merchants and traders. It was not created by and it did not depend upon great armed forces. Indeed, Britain never had them. And the profits from trade, not the spoils of war, poured back into the home islands to spawn the factories and build the City of London. More different kinds of people live and feel at home there than in any other great city.

This was not an Empire conceived by some mighty prince, dictator, or ambitious government. At every step along the road of its accidental growth the Government was led, begged, cozened and bullied by the merchants of her seaports and the bolder spirits out on the fringes. There was brisk and open opposition at home all along the way. The Parliament and taxpayers never willingly or happily provided the funds for the few soldiers and the always inadequate and frequently obsolete warships which policed the result. It was policed not ruled. There was never enough military power to rule it.

The nature of the origin explains the residual form now emerging. The Union Jack comes down and the plumed Royal Governor is replaced by a business-suited High Commissioner, but the trading web survives. More British live in India today than under the Raj. They prosper and are welcome. The jungle tribe turned "independent nation" sends a delegation to the UN speaking flawless Oxford English. Its politicians may dally with Moscow, but its army is officered by Sandhurst cadets. It may choose to put its own flag on its new airline, but it is neatly tied in with BOAC. Its radio and television network leans on the BBC and its communications channels somehow center on London. The trappings of Empire are gone. It is now what it was before the trappings—an informal, unofficial and ever-shifting community of trading interests. The dingy tramp freighter is the principal surviving link and the merchant is the real ambassador. But this was always the backbone of the relationship. Its future is precisely as valid as the prospects for survival of the breed of British trader.

One may say if one likes that this is the end of the British Empire, and hence of British capacity to influence the course of events. But it is necessary to make still another adjustment in perspective. Britain has never wielded decisive power. She never had the power to coerce even her colonies (we proved it) let alone the great continental nations which have risen and declined throughout the long span of British history. She has survived not by power but by the judicious and economical placement of her small weight in the balance between far mightier rivals.

Events have stripped away the illusion of "Empire." It discloses what was there all the time, and from way back—not the wreckage of a once world-ruling force, but a tight little cluster of islands in which people live now as they always have, much more by wit than by planning handed down from the top, and are less concerned with dogmatisms than with new ideas possessing practical application.

In Britain, Government is still surprisingly "small." Most of it still works in the half-mile square of "Westminster" and the whole of it could be housed in the Pentagon—with ample space to spare. The top men of all departments know each other personally, work in close physical proximity, and lunch together in their Pall Mall Clubs at a ten-minute walk from their offices. The cuisine is not remarkable.

It has to be thus. The British could neither exist nor survive on any other basis. There is not enough money in the Kingdom to support either massive government or massive power. The survival of the trader is the essential goal both of people and of the state. There are many reasons for the survival of the Monarchy, but the decisive reason is that it more than earns its way as a tourist attraction. Necessity, not theory, tests and shapes the end product of policy. Britain will join, or not join, the continental "common market" depending in the last analysis upon which course will be best for British trade. It causes her to be called "perfidious Albion." Her foreign policy is as adaptable as her commercial policies.

Those who can afford the luxury may indulge in crusades. For Britain, it is hard enough just surviving. She is adept in the art. Of course she knows that the word "crusade" has a market value. The palpably "good" cause usually in the end attracts more allies. She prefers to be on the "good" side, and usually is. Only the very powerful can afford to be evil.

There are more illusions to be stripped away before the present Britain is seen in accurate outline. The outside world thinks of British society as being caste-ridden. Nothing could be more mistaken. The rise from "rags to riches," and quick descent therefrom, is and always has been the normal rule in Britain. The system of titles tends to cloak the process, but younger sons have been disappearing into the indistinguished masses with a callousness on the part of the survivors which outsiders neither see nor could accept. No other society so ruthlessly discards the misfits and the failures, even when sloughed off from Royalty.

To a Britisher, the American social system seems more inflexible and caste-ridden than his own. It is the difference between appearance and substance. Substance is on the side of the British view.

The gap in Britain between the living standards of the rich and the poor is still by American standards shockingly wide. It is bridged by the ease with which the able and unscrupulous rise from poverty to wealth. Charles Clore, one of the currently richest men in Britain, came from the slums of Whitechapel. In America he could never hope to break into the "high society" of Boston, New York, Philadelphia or even Toledo. In Britain, members of the Royal Family attend his parties. Lady Docker's yacht and gold-plated Daimler are not resented by the barmaids of the world from which she came. Rather, they are an example of what, with equal luck, they might attain.

The gleaming Rolls, and its mink-coated freight, is not resented on its incongruous passage through London's East

End. The poor know that it is based on an "expense account" and its possession highly precarious. The robes of nobility are usually rented for grand occasions from "Moss Bros."

Then take the prickly matter of "Socialism." The British acquired a substantial dose of it in their emergence from the strains and privations of the last great war. But it is an extraordinary variety of Socialism. It nationalized those industries which had ceased to be profitable to their owners, but has never yet shut capital out from an opportunity for lush profits. It would be more accurate to say that capitalism in Britain managed to unload its liabilities onto the taxpayer than to say that Socialism ever seized anything which the capitalists truly wanted to keep.

The years of Socialist rule were also the years of blossoming of the new rich. The Socialists provided "socialized medicine" and "cradle-to-grave security," but they also left a score of loopholes in the tax laws through which the bright, the energetic, and also the unscrupulous have poured in thousands. To this day there is still no capital gains tax in Britain. There is a better chance that it might someday be imposed by Tories than by Socialists. One reason is that to tax capital gains would mean also taxing gambling winnings. The British workingman is an inveterate gambler. The party which closes to him his chance of making his tax-free fortune on "the football pool" is going to lose a lot of votes. Socialists, too, are practical, in Britain. Union funds are heavily, and profitably, invested in private business.

And do not shed too many tears for the plight of the British doctor who has been "dragooned" into "socialized medicine." It is miraculous how many of them drive Bentleys and Lagondas. One possible explanation could be that there is little rendering of bills for medical service. The doctor with his panel of national health patients does an assembly-line business during his "nationalized" working hours. The fee for each patient may be small, but it mounts up. And once established, he has his private practice on the side. The private patient pays cash. And there is no one watching the transaction.

The rule of "live and let live" takes precedence over any obligation to watch a neighbor's morals. The British are, by and large, law-abiding, but seldom legalistic. It is not without significance that the British school system penalizes those who are caught, not those who are clever enough to get away with an infraction of the rules. This applies even when authority is well aware of the identity of the culprit. The system also treats the informer, the "tattletale," with contempt and loathing.

It is relevant that the Puritans migrated massively to America, became highly respectable there, and for the most part are Republicans today. The few who stayed behind in Britain now largely survive in the left wing of the Labour Party. "The establishment" is anything but puritanical. This is one reason why Americans find it so difficult to identify their own political parties with those in Britain. Labour may be "left" in Britain, but its own left wing is the only place where one can find those who would if they could legislate morals for the masses. ˙

The mood, though not all the specific policies, of American Republicans finds its true counterpart in Britain among protest marchers and the perfectionist preachers of the Socialist left. There alone in Britain does one find conscious "righteousness," and confidence in the perfectability of man. It is not accident, but mutual Puritan heritage which locates isolationism in America on the Republican right and in Britain on the Labour left. The line of descent from the Puritans is in both cases authentic. Tories and most British Trade Union leaders, like Democrats, profoundly doubt the achievability of the millennium or the perfectability of man. In Britain, the majority of people not only doubt the doctrine of perfectability, they regard it as heretical.

Between Tory peer in his castle and workingman in his "pub" is the unseen but powerful bond of mutual loathing for the moralist. The political division by economic class is more presumed than real. A good third of the working class votes Tory. Labour is more a lower middle and white collar clerical grouping than it is a bona fide working-class movement. The "down-trodden masses" of Britain may battle their company foremen and managers, but the latter frequently vote Labour. Envy of the rich or titled is far less frequent than the desire to "make a packet." And besides, one of their own best-loved lads, " 'Erbie" Morrison, is now Lord Morrison of Lambeth, and a Peer of the Realm.

British-style Socialism has not sapped the vitality or resourcefulness of the British. They have adapted it to their system and their needs. Probably the worst thing that can be said of it is that it released too large a class of new rich too fast. It most certainly has not stamped Marxism upon the British character or political mind. Marxism is far too puritanical, and too much concerned with morals for the masses, to suit the British islander. He did use Socialism, successfully, to get rid of too much social and economic inequality left over from the nineteenth century. The Britisher is equalitarian at heart. The idea that one man is as good as another was not invented in the Thirteen Colonies. It was damaged in Britain in the Victorian nineteenth century, which was also the least British century Britain has been through.

This is one reason why the British people have not been particularly or perceptibly distressed over the passing of the Victorian Empire. They had a better life before it happened, and it is better again now. The Empire already begins to look like a brief aberration in the stream of British history. It happened to coincide with the roughest and ugliest phase of the industrial revolution. The association left a bad taste in the mouth of those at home. The vast expanses of pink on the map may have been a source of some pride, but the essential thing for them is to trade with, not to rule over, strange and faraway places. They are getting back to what seems to them their normal role in the world. South Africa, and Ireland, have left the official family. They have not left the trading community.

What emerges from this process of evolution from Empire back to being Britain is not power in the sense that the Kaiser's army was power in its day, or in the sense that Russia is power today and China may become power tomorrow. Britain never did dispose of that kind of power. Her honorable role in many a war was never that of the wielder of the decisive weapon. America provided the decisive weapon in World War I, and America and Russia together did it in World War II. Incidentally, it was Russian power which finally and decisively turned the balance against Napoleon a century and a half before.

In all the great struggles in which Britain has fought, her role was to hold the line until others of greater strength saw the issue, brought their forces into action, and took over the major burden of the struggle. Winston Churchill did not carry on the fight after the fall of France because he hoped or expected to beat Hitler by Britain alone. At most, he hoped to hold Hitler at bay until the effective weight of America and Russia might be brought into action. This was in the British tradition. It repeated the story of Britain's role against Napoleon and the Kaiser.

When inclined to downgrade the British it should be remembered that there would be no "free Western world" to defend had it not been for British stubbornness on those occasions. Hopelessly outclassed in measurable military might, they refused to recognize that they were beaten. In each case they won the time for bringing up the larger battalions. It was fortunate for them that the larger battalions finally did come up. But it was fortunate for the rest, too, if one accepts the premise that it is a better world for having escaped so far the imprint of a single authoritarian doctrine, or even domination imposed by force of arms from any one place. Britain is the principal reason why the hallmark of Western civilization today is diversification of religion and doctrine. Tolerance is the only doctrine she instinctively defends.

To summarize the actual condition of Britain in the early sixties, in the twilight of her Victorian Empire, and at the time of re-emergence of her true proportions, she is a small country in size and population, outclassed in power by America and Russia, backward by the standards of others in social development, her economy balanced on a razor edge, possessing a low rate of economic growth, and unable to afford mass higher education or massive power. But she is also the center of a vast trading and communications web, enjoys easier relations with more different peoples around the world than anyone else, possesses an extraordinarily stable political system, and is much respected for her tolerance, her vitality and her common sense.

That is enough to sketch out the background of John Kennedy's British problem. Now let us turn to the problem itself.

Getting along with the British is no easy task. Of course, we get along well enough with them as fellow tourists in odd places, we like to go to their schools and universities and they like to come to ours, and no great problems arise. We trade with each other largely to mutual satisfaction. These are not problems. But when it comes to co-ordinating foreign policy in a period of a tense, dangerous and perhaps long-enduring power struggle with the Soviet Union, we do have difficulties.

The first and the greatest of these difficulties arises out of the disparity between their physical power and ours. We have a great deal more power than they do, and not unnaturally feel therefore that the decisions should lie with us. This they do not accept. They recognize the difference in power, but by their lights it is offset by a difference in experience and wisdom, where they feel they are more richly endowed. They feel that between the two countries should be an equality in decision within a partnership of equals.

This view is not pressed unduly in the higher levels of British Government, but is deeply embedded in the mass of people and comes out in politicians. It would be as fatal for a British politician to recognize a lesser British role in the partnership as it would be for an American politician to do the same in reverse. Both Harold Macmillan and Hugh Gaitskell know what it is to be denounced on the hustings as a "stooge" of America. Votes can be made in Boston or Chicago by fulminating against the British. The best ammunition for the British demagogue is anti-Americanism. It is used on both Tory right and Labour left. The London *Daily Express* uses it to build circulation as successfully as Colonel McCormick once built circulation for the Chicago *Tribune* on a policy of "keeping King George out of Chicago." Communists are not the only people who feed upon exaggeration of Anglo-American problems and differences. Money is to be made, and has often been made, on both sides of the Atlantic from exploiting the differences.

A related difficulty arises out of the very different economic condition of the two countries. America does not, at least yet, have to export to live. Britain does. Hence, Washington will reach with alacrity for the embargo weapon against its enemies. To Britain the embargo is a weapon to be used only as a last and desperate resort. We yearn to use embargoes against Communism, and consistently since the cold war began have attempted to bind the alliance to a policy of no trading with any Communist country, but particularly with China. Britain yearns to trade with anyone, and shuns the embargo which hurts her more than it hurts the intended victim.

This bears on the matter of recognition of governments one does not like. We believe in nonrecognition. The British see no reason to withhold recognition from a government just because they do not like its political policies or religion. They have always been most happy to trade with anyone, regardless of race, creed, color or condition of servitude. The two countries can no more reconcile their recognition policies than their embargo policies.

To us, nonrecognition and nontrade are moral positions when dealing with enemies we regard as immoral. The British have always done some trading with their enemies, even during war, and never regarded morals as a factor. During World War I they needed optical lenses and the Germans needed rubber. The transfer was arranged through Switzerland. There were controlled exchanges of a similar nature during World War II. Napoleon contemptuously called the British a nation of shopkeepers. He was wrong. They are a nation of traders.

Out of the above arises another difficulty. To us, our enemies are immoral. We see the struggle against Communism as a struggle against total evil which should be totally destroyed. To them, the moral issue in the struggle is less easy to determine. As a religion, they have little fondness for the teachings of Mohammed. But they have long traded with Mohammedans. To them, Communism is another religion like Mohammedanism. If Russian, and other, peoples prefer to believe in Communism, that is their problem. It touches the British only when Communist doctrine leads to attempted conquest or interference with trade. They are hard put to it to show that their prompt recognition of Communist China has produced any benefits, but they can see no harm having come from it. They recognize a new government automatically, and cite the flow of information sent back from their Embassy in Peking as sufficient justification.

Another difficulty arises out of difference in size in this nuclear age. Our own people are not too happy about the prospect of a nuclear war. We have been told that it could mean the loss of some twenty of our key industrial cities, and casualties running between twenty and eighty million persons. It is enough to cause our successive governments to be hesitant about using nuclear weapons. But in theory we could sustain a nuclear attack, survive as a nation and even keep up the struggle. The British have no such comfort. With their size, there would not be enough left from a nuclear attack to be worth thinking about. They are sensitive to any word or gesture from Washington which sounds like atom bomb rattling. The word "deterrent" conveys to their ears an overtone which is both menacing and, in this case, truly immoral.

History injects another disparity in reactions to Russia. We are not conscious of owing any historic debts to Russia. The British remember that it was Russian weight which turned the tide against Napoleon, and Russian refusal to be satisfied with Hitler's policies which drew the weight of the *Luftwaffe* eastwards from the Battle of Britain. The two of us do not see eye-to-eye about Russia, or China. It is not likely that we ever will.

Also, back in 1917 they wanted, as Winston Churchill put it, to "strangle Bolshevism in its cradle." We refused to help them. They feel that in part the result is our fault. And during the last war Churchill vehemently opposed Roosevelt's China policies. It was our idea to arm, unify and liberate China, not a British idea. Again, they incline to attribute the ultimate and unfortunate result to us.

Had they had their way, Russia would not be Communist today and China would not be united. They also deprecated our determination of 1918 to dismember the old Austro-Hungarian Empire. The practical results of some of our most high-minded past policies do not encourage the British,

with their long historic memories, to assume that we necessarily have the best answers to all of today's problems.

But how then can we merge and blend our policies in the
power struggle? It would almost seem that it would be easier
to go our separate ways, and not even try. But that would be
difficult, too.

While the British approach the tactical use of such devices
as embargoes, diplomatic nonrecognition and nuclear weapons from a very different point of view than we do, they do see
at one with us on the basic proposition that Moscow should
not be allowed to master the world. London and Washington
are unanimous about the strategic objective, in spite of very
grave differences over how to move toward that objective.

And suppose that in a moment of exasperation with the
British we were to decide to cut our policies loose from them
and "go it alone"—what then would be the practical consequences?

We would immediately lose our military bases in Britain
which they have unhesitatingly put at our disposal regardless
of the political persuasion of the government of the day.
Clement Attlee was Labour Prime Minister when the bases
were first promised. Even the shock of Suez did not shake away
the bases. Macmillan granted the Polaris submarine base re-
quest at once, without hesitation. Britain is the only ally in
Western Europe which always has given us what we want in
the way of military bases.

Britain is the only other country in the alliance with interests all over the world, and hence the only other one which
sees the struggle as a whole, and can discuss with us the
weights and pressures in one place as they affect those in
others. We may disagree, as we do, over the best way to re-
strain Communism in Laos, but we are equally interested in
what does happen in Laos.

While there are factors which make agreement on tactics

and use of weapons extremely difficult, there are also factors which pull toward attempts to agree. It is not only Shakespeare, thatched cottages, and Coronation processions which attract Americans to Britain. British tolerance for dissenters also draws them, with sometimes interesting consequences. Some Republicans sought haven in Britain during the New Deal. After 1952, a far larger number of political emigrés from Washington included Britain in their wanderings. Ex-New Dealers found a congenial mental atmosphere in Oxford, Cambridge and London. It has been observed, accurately, that a high percentage of the New Frontiersmen who trooped to Washington in 1961 arrived there knowing Whitehall better than Pennsylvania Avenue. There is many a personal relationship between individuals at all levels of government in Washington and London.

It is a footnote to the above that in November of 1960 the victory of Democrats over Republicans came as something of a surprise to most foreign embassies in Washington, and hence to their respective governments at home. To most, it was disastrous. London was as unprepared as any, but to the British it did not matter. Harold Macmillan may have courted Nixon, but a score of British politicians, diplomats and journalists happened to be on excellent personal terms with John and Jacqueline Kennedy. Far larger numbers were on equally close personal terms with the bulk of the New Frontiersmen. Mr. Macmillan met Mr. Kennedy for the first time when he went to Washington in the third month of the new Administration, although John Kennedy could call several younger members of the British delegation by their first names. They could have used his first name but they did not. In less responsible times they had "done the town" together.

Add to the above many small things. An English novel does not have to be translated for the American market. It is enough to give it a more lurid title. American law derives from English common law. What we call advertising originated in Britain, although it is done with rapier rather than meat ax. The British have been advertising themselves by understatement since William Shakespeare. He is still the best show window display any country ever invented.

Britain and America have become somewhat "mixed up" with each other. They do influence one another. It would be hard to say which influences the other the more. It would not be easy to unscramble the relationship.

Others have noted this and revised their appraisals of Britain's importance in the process. When Japan came back into the world after the peace treaty of 1952, she put together the biggest and best Embassy staff she could manage for Washington and sent a token mission to London, but after testing the waters in Washington, hastily upgraded her London mission. Japan had momentarily assumed that Britain was finished. The episode is not isolated.

Harry Truman did a "reappraisal" of the British relationship when he took over in the White House. One of his first official acts was to cut off "lend-lease" to the British, as well as to the Russians. Later he brushed aside the British contribution to "the bomb" and claimed it as an American monopoly. But the time came when he thought differently. His proudest hour was when he took his honorary degree at Oxford. He and Mrs. Truman became rather fond of a young lady who happens to live in Buckingham Palace.

In the early Eisenhower years there was another "reappraisal" of Britain's value to the United States. John Foster Dulles was never a particular favorite with the British, or they with him. One of the curious things about the Suez affair is a vague residual feeling that somehow America was more disloyal to Britain than Britain to America. The facts do not entirely support this feeling, but it exists.

Britain, too, is periodically tempted to cut loose and "go it alone." The relationship between father and son is never easy. It is less easy when the son has struck it rich.

In the long run the ultimate relationship between the two will turn on the real value of each to the other. Should Britain become another Sweden or Switzerland, it would become just that, and in effect become a minor pawn in Washington's hands. Because of geography, it would have no other place to go.

But this has not happened yet, nor could any prudent person base his calculations on an expectation that it will happen. It depends on the survival of the British breed of merchant traders. As long as they range the world, know its every nook and cranny, and retain their trading and communications network (whether it be called Commonwealth, or not) their voice, their councils and their influence on the world will be an asset to their friends and a danger to their enemies.

Power and influence are not identical. There is little material reason why the voice of America should speak with more authority when it is supported by the voice of Britain, but it does. American influence has, if anything, declined with the increase of American power. The same can be true of Russia and China. Britain's influence has not declined in proportion to the decline of her visible power. If anything, it has increased. The weight of Britain and America together is greater than the sum total of the two parts.

One reason the weight of the combination is greater is because Britain is too small, her people too few, and she lives on too narrow a margin of reserves, to be able to afford the luxury of sweeping ambition. She has never dreamed seriously of world conquest or world dominion. This is something all the world recognizes, subconsciously if not consciously. Britain is not a menace to others, or to their beliefs. Her posture of "nonmenace" balances off her physical weakness. It is one of her greatest intangible assets.

Two arguments bear on Mr. Kennedy as they have borne upon his predecessors against according any special place to Britain in Washington's councils. One is that it makes others—principally the French and Germans—jealous. The other is that Britain is a drag on the decisiveness and effectiveness of American policy.

If he rejects these arguments, as his predecessors have ultimately rejected them, he is left with the problem of reconciling Washington and London policies. It can be an exasperating process. It can lead to explosions, like Suez. Washington must remember that no matter what the evidence that Britain is finished, the British themselves do not accept it. It is absurd to think that Britain would ever cut loose from America and seek another major relationship for herself. It is absurd—almost, but not quite.

In March of 1960, Harold Macmillan went to Washington with a grievance heavy in his mind. Washington at that time was strongly supporting the "common market" of France, Germany, Italy and the Benelux "low countries" and refusing comfort or even recognition to the rival European Free Trade Area which Britain had organized in economic self-defense. The continent seemed to be moving toward a trade war with Britain, and Washington was backing the continent against Britain.

Many a Briton felt that once again his country's very survival was being threatened, for her life does depend on her freedom to trade, and once again America was consorting with her enemies, as in 1812.

The classic British response in such a case has been to seek to engage some other outside power "to redress the balance." She had in fact invoked Russia against Napoleon. At the Foreign Office it was noted, factually, that the classic response to the developing situation of early 1960 would be to seek in Moscow the counterweight to the imbalance.

If ever Washington policy should appear to threaten Britain's survival there is scarcely a man among them who would not turn to Russia. If it were the last chance for survival, the staunchest Tory would be leading the delegation to Moscow and the ranks of Labour would be cheering from the side.

I was dining quietly and pleasantly one night four years after Suez with an old and close friend whom I had not seen since before that event. He is now an ambassador, had served in Washington earlier in his career, was always a good friend of America. I mentioned Suez. His face went white. With deep emotional intensity and absolute finality he said, "I'm sorry, I cannot discuss that with any American. I shall never, as long as I live, be able to forgive you for what you did to my country then."

Two conditions could drive the British to an act of desperation. The first would be a decisive Washington policy which appeared to threaten Britain's economic life. The second would be a visible inclination in Washington to engage in "preventive war." If one assumes that Washington would never commit itself to either, then one can take Britain's loyalty to the American partnership for granted. Those two exceptions remain. Within Mr. Kennedy's first two months he had reassured the British on both counts—whereas John Foster Dulles had alarmed them on both counts. That is the main reason why even the Cuban affair did not seriously shake Britain's continuing welcome for Mr. Kennedy.

One last question remains regarding Britain's value to America. Does Washington expect and intend, as it has in recent years, to build a European bastion against Russia upon the French-German combination and thus find the freedom to draw back out of Europe and leave it to take care of its own defense needs? If that is the long-term strategic plan, then Britain is not particularly important or necessary. She can have her choice of joining Western Europe or floating off to her own devices.

But would that concept any longer be sufficient to the needs of American security? Some longer thinkers in these days begin to doubt. They talk increasingly again of an "Atlantic community" in which there must be a far tighter pooling of Western resources if we of the West are to be able to match, and stand up against, the rising Empire of the East. If this is to be the trend of the future, then Britain's value increases greatly. She lies, physically, between us and the continent. Our personal and our cultural ties are closest and strongest with her. She is the logical base and channel of communications between Washington and the continent. She is tied in with the commonwealth countries.

Mr. Kennedy very probably will make the decision while he is in office which, in the long run, will determine whether we hand Europe and its problems to the French and Germans, or find ourselves someday living in an "Atlantic community." To do the latter, he must build on Britain. To do that he must be considerate of Britain's need to trade, and must shun anything which even begins to sound like "preventive war."

The time has not before been ripe for setting forth upon any such project as the "Atlantic community." It may not come again.

This is Mr. Kennedy's biggest British problem.

—JOSEPH C. HARSCH

JOSEPH C. HARSCH, Senior European Correspondent for NBC News, makes his base in London and has long been known as one of this country's foremost diplomatic reporters. A native of Toledo, Ohio, he was educated at Williams College and Corpus Christi College, Cambridge. Ever since graduation from Cambridge in 1929, he has been associated with *The Christian Science Monitor* and still writes a twice-weekly column for the newspaper in addition to his duties for NBC News. He is the author of books on Germany and on Eastern Europe, has lectured widely and written extensively for several magazines and leading newspapers both in England and the United States. Since joining NBC News, he has covered every major story concerning American-European diplomacy. He is a thorough student of the British scene.

# 3.

## FRANCE:
## *"Valuable if Troublesome Ally"*

WHEN John Kennedy took the oath of office as President of the United States, the President of the French Republic, Charles de Gaulle, sent him a congratulatory cable. It said: WELCOME, DEAR PARTNER. With those three words, de Gaulle distinguished France from the other countries of the Western alliance. France's self-election to partnership is not accepted by the United States (or by Britain). That leaves France the only member of the alliance actively trying to alter its terms and dispositions, and also to change her place within it. Since the present arrangement is not satisfactory, France also bases her policy more frankly than any of the others on the possibility that the alliance, as presently constituted, will in the not very distant future come to an end.

It should be a mistake to attribute this outlook, and the actions that flow from it, entirely to the President of the French Republic, Charles de Gaulle. The dissatisfaction existed before de Gaulle returned to power in the critical but oddly low-keyed days of May, 1958. Prime Minister Félix Gaillard complained in January, 1958, that France was being treated as "a subordinate partner."

The disinclination to follow wherever the United States might lead existed, too. As long ago as 1946, France was speaking of mediating between the Russian and American blocs. The idea did not survive the Communist coup in Czechoslovakia two years later, but reservations toward the United States persisted. In January, 1958, Gaillard's foreign minister, Christian Pineau, refused American nuclear weapons in France except under French control; de Gaulle was to take the same position later on.

De Gaulle's contribution was to expound the dissatisfaction more cogently and to expand the disinclination to follow into an inclination to go off in another direction. He spoke with bitter amusement of the postwar "illusion of the Western nations—in any case of the Americans—to bring the Soviets to co-operate with the West," and added sententiously, "We know what has happened." He lumped together the United States and the Soviet Union as "rival camps" toward which France turned a wise, aged and slightly cynical eye.

This does not mean that one fine day de Gaulle will order American forces out of the country or pull France out of the North Atlantic Treaty, or conclude a separate treaty with Russia. That is unlikely. In April, 1961, de Gaulle himself said, in one of his magisterial news conferences, "What I question . . . is not the Atlantic alliance, but the present organization of the Atlantic alliance."

What will happen is that France will offer her co-operation always selectively, often reluctantly, and sometimes not at all. Thus her refusal to allow American missile bases on French soil, or stockpiles of American nuclear bombs, unless she, France, controlled them. Thus the withdrawal of part of her Mediterranean fleet from NATO command. Thus, in the

spring of 1961, her attitude toward Laos, when Foreign
Minister Maurice Couve de Murville went to the Southeast
Asia Treaty Organization meeting in Bangkok, Thailand, and
got a softer resolution than the United States wanted. Thus
her refusal to share the cost of United Nations operations in
the Congo because she believed that the UN (and the United
States) was following a futile course there, because de Gaulle
considered the UN to be "a scene of disturbance, confusion
and division," insanely weighted in favor of the smaller
powers, and because France believed in supporting her ally,
Belgium, just as she wanted her allies to support her.

In short, France will co-operate at times, but not on any
terms. She expects to have something to say about the terms.
If she does not, or the terms are unsatisfactory, she may choose
to stay out.

De Gaulle realized from the first that the United States was
the logical and inevitable leader of the West, but in the
absence of American leadership, he was perfectly prepared to
supply his own. Equally, he did not consider that even in the
presence of American activity he was obliged to step aside.
Leadership, in de Gaulle's view, has always been competitive.
How much France could exercise depended at least in part on
her own efforts.

Apart from that, de Gaulle believed that the balance within
the alliance had changed. In his news conference of April,
1961, de Gaulle asserted "the right and duty of the European
continental powers to have their own national defense." He
went on, "It is intolerable for a great state to leave its destiny
up to the decisions and action of another state, however
friendly it may be."

When he said that, de Gaulle was not asking merely that
some Americans in positions of command within the alliance
be replaced by Europeans. He was opposing the integration
of national armed forces under the alliance, for "the inte-
grated country loses interest in its national defense, since it is

not responsible for it." He was also demanding a larger voice in the decisions of the alliance about going to war and which weapons to use. "It is necessary to clarify thoroughly," he said, "the question of the use of nuclear weapons by the two Western powers which possess them, and also the question of the use of their other arms. For the European states of the continent, which are by far the most exposed, must know exactly with which weapons and under what conditions their overseas allies would join them in battle."

Nor was this all. De Gaulle, as a prudent man, hedged. He knew that the world changed and that public opinion in the United States might swing violently. He therefore hedged against the possibility that the Western alliance would break up, or that the United States would one day leave Europe. That was one reason that his devotion to the alliance did not always seem to be everything it should be. De Gaulle wanted to be ready for anything that might come if the alliance were no longer there.

De Gaulle believed also that the alliance was unfortunately incompetent to deal with threats of war that "extend over the entire world, Africa and Asia in particular." His military and diplomatic moves took these points into account, so far as France's resources permitted. His insistence on France having her own nuclear arsenal was explicable in those terms. "As long as others have the means to destroy her, it is necessary for her to have the means to defend herself."

De Gaulle also, with his awareness of the great tides of history, always tended to think in terms of the old world and the new. He wanted Europe to succeed "in organizing itself and consequently in asserting its power, its reason and its experience in the world." He pictured Russia as a white and essentially European nation, with interests separate from and conflicting with those of China. He did not believe that the United States, a North American country, should have primary influence in deciding "European" questions.

These are the ideas, some purely de Gaulle's, some belonging to the French nation, with which, in a variety of combinations, any American President must deal. They will make any man wonder what real strength lies behind French stubbornness, and whether it is worth it. The answer will undoubtedly be that it is. France is a valuable if troublesome ally.

Since the end of World War II, it has often seemed that what troubled France was chronic and incurable. Politically, economically, militarily, socially, it seemed that everything had gone wrong and nothing could be done about it.

World War II and the period that followed it are not a time that the French take any pleasure in remembering. The Resistance and the Free French forces did something to diminish the national shame, but not enough. That sense of shame, and the knowledge of overwhelming and humiliating defeat, help to explain why some Frenchmen, especially those in the armed forces, so badly wanted victory in Indo-China and Algeria, and why they resented so fiercely the surrender of sovereignty over Tunisia and Morocco. They help to explain also why the regular armed forces were regarded with something like contempt by many Frenchmen, and this in turn is one reason the French armed forces have such bitter feelings toward the civil government and themselves take a hand in political matters. The uprising in Algiers in May, 1958, which brought Charles de Gaulle back to power, and the uprising of January, 1960, were in part revolts of the military, and the uprising of April, 1961, was an insurrection of the generals.

The division between the armed forces and the great mass of Frenchmen was paralleled by another even more basic —between those who resisted the Germans and those who collaborated with them. The final victory in which the French shared when the Germans collapsed may have been

sweet, but it was not sweet for everybody. There were echoes
of this in May, 1958; some of those who had a hand in the
Algiers uprising were former followers of Pétain. De Gaulle
personally may have been anathema to them, but they were
attracted naturally to the strong, authoritarian military hand.

It is fashionable to regard de Gaulle as outstandingly
prescient because he resigned in 1946 and then waited, more
or less serenely, for his country to call him back. Obviously
it helps a man's reputation for foresight to have been proved
right after twelve years. Unfortunately, de Gaulle was not
peering that far ahead. He expected political chaos and his
consequent return to come quickly. The chaos did not reach
the required pitch until 1958. It may be argued that this
demonstrated his ability to read the future; it also demonstrated his inability, in 1946, to understand the present.

It is nevertheless useful to see de Gaulle's return as an
inevitable turning point toward which all events from the
time the first new constitution was drawn up, in 1946, con-
spired. France moved through crisis and disaster almost as
though she were deliberately building up the tension to
make de Gaulle's hour of triumph more dramatic. The immediate cause of his return was Algeria. There were, however,
others equally important.

One of these was the absence of a workable political system. This often stood in the way of necessary decisions; it also
had a way of making things look even worse than they were.
A second cause was the absence of a social revolution and the
uneven distribution of economic benefits. A third was the
disintegration of the French Empire, which left much of the
population, especially the armed forces, in a state of disaffec-
tion. A fourth was France's failure to achieve the place she
thought she should have in the Western alliance, whereas
West Germany was achieving a place many Frenchmen
thought she should not have. All of these things helped to
explain why there was so little opposition to de Gaulle in

May, 1958. There was also general confidence in his recti-
tude and good intentions, and a feeling that he had to be
better than the army. So de Gaulle came back.

The political system was a prescription for instability and
inaction, and to achieve even that took a good deal of doing.
The first new constitution for the Fourth Republic, written
for the most part by Communists and Socialists, and worded
to suit parliamentarians, placed all power in the Assembly. In
May, 1946, the voters rejected it.

The second new constitution, drawn up mainly by the
Catholic MRP, again placed all power in the Assembly; so
much so that de Gaulle, who had been against the first constitution for this very reason, also came out against the second.
He noted correctly that it risked "pushing the State into
a confusion of powers and responsibilities even worse than
that which led the preceding regime into disaster and abdica-
tion."

By this time, however, most people wanted the matter over
and done with. The draft squeaked through.

This was the constitution by which France was governed,
or failed to be governed, for almost twelve years. The parliament was the dominant power in the state. In parliament,
because there were so many parties and "groups," and because
the Communists had such a large bloc, the only way to govern
was by compromise and coalition. This led to constant jockey-
ing and intrigue; parliamentary politics became a game;
the result was a situation called *"immobilité."* The Assembly
was able to cripple any government but unable to do anything
itself.

During the twelve years of the Fourth Republic, there were
twenty-two governments, spread over seventeen premiers.
Because these men were drawn from a relatively narrow range
of political beliefs (Pierre Mendès-France was the only one not
in the tradition) and because, from 1947 to 1952, there were
only two foreign ministers (Robert Schuman and Georges

Bidault), some students have argued that there was continuity and stability in French policy.

It is, I think, a poor argument. Some men were more adept than others at patching up the coalitions that could, for brief periods and for limited purposes, win a majority in parliament. The price paid for this majority often was a tacit recognition that if the limited purposes were exceeded, the government would fall. Nor did the fact that Schuman or Bidault was constantly at the Quai d'Orsay mean that they were any freer to act. The failure of the French political system was genuine. It was at the mercy of vested interests and pressure groups enormously powerful in protecting farmers, in restricting imports that might upset inefficient home industries, and in blocking anything that might cure tax evasion. It fell to the civil service to maintain continuity of government, and the civil service in France is a musty, ill-paid, stodgy group badly in need of renovation. The French people were given neither leadership nor unity. De Gaulle was able to slay parliamentary government not because it was itself wrong, but because the distortion of it that the French adopted was hopeless.

The economic picture was less unrelievedly gloomy than the political. Economically, there were even some triumphs.

At the end of the war, France had to be reconstructed. No part of the country had escaped some degree of devastation. Some parts, such as the Channel and Atlantic ports, had been laid flat. The city of Brest, for example, had handled 750,000 tons of import traffic annually before the war. When the war ended, its capacity was nil. On the railways, 9,000 of 12,000 steam locomotives were gone; 7,500 passenger cars and 55,000 freight cars. On the roads, 2,500 bridges were down. In agriculture, six and a half million acres had been made uncultivable, and livestock was down to a minor fraction of the prewar totals.

This did not tell the whole story. For years, there had been no new investment. Capital equipment had run down. The economy had been stagnating before the war.

In spite of this, recovery was swift, and perhaps we should now acknowledge this as a well-established pattern in the West. By 1946, total production was back to about 90 per cent of prewar levels, helped, no doubt, by the fact that those levels were low. In 1946, the Government took a vastly significant step. This was the plan named for the man who ran it, the apostle of a United Europe, Jean Monnet. It determined which sectors of French industry should get the most investment and then gave it to them. Steel, transport, coal, cement and electricity were singled out, and agricultural machinery. France's economic renaissance is largely traceable to the $12,000,000,000 thus invested, plus the help supplied by the United States.

By 1949, industrial production as a whole was about 30 per cent over the prewar level; by 1959, it was twice the prewar rate. The trend is still upward.

The picture in agriculture was less favorable. In 1949, farm production was still below the prewar rate; it only passed it a year later, and the significant increase did not begin until 1954. Even now, agricultural development lags behind industrial development; the system of food distribution is still stuck in the ways of yesterday. Farms are too small to be efficient, however desirable from the social and political view individual proprietorship may be, and, as in other countries, there has been a drift from the countryside.

In spite of undoubted economic progress, the benefits were unevenly spread. Inflation was victimizing almost everybody, but especially wage and salary earners. (There were seven devaluations of the franc after the war: from 50 francs to the dollar, it went to 493 in December, 1958.)

The housing situation was miserable, and here the principal victims were people who were forming families and were obliged to pile in with relatives. World War II destroyed 420,000 houses and damaged a million more.

This was piled on top of a low building rate between the wars, and it was exacerbated by a suddenly rising birth rate, and a deplorable failure to meet the need. In 1951, only 75,000 new houses were built. It was not until 1958 that the annual rate reached 300,000, and if the arrears are to be cleaned up, it will be necessary to continue this rate until the year 2000.

The picture in education was not much better. French education never paid much attention to science and technology, but what was chiefly wrong was the class basis of education. In practice, only the well-to-do reached secondary school or the university.

There was nothing peculiarly French about this. Other countries spread the benefits of their economic progress unevenly, and had class systems as rigid. The difference was that the situation in France was particularly explosive. The humiliations of World War II had made it so. The spectacle of governments rising and falling, while the world made jokes about it, also contributed. So did the loss of Empire.

The middle part of the twentieth century has seen all the European colonial powers, with the no doubt temporary exception of Portugal, begin and largely complete the involuntary liquidation of their empires. Once begun, the process cannot be stopped. Let the colonial powers give independence to those they concede "deserve" it and the "undeserving" will expect it, too, and set about getting it.

The loss of Empire was particularly hard for the French because it seemed to them that their allies, who should have been helping them to hold their colonies, were instead forcing them to give them up. The process began during World War II, in Syria and Lebanon, which were French mandates. The French yielded them with the greatest reluctance; at worst, they hoped to maintain military bases there. They were forced out as much by a British ultimatum (at that time, the British were hoping to reap the benefits of friendship with the Arab League) as by anything the Syrians and Lebanese did, and they left no bases behind them. American policy at that time also favored a French departure.

This is not the sort of thing that is readily forgiven. De Gaulle wrote in his memoirs that the British were trying to be the only power in the Middle East; he told the British Ambassador on June 4, 1945, that Britain had "insulted France and betrayed the West." He also wrote that "eventually the British and Americans will pay dearly for the enterprise they had launched against France."

After Syria and Lebanon came Indo-China. By the end of 1946, having tried to restore the prewar colonial regime, the French were at war there against the nationalist Viet Minh movement. The Viet Minh was Communist. Whether it might have become independent and Titoist, if France had behaved differently, is an open question. In any case, eight years after the fighting began, a hundred and fifty years after she entered Indo-China, France was out.

Here, too, there was French bitterness against her allies. The United States began by being reluctant to support a "colonial" war, although the French insisted that it was no more colonial than the Korean war had been and was, in fact, a key part of the struggle against world Communism. Only after the Viet Minh formally threw in with Russia and Communist China, did the United States put in vast sums in money and arms to demonstrate that the war had changed its aspect.

Beyond that, however, the United States would not go. In the spring of 1954, when French Foreign Minister Bidault asked for an American air strike at Dien Bien Phu, Secretary of State Dulles, after going this way and that (and after Vice-President Nixon had spoken publicly of "putting our boys in" to stop further Communist expansion in Asia), decided no. The principal reason was that British Prime Minister Winston Churchill and Foreign Secretary Anthony Eden would not go along. Some Frenchmen were deeply grateful; for others, it was simply added cause for resentment, especially against Washington. The British had never intimated that they would do anything, but Dulles had given the French reason to hope that they would be rescued from disaster.

Indo-China left a far deeper mark, particularly on the armed forces, than did Syria and Lebanon. The military were deeply disillusioned. They felt they had been given a job without being given the means to carry it out, and had then been abandoned. They felt that France's allies had neither understood what was at stake nor the nature of the Communist conspiracy, and when they got to Algeria, they felt the whole drama was being played out again. That helped to account for the moods of desperation that at times seized the armed forces in Algeria, leaving some of them ready to plunge the country into civil war. The resentment against the United States often expressed itself in personal terms. One night, during the uprising of May, 1958, in Algiers, I arrived at the radio station to do a broadcast. "You are an American?" asked the paratrooper on duty. I said I was. "Take the door," he said.

After Indo-China, Tunisia and Morocco went in 1956. In both countries, the French tried to hang on. In Tunisia, they began, characteristically, by refusing even to grant home rule. Thousands were thrown into prison (including Habib Bourguiba, who was to become Tunisia's first president); Bourguiba's close associate, trade union leader Ferhat Hashed, was murdered, apparently by the French terror organization known as the Red Hand. The attempt was made to hold Tunisia by force. Inevitably, it failed. When Mendès-France became prime minister in 1954, he began to negotiate home rule for Tunisia. The job was completed by his successor, Edgar Faure. By March, 1956, France had recognized Tunisia's independence.

In Morocco, the performance was even more tortured. Sultan Mohammed was a nationalist; the French encouraged their creature, the Berber leader El Glaoui, to depose him in 1953, and choose a new sultan, Moulay Ben Arafa. That brought the nationalist movement to life. Terrorism and counterterrorism set in. The French tried various devices to make it appear that they were giving Morocco some degree of self-rule. None worked. In the end, Mohammed was recalled from exile in Madagascar and restored to the throne. By the spring of 1956, Morocco was independent.

None of the agonies France went through elsewhere quite equaled those experienced in Algeria. The war in Indo-China was perhaps more bitter, and the Viet Minh probably was superior, militarily, to the Algerian rebels. Indo-China, however, was far away. Algeria was just across the Mediterranean; administratively, the fiction was maintained that it was part of France. More than a million Europeans lived there, many of them with personal ties to France, some of them members of families in Algeria since 1830. The richer "colons" had long controlled Algeria and at times they also controlled the government in Paris. Algeria not only had some oil and gas and minerals of its own, but it was the gateway to the greater resources of the Sahara, farther south—key factors in plans for the French economy and for the economies of all the French-oriented territories of Africa. Finally, it was the end of the line. The disappointed hopes, the anger with allies, the feeling that France was shouting the truth but nobody was listening, all of these accumulated there.

The first nationalist uprisings in Algeria came in 1946, and were brutally put down. For the next eight years, reforms were refused that might have postponed the blowup, or at least made transition easier. The fiction that Algeria was part of

France was used to deny that Algerian nationalism existed, or that the 90 per cent Moslem population might legitimately have different feelings about things from the French. The French even appeared to believe that the independence of Algeria's neighbors, Morocco and Tunisia, would have no effect on the Algerians.

Then, at the end of October, 1954, armed attacks on military posts and against civilians started. On November 1, 1954, Prime Minister Pierre Mendès-France rose in the National Assembly to say that "the Departments of Algeria" were part of the French Republic and devoted to France. "Never will France, never will any parliament, never will any government, yield on this fundamental principle."

It was the sort of empty oratory that French officials habitually felt called upon to employ whenever Algeria was mentioned. Now began more than six years of wildly dramatic events. Governments in Paris rose and fell. Tens of thousands died and more were maimed and wounded. A million Algerians were uprooted from their homes and placed in camps. Thousands of others sought refuge in Morocco and Tunisia. The French used torture against some of their prisoners, Moslems and Frenchmen who sympathized with them. The rebels burned farms (and sometimes the people on them), cut out the tongues of Moslems they thought were collaborating with the French, stopped buses on lonely roads and machine-gunned people to death. In late 1958, the rebels carried terror into France, firing at random at policemen and soldiers and carrying out an unsuccessful assassination attempt against the politician Jacques Soustelle.

The French constructed electrified barbed-wire fences along the borders of Morocco and Tunisia. Men and cattle died on them. Areas controlled by the French during the day were taken over by the rebels at night, while French administrators spoke of the war as being in its "last quarter hour."

Over the years, France's military forces in Algeria were built up to half a million men, while French contributions to European defense dwindled to the symbolic. At home, some young men refused to serve in the army, and some of their elders, politically on the extreme left, encouraged them. Civil liberties were restricted; opposition to the war became highly impolitic and sometimes dangerous.

The rebels used Tunisia and Morocco as "privileged sanctuaries" for training, medical treatment, and headquarters. The French Air Force bombed the Tunisian village of Sakiet in February, 1958, and thereby effectively internationalized a war the French Government insisted was a purely domestic affair. The United States and Britain supplied their "good offices" to settle the ensuing dispute, and millions of Frenchmen were outraged that the Americans and British should equate their ally in two World Wars with a few million Tunisians who were sheltering enemies of France. This led directly to the return of Charles de Gaulle.

Hand in hand with the fighting and brutality went a remarkable effort by the French to help the Algerian people. Special units were sent into the villages to live with the people, educate their children, provide medical care, improve their farming, protect them from the rebels, and bring them water and supplies. This was perhaps the most poignant aspect of the war, for the French had a genuine, paternal affection for the Moslems with whom they were working. For these Frenchmen, most of them young army officers, leaving Algeria would mean leaving these people to the mercy of the rebels. It was not an enjoyable prospect.

In the spring of 1958, the Assembly overturned the government of Premier Félix Gaillard, who had accepted the British and American good offices in the Sakiet incident. Georges Bidault, candidate of the right, failed to form a government and Pierre Pflimlin took over. Pflimlin hoped to end the war by social, economic and political reforms. For the Europeans in Algeria, settlers and some army men, it was a danger sign and a signal.

On May 13, 1958, the day Pflimlin formally took office, insurrection broke out in Algiers. Even now, what happened is far from clear. Some investigators have found as many as thirteen conspiracies, all functioning at the same time. There was, in any case, a march on government headquarters. The main military commanders, Generals Massu and Salan, decided to go along with the uprising against the Paris Government, partly to contain it; partly because they, too, foresaw the loss of Algeria if Pflimlin remained in power; and partly because they probably had no control over the paratroopers who held the key to Algiers. Among the plotters, the most skillful was Leon Delbecque, emissary of the former defense minister, Jacques Chaban-Delmas. It was he who initiated the clamor for de Gaulle. In a few days, Jacques Soustelle, a devoted de Gaulle follower and wrecker of governments in Paris, flew in from Switzerland, having evaded a suspiciously lax Paris police force. Soustelle supplied the political direction that turned the uprising against Pflimlin into an uprising for de Gaulle.

During the middle of the uprising I stood with Soustelle on the balcony of government headquarters, watching thousands of Moslems file into the square below to demonstrate their solidarity with the French. "Don't ever let anyone tell you," he said, "that this is staged, that it isn't spontaneous." My own conclusion was that it was both.

In Paris, meanwhile, the Assembly was voting its confidence in Pflimlin and preparing to give way to de Gaulle. Skillful radio broadcasts from Algiers unsettled nerves in Paris. There was considerable fear of paratroopers from Algiers dropping into the Place de la Concorde. President René Coty insisted that de Gaulle be brought in, and threatened to resign if he were not.

While indecision reigned in Paris, there was at least outward confidence in Algiers. "We shall land in Paris in two transport planes," Delbecque told me, speaking of the leaders of the uprising, "and the entire country will be with us."

Nobody has ever been able to demonstrate that de Gaulle was behind the uprising, or behind the use that his devoted followers, Chaban-Delmas, Soustelle and Delbecque, made of it. He was, nevertheless, happy to grasp the opportunity it offered. On May 15, he issued a statement saying that he was "prepared to assume the powers of the Republic."

There was much political coming and going after that. The niceties of party procedures were observed; calculations were undertaken on how to establish an alternative to de Gaulle, and how to restrict him if he did take over. Antoine Pinay of the Independents questioned him about his intentions. Guy Mollet of the Socialists questioned him. So did Pflimlin. It was all in vain. I was in Paris in those early days, and while there was no enthusiasm for de Gaulle, the Government it-self was plainly a lost cause. For the plotters in Algiers, who often seemed confused about how to proceed, de Gaulle be-came a way out. For the politicians in Paris, unable to gain public support, he was a way out, also.

On May 19, de Gaulle held a news conference in which he spoke about the "modalities" by which he would take power. On May 20, he remarked that it was "profoundly natural and normal that the Algerians cry 'Vive de Gaulle' as do all Frenchmen in agony or in hope." On May 27, he announced: "Yesterday I began the process necessary to the establishment of my government." On June 1, de Gaulle was invested as prime minister by a vote of 329 to 224.

De Gaulle brought to France exactly what he said he would, a government that would go on governing. Not everything he did was unassailably correct, nor was his judgment infal-lible. The constitution he imposed on the country in a referen-dum in September, 1958, was complicated and frequently obscure, especially in dividing power between the president and the prime minister; it provided means for the suppression of liberty, as well as for its protection. It was also tailored to the needs and personality of de Gaulle himself.

Equally, in the election in the fall of 1958, he allowed his name to be shamelessly exploited by Soustelle and his new party, the Union for the New Republic. The UNR was essentially an antiparliamentary body, inspired by de Gaulle's denunciation of "the regime of parties." Men ran for a parliament that they argued should have as little power as possible. When they reached office, they found their power-lessness less attractive.

The election law was loaded against the Communists. They got 19 per cent of the popular vote and fewer than 3 per cent of the seats. The UNR, with 18 per cent of the popular vote, got about 40 per cent of the seats.

This, however, was incidental. De Gaulle's constitution had largely destroyed the parliamentary system. The election largely destroyed the old parties. Essentially, this was what de Gaulle wanted—the power to govern without interference. The French people were willing to have him do it. They knew that he would conduct himself honestly, and with a reasonable respect for their liberties and a genuine concern for the nation's well-being. Moreover, with de Gaulle in power, it was possible to ignore politics and still feel patriotic.

One of de Gaulle's first and bravest reforms concerned the French Community. In the referendum of September, 1958, de Gaulle gave all the colonies of France the opportunity to break away. With the exception of Guinea in West Africa, where Sekou Touré headed an ambitious Marxist party (the only party in the country), they all voted to remain. It was a clear demonstration of the extent to which individual leaders influence affairs in backward countries. Guinea went 97 per cent for independence. In the other twelve African colonies, the vote for de Gaulle ranged from a low of 77 per cent in

Madagascar to a high of 99 per cent in the Ivory Coast, Upper
Volta, Ubangi-Shari, Middle Congo, and Chad. These twelve
colonies now joined France in the Community. (Other
colonies, such as New Caledonia, Reunion, Martinique, and
Guiana, chose to continue under direct French rule.)

De Gaulle began by believing that the Community could
have a number of common institutions governing economic,
financial, and defense matters as well as foreign affairs, with
France having the predominant voice. He saw the Community
as a channel to independence for the Africans, but he thought
that even when they eventually chose independence, they
would remain in community with France. He saw France as a
big brother, leading them through a complex, difficult world.

It was a noble enough idea. But even when they voted to
remain with France, for some of the African leaders it was
only to avoid too precipitous a break, to avoid affronting de
Gaulle, and to keep the assistance that France offered. When
Guinea voted "No," the other political leaders had to go
the same way. The various institutions of the Community
never really functioned. A number of defense and assistance
arrangements still exist. There are ties of culture and sentiment. The new African Republics are tied to the franc zone.
That is all that remains.

It always seemed to me that de Gaulle must have expected
this, though perhaps not nearly so soon, but that he had to go
through certain motions so as not to appear to be simply
casting Africa away. He also wanted to keep the transition as
friendly and nonviolent as possible, so as to give the Communists no opportunity to profit from it. The Community
did serve that purpose.

Domestically, de Gaulle's government did something almost everywhere, though often it was only a continuation of
work already under way or planned. The franc was again
devalued and strengthened, and a new heavy franc created.

Tax reform was begun. Exports were encouraged. A wage freeze was imposed. The command structure of national defense was reorganized, the courts modernized, local governments given more independence, urban development and slum clearance encouraged, technical education expanded, profit-sharing in industry promoted, farm subsidies reduced, depressed areas helped, barriers against foreign competition lowered, schools built, parochial schools given government assistance, the school-leaving age raised from fourteen to sixteen (though most children were remaining until sixteen, anyway). There was also a strong attack on alcoholism and prostitution. The attack on the first shows more signs of success than the attack on the second.

In the economic field, de Gaulle relied on businessmen and classical economists and his policy was conservative in the extreme. Inevitably, the wage earner was penalized. In spite of this, there were almost no strikes. The unions were too weak and de Gaulle's prestige was too strong. Moreover, the constitution gave the government power to impress men into the army, if necessary to keep key industries going. Deflation had its victims, just as inflation had had, but de Gaulle got away with it.

These things were, however, to some extent sideshows. De Gaulle's main preoccupation was the one that had brought him to power—Algeria. His actions on Algeria, I believe, can be understood only if they are seen as part of a plan to let the country go. There were, however, a number of conditions:

First, that the European population and those Moslems who had stood by France should be protected as far as possible.

Second, that the oil and gas and other resources developed by the French should continue to be at France's disposal and, wherever possible, in her possession.

Third, that departure should not be ignominious but in

fact should look like a military victory, so that the armed forces would not revolt and, in turn, upset France.

There were those who said that de Gaulle missed the psychological moments, that he could have acted radically after taking power, and again after he put down the revolt of January, 1960, by settlers and servicemen who felt that his September, 1959, offer of Algerian self-determination had betrayed them. Evidently he did not see it that way. Obviously, he wanted to avoid being accused of abandonment. He may also have thought of France as a patient that first needed to be given stability and confidence in the course of treatment. Once that was established, more radical measures could be used; the patient could stand the shock of losing Algeria.

In any case, there was never any doubt that he would offer Algeria its independence. He could hardly do otherwise once he had offered it to the members of the Community. In April, 1961, speaking of his conviction that the Algerians would choose to become a sovereign state, he said, "I do not deny that the rebellion has confirmed, affirmed in my mind that which was already my thought well before the rebellion broke loose."

However, he felt that he had to avoid giving the rebels everything they wanted before talks began. He had to keep some bargaining power to ensure fulfillment of the three conditions. Also, he had to wait until the French army had established its military superiority beyond any sort of doubt. He gambled that, even though he kept the rebels waiting, they would want, once independence was achieved, to retain some ties with France. His much publicized Constantine Plan of social, economic and political improvement for Moslems was a promise of rewards for good behavior. His threat of April, 1961, of what would happen if Algeria broke with France, was addressed to the same point: "Naturally, we shall cease immediately to sink in a henceforth hopeless enterprise our resources, our men and our money. We shall invite those of our nationals who are there and who truly run too many risks, to leave the territories concerned. On the other hand, we shall send back home those [400,000] Algerians living in France who would cease to be French." He added an implied threat to partition Algeria, holding certain areas for those Europeans and Moslems who wanted to remain French.

To say all this is to suggest a neat plan, consistently carried out. It did not work that way. Progress, or to put it more accurately, retreat, may have been inexorable but it was not smooth. Public opinion had to be watched; the rebels themselves were able to shape events from time to time. I suspect, too, that de Gaulle hoped that he might talk the rebels into stopping fighting and that, if he did, the terms France could expect would be greatly improved. Finally, and always, there was the Army. (It was hard, at times, not to sympathize with the Army in its feeling that it had been deserted by the nation. France had not even introduced conscription during the Indo-China war; the burden was borne by the regulars, the Foreign Legion, and colonial troops.)

Sooner or later, then, France will turn Algeria loose. French forces there will be reduced, and increased in Europe, and that will increase French pressure for more influence within the alliance. Some new NATO commands might help de Gaulle, and he will hope to appease the army also by modernizing French defenses which were allowed to run down during the Algerian war. Money released from the fighting will go into research and development, and into the procurement of new weapons, especially nuclear weapons.

As for the settlers who cross the Mediterranean, I would expect them to be swallowed up in the French population. Enthusiasm for the Algerian war waned in France in the late fifties; the mass of French people long ago stopped looking for ways of prolonging it or, if it should end, restoring it to life.

They were too busy with prosperity and other factors making France increasingly middle-class.

The return of large numbers of men always, of course, creates economic difficulties. France's full employment—the most complete in the Western world—was assisted by the occupation of hundreds of thousands in Algeria. Other stimuli will have to be found.

I would, nevertheless, expect France to go on spending money in Algeria for civil purposes, though less than she has been doing, and on stricter terms. The alternative is to leave this spending to the Americans, the Communists, or the West Germans. De Gaulle announced in April, 1961, that France would provide assistance only if the Europeans were well treated, and if France were given economic and cultural preference and military bases. He also said that if France withdrew, some people believed that, "Either the Soviet Union or the United States—or both at once—would try to take France's place." He went on to say, "I wish them joy."

In spite of this, I believe that under almost any conditions France will want to keep such influence as she can in North Africa. Spending money is one way to keep it, especially if that protects France's hold on the oil and gas in Algeria and the Sahara.

France's debt to de Gaulle for what he did in World War II was almost inexpressible. Its debt to him for a satisfactory settlement in Algeria may be just as great. Unfortunately, de Gaulle's indispensability leads to speculation about the time left to him, and such speculation about a man of his age always has a nightmarish quality, especially in a country as conspiratorial as France. For a long time, I assumed that if he disappeared from the scene, the armed forces would take over in the ensuing scramble. The generals' revolt in April, 1961, because it failed, made that seem less likely, but it also demonstrated that the armed forces were as politically minded and as bitter as before. More than that, although de Gaulle received overwhelming and active public support, he passed up the opportunity to give it political organization, to restore parliamentary life.

De Gaulle has spoken of altering the constitution to provide for direct election of the president by universal suffrage, rather than by the college of elected officials that voted him into office. Such a change might help toward a more or less normal political succession. So would a settlement in Algeria. Nevertheless, at the time of writing, de Gaulle's lack of provision for the political future was his worst omission.

The relationship between France and the United States is a happy hunting ground for amateur psychologists. Phrases like "love-hate relationship," "ambivalent feelings," "jealousy," "resentment," and "frustration" are commonly uttered. Amateur psychologists in Britain use the same set of phrases to describe relations between France and their country. With Germany, the situation is somewhat different. Love does not come into it on the side of the French, though admiration does. The United States, in other words, is not the only country that finds getting along with France a problem. Other countries do, too, and how they get on with France also affects how they, and France, get on with us.

Take West Germany. At the end of the war de Gaulle, and other Frenchmen, wanted to divide Germany into small states as in the past. This was never a practicable idea, and it had to be abandoned. So did France's hope of a long and stern occupation; of detaching the Rhineland, the Ruhr and the Saar; of keeping Germany disarmed; of keeping her economic recovery within bounds. By 1946, when the United States started turning Germany into an ally, French resentment against the United States began to form.

Once the change in Germany's status became irrevocable, France adjusted to it. De Gaulle himself made friendship and co-operation with Germany a key part of his policy. This had a practical side, for de Gaulle had ideas about leading a European bloc of which Germany would be a part and in which Germany would supply money for investment in Africa and in Latin America. It also provided a means by which Germany might be kept in check. The European Coal and Steel Community, the Council of Europe, the European Defense Community, Western European Union (which watches over the ban on German production of atomic, biological and chemical weapons), Euratom and the European Common Market may be interpreted as part of France's attempt to do that.

This is also the key to France's attitude toward the unification of Germany. The French considered it hard enough to control West Germany without adding East Germany to it, and de Gaulle personally believed that Germany had to be held firmly within the Western system for at least twenty-five years before it could be trusted.

The French want Germany to be prosperous enough to help in projects that Paris approves of, but not so prosperous as to dominate Western Europe. They want Germany to be powerful enough to take part in Western defense and to join France in a variety of arms manufacturing projects, but not so powerful as to threaten the rest of the continent. They want to be friendly with the Germans, and have made a sustained and generous effort to do so, but at times they cannot help feeling that they are being made fools of. Their feelings toward Germany, in short, are exactly those of the rest of us, but perhaps more acute.

Toward the British—ancient enemies, less ancient allies— the French attitude is more subtle. The French have always to calculate whether they can hold Germany in check without the help of the British. At times, they appear to think that they can, and then they form such purely European conceptions as the Schuman Plan and the Common Market. (These European conceptions have the additional advantage of not leaving the United States as the sole effective Western influence on Germany.) At other times—in 1954, for example —the French swallowed German rearmament only because of the British promise to maintain certain ground and air forces on European soil. Nor have the French ever been willing to slam the door shut against the British. Essentially, the French find themselves in the position of the boy who goes out to challenge the town bully and wonders whether to take his brother along. Victory without his help would be far more glorious, but would it be won? The French never quite make up their minds.

So far as France's attitude toward the United States goes, I never felt quite so pleased during my two and a half years in Paris as in September, 1959, when President Eisenhower arrived there. It was a particularly beautiful day but what happened on that day was far more important. Relations between France and the United States had been extremely difficult. There were residual reasons that went back to World War II; there were the differences over France's place in NATO; there was our failure to help France make nuclear weapons— help, by the way, for which French pride never allowed her to ask. There was our assistance to Tunisia, especially arms shipments, which the French deeply resented. There was our frequent lack of support for France at the United Nations over Algeria.

That does not exhaust the catalogue. There were disputes over basing American missiles on French soil, over France's refusal to join a NATO fighter defense force, over her failure to maintain ground forces in Europe at promised levels. There were other reasons as well, including doubts in the capacity of the United States brought on by the Russian sputnik, and American conduct during the French and British invasion of Suez in 1956.

Whatever one may have thought of what the French and

British did, it was for them an act of desperation brought on
by the feeling that they were being used by the United States
in some devious American game in the Middle East. Britain's
prime minister, Anthony Eden, was obsessed by Egypt's dictator, Gamal Abdel Nasser, and there was a large emotional
element in his actions. With the French it was coldly calculated, the theory being that if the action could be carried
through, the entire trend in the Middle East could be reversed, the trouble in Algeria ended, and the buccaneering
activities of upstarts like Nasser put down. Still, there was
also anger behind it, and when the Americans stepped in at
the United Nations and stopped the French paratroopers on
the verge of finishing what they had started, the anger shifted
to us.

So, when Eisenhower stepped off his airplane and de Gaulle
spread his long arms and said, "Ah, Mister President, how
welcome you are!" and they drove past the cheering crowds,
with the red, white and blue of the United States flying next
to the red, white and blue of France, it was impossible to
suppress a feeling of relief or the conviction that this was as
things should be. Those of us who had watched the situation
grow steadily worse felt, certainly, that it was about time. We
knew that the good will generated by the visit would not last
forever and that it had to be turned into concrete agreements
and mutual understanding. I had said on the air that, with
the way things had been going, Eisenhower would have to
make trips of this kind every three months to undo what had
gone wrong in the interval.

Unfortunately, the visit produced nothing concrete.
Within a matter of weeks, things were as bad as they had
been before. It was a simple matter to flatter de Gaulle. When
the flattery ended, he still wanted what he wanted when he
wanted it. One might not have given it to him, but one had to
know, at least, what it was and to have been prepared to talk
about it.

I never felt that the Eisenhower Administration made a sustained effort to meet de Gaulle or to understand his preoccupations. Understanding will not necessarily eliminate them; some of the conflicts are fundamental and will be ended only by the passage of time. What is important is to make de Gaulle feel that he and France are being treated with the seriousness they deserve. That can be done only by treating them seriously. Visits to Paris by American Presidents, such as the Kennedy visit of June, 1961, play their part. They can, however, be only an incident in a continuing process. It should be made as easy as possible for de Gaulle to communicate with the American Government. He wants to be able to pick up the telephone and speak to the American President, as the British prime minister has been in the habit of doing. An ambassador as fluent in French as in English (British ambassadors are) would be extremely helpful, and from that point of view General James Gavin was not the best possible choice as ambassador, although his other qualities may overcome this disability.

I do not suggest that the rest of the world be ignored for the sake of France and de Gaulle, or that de Gaulle is some sort of superman. He is prey to the same pressures and forces that beset other politicians, even though his style enables him to suggest that he is not. The point is that France and de Gaulle can be ignored, or patronized, or brushed off, only at peril.

—EDWIN NEWMAN

EDWIN NEWMAN, Paris Correspondent for NBC News until February, 1961, is a veteran of overseas service. Now assigned permanently to New York, he has been stationed in London, Rome and Paris at various times, and has covered other assignments in all parts of Western Europe, North Africa, Egypt, Israel, Kenya, Ghana and Guinea. A native of New York City, he was graduated from the University of Wisconsin and did graduate work at Louisiana State University. He worked for United Press and International News Service in Washington prior to World War II and the newspaper *PM* after it. In 1949, he began special work for NBC News in London and joined the staff three years later. His articles have appeared in magazines here and abroad.

# 4.

## GERMANY:

## *"Story of Contradictions"*

A FEW weeks after Nikita Khrushchev's Berlin ultimatum in 1958, Soviet sentries halted an American Army truck on a minor technicality at the check point on the outskirts of West Berlin. The American commandant immediately protested to the Soviet command in East Berlin. After hours passed and the truck was still detained, an alert went out from U. S. Berlin Headquarters. American infantrymen grabbed their armored vests; the heavy motors of the Patton tanks were revved up. Berlin's tiny American garrison was on the verge of sending a task force down the autobahn to rescue the truck and crew, by force if necessary, when the Soviets relented and set it free.

Again, in October, 1959, the Communist East Germans ran up their new hammer and sickle flags in elevated railway stations all over West Berlin. The West Berlin police ripped some of them down, but then found themselves outnumbered by East German railway workers. Policemen were beaten. Major violence seemed unavoidable. The Western military commandants calmly but firmly warned their Soviet counterparts that if more flags appeared, Allied soldiers would intervene to remove them. At the same time a battle group from U. S. forces in West Germany donned combat gear and prepared to board transport planes to fly to Berlin. At this critical moment the Soviets stepped in, reined back the cocky East Germans, and no East German flag has appeared since in a West Berlin station. One more possible explosion in Berlin was averted.

On any morning, John F. Kennedy may wake up to find himself facing another such crisis in Berlin.

He has inherited the legacy of an unfortunate mistake made back in 1945, when the United States and its Allies took on a job of occupation in a city 110 miles within the Soviet zone, without receiving in writing a right of transit to and from the city. Few then, of course, could foresee the speed with which the cold war has developed, but one of the rules every soldier is supposed to learn in basic training is to keep his supply lines open.

Berlin is a city where the Soviets now hold all the high cards. They could pinch off the 10,000-man Allied garrison in a matter of hours. Five Communist divisions are stationed within artillery range of the city. Even the locomotives that pull American military trains to and from Berlin belong to the East German railway and are run by East German engineers.

The main recourse for the West in Berlin is the threat of nuclear war, which it has said it would wage if attacked—a nuclear war that would probably destroy us as well as most of the rest of the world. The terrible consequences of such a war make it less likely that we would ever resort to such a measure, and this, in turn, reduces the effectiveness of our main deterrent against aggression in Berlin.

Yet, we can hardly afford to back down on Berlin. We have

staked our honor and prestige there. Few Americans realize how deeply committed we are to defend this alien capital that we ourselves so recently were trying to destroy. Berlin is another example of the postwar shifting of alliances that sees us binding ourselves by treaty to Japan, stationing in former-Axis-partner Italy our intermediate-range missiles aimed at our wartime ally, Russia, and hosting a former Hitler general in Washington as head of the NATO military committee.

At the end of the war who could have foreseen that American and German soldiers would be standing as allies, shoulder to shoulder, along the hills and valleys of Bavaria and Hesse? Who could have dreamed then, standing in the rubble of shattered Germany, that an American Secretary of the Treasury would fly to Bonn to ask the German Government to buy more American-built tanks, jet planes and missiles?

The story of Germany is a story of contradictions. The wartime Allies set out to destroy Germany, yet through their own bickering they have succeeded in recreating many of the very things they set out to eliminate—among them a powerful military machine and a mighty industrial complex.

The Soviets began by arming the East Germans; then the West, the United States more than anyone else, forced the West Germans to rearm. The first West German draftees were conscripted reluctantly in 1957. Initially we insisted that the West Germans put half a million men in uniform. Now our Allies, and lots of Americans as well, shudder because West Germany is approaching a modified goal of 350,000 men.

Following the war, German industry was a pitiful heap of twisted, rusting machinery. Now it dominates the continent of Europe. East German industry is second only to Russia's in the entire Communist bloc. West German output tops anything in the West except our own. The flight of foreign capital to West German banks has become an embarrassment to German financiers.

Totalitarianism, something we promised to crush, still thrives in Germany beyond the Iron Curtain, where life under Communism varies very little from that which the people lived under Nazism. West Germans can thank the cold war for their refrigerators, TV sets, and their rapid acceptance back into polite society, but they must also blame it for the continued entrapment of seventeen million of their countrymen behind the Iron Curtain.

Long before the first landing craft set out across the Channel, bound for Normandy, planning for the German occupation had begun. The trouble was not in starting late, but in the inability of the Western Allies to agree on the sort of postwar Germany they wanted. Josef Stalin knew what he wanted. It was a bit like the postwar rival space programs. While United States agencies bickered over programs and priorities, the Soviets plowed ahead on a fixed schedule to new accomplishments. So it was with Germany. Stalin set out to build a Communist state in all Germany and before we awoke he had almost succeeded.

It makes fascinating reading to look back over the Western proposals put forward in the closing days of World War II for treatment of defeated Germany. They range from the extreme of genocide to complete disarmament as a minimum. Secretary of the Treasury Morgenthau nearly succeeded in gaining acceptance for his plan to turn Germany into an agricultural society and split it up into independent states.

Even before final victory over the Third Reich, the Allies began squabbling over the spoils. At Teheran, and later at Yalta, the differences became clear. At Yalta important decisions were postponed because the Allies could not agree. Nevertheless, the Allies could hardly afford to break openly while the war was still being waged. They did succeed in agreeing on postwar zones of occupation and here the West made one of its greatest blunders.

President Roosevelt had at first desired an American zone of occupation in North Germany, with the easternmost end of it touching Berlin. A northern zone would have been convenient for getting our troops out after the fall of Germany and shipping them to the Pacific to fight against Japan. Roosevelt is believed to have dropped this under British pressure.

At Yalta, Stalin, Churchill and Roosevelt accepted the recommendations of the European Advisory Commission on postwar zones of occupation in Germany and Berlin. The EAC, set up in London in 1944, was a body of Big Three experts charged with studying European problems as they developed. The document brought in by the EAC at Yalta placed Berlin smack in the center of the Soviet zone but said not a word about guaranteeing Western road, rail and air access to the city. It was studied by the Joint Chiefs of Staff, approved and finally adopted by the Big Three. Here was the root of the present Berlin dilemma. It could have been avoided had someone insisted on pie-shaped zones with their points contiguous in Berlin.

Even though we had agreed to specific zones of occupation and were bound by treaty, it might have strengthened our hand had Western troops reached Berlin ahead of the Russians. Field Marshal Montgomery begged General Eisenhower to give him the men and support for a swift push across North Germany to Berlin. Winston Churchill, although he bears his share of blame for permitting Berlin to be placed in the middle of the Soviet zone, also pressed, after Yalta, to get Western troops there ahead of the Russians.

Eisenhower, responsible for the whole wide front, disagreed. At the time, the Western Allies stood on the banks of the Rhine with Berlin 300 miles away and the Elbe River between. The Soviet forces of Marshal Zhukov were at the

Oder, only thirty miles from Berlin. Eisenhower reasoned that a thrust at Berlin might not only weaken the whole front, but that it might get there too late anyway. He wrote in his book *Crusade For Freedom:* "This, I felt to be more than unwise; it was stupid." Eisenhower also had the backing of General Marshall and the military Joint Chiefs in his decision.

There was one further Allied plan to reach Berlin, which might have worked: a paratrooper- and glider-borne attack on the city itself. Major General James Gavin, who was commander of the 82nd Airborne Division, has told me that his unit rehearsed the operation and was ready to go as early as March, 1945. It never came off.

There was a last-minute plunge of Western troops across the North German coast to head off the Soviet armies from occupying Denmark and controlling the mouth of the Baltic Sea. As it turned out, Montgomery got to Lübeck only half a day ahead of the Russians and barely thwarted them from gaining a foothold on the North Sea. Russian armies still sit there, fifty miles from Hamburg, within easy tactical rocket range of London.

At Potsdam in July, 1945, that odd meeting of Stalin, Harry Truman, and the British duo (Clement Attlee replacing the defeated Churchill in the Hohenzollern villa) really set the future tragic course of postwar Germany. Here the West found itself faced with a *fait accompli*. Stalin had already set the western borders of Poland at the Oder-Neisse rivers and handed the territory over to Polish administration. Harry Truman described it as a "highhanded outrage," but the West could do no more than acquiesce and insist that the final disposition of this land must be settled at a future peace conference, which still has to be held. The question of the Oder-Neisse line, not yet accepted by West Germany, remains to plague a new American President.

Potsdam spelled out principles for controlling Germany

during the first occupation days and answers to questions of reparations, decentralization of the economy, disposal of the navy and merchant marine, and the trial of war criminals.

Nikita Khrushchev based his proposal of 1958, calling for an end to the Berlin occupation, on the grounds that since Four Power occupation had been established at Potsdam and since that agreement had been violated by the Allies, it was now null and void. The West was not long in reminding him that Allied rights in Berlin stemmed not from Potsdam, but from separate agreements reached previously by the European Advisory Commission. The EAC had worked out an agreement on the postwar status of Berlin which was approved by the Western governments, lastly by the USSR on February 6, 1945. It was on this EAC agreement, plus its rights as victor over the German Government, that the West has based its stand in Berlin. Unfortunately, although the EAC document spelled out the specific occupation sectors in Berlin, there was not a word in writing about Western access.

Incredibly, nothing was done about the question of how Allied forces would get to and from the city until General Clay, Eisenhower's Military Governor, flew there on June 29, 1945, to prepare for the entry of the Americans later the same week. At first only a single air corridor twenty miles wide was assigned; its free use was to be subject to one hour's advance notice being given to the Soviets. This restriction still pertains.

In later meetings with Marshal Zhukov, General Clay and his British counterpart accepted temporary arrangements on further access routes—the autobahn, a rail line and other air corridors, but they reserved their right to take up the matter later in the Control Council. No record was kept of the meeting. Clay said: "I must admit that we did not then fully realize that the requirements of unanimous consent would enable a Soviet veto in the Allied Control Council to block all our future efforts." In his book, *Decision in Germany,*

Clay confessed that he had revised his views and considered it an error not to have made Western withdrawal to agreed occupation zones contingent on free access to Berlin.

At that time, however, Clay took the position that Ambassador John G. Winant did at the EAC meetings in London. Mr. Winant then felt that an agreement in writing might have prejudiced our basic position, which was to insist on full rights of unrestricted access to the city. Compare this concept of "unrestricted access" to what happens when an American airliner has strayed out of the twenty-mile limit of one of the three corridors, or climbed above 10,000 feet—even though there never had been any understanding on altitudes in the corridor. Soviet jet fighters would appear off the wing-tips and Moscow would warn that through past practice the air corridors had become limited to a ceiling of 10,000 feet.

Some of General Eisenhower's remarks on early postwar Berlin thinking are revealing now. ". . . We felt," he wrote, "that a record of local achievement would have a happy and definite effect upon the whole question of whether Communism and democracy would find a way to get along together in the same world." Berlin still stands as the most graphic and potentially explosive monument to this inability to get along.

The original strengths of the Western occupation units in Berlin were at first set at 25,000 men for each nation. The three Western Allies now have a combined total of only about 11,000.

France got into the occupation when the British and Americans decided to allot her zones from their own territory in both Berlin and West Germany. General Charles de Gaulle was in a familiar role. He was not co-operating with his Western allies. Even then pursuing grandeur, he was demanding for France rights from one end of the Rhine to the other. De Gaulle also saw the possibility of using Russia to get a larger voice for France with his own Western allies. It was he who said in 1944: "The Russians and the French are united by history and geography in an indissoluble community of interests." De Gaulle has been the only Western statesman since the war to endorse the Oder-Neisse line as the best permanent boundary between Germany and Poland.

Since 1945, there have been ten Four Power Foreign Ministers meetings and two Summit attempts to solve the German question and write a peace treaty. Progress has been nil.

In 1945, an Allied Control Council in Berlin tried to administer postwar Germany, but it ended in a shambles for the familiar reason that the Soviets had a veto. The trial of war criminals seemed the only thing on which the victors could agree. At Nuremberg, twenty top Nazis were tried and twelve were hanged. Three still serve jail terms within the dismal brick walls of Spandau Prison in West Berlin. A Soviet officer is one of the four prison wardens; for one month out of four a platoon of Soviet soldiers trucks in from the East sector to assume guard duty. The aging, haunted three remnants of the Thousand Year Reich are Rudolf Hess, now half mad, the Hitler deputy who parachuted into Scotland; Albert Speer, munitions czar; and Baldur von Schirach, Nazi youth leader.

Spandau is a vast, exclusive prison and the three men its only inmates, but so far the four former Allies have been unable to agree on less costly quarters for them.

Besides Spandau Prison, the only other center of Four Power co-operation in Berlin has been the Air Safety Center where flight plans for the air corridors must be filed with Soviet officers.

After the war, reparations became an immediate bone of contention. The Soviets, as they did in Manchuria, dismantled factories, piled them on railroad cars and started them eastward. While the West pumped food and assistance into its zones, the Russians were removing it from the other side. Germans relate how Soviet soldiers yanked out water faucets

to take home to houses without plumbing. Returning prisoners of war found Poland strewn with discarded pianos and
easy chairs, and here and there carloads of rusting machine
tools. Berliners have not forgotten the rape of that city prior
to the arrival of Western troops. On the day the Russians sent
their first Sputnik into the sky, I announced it to our German
maid. Her only comment was: "Now maybe we'll get our
wrist watches back."

Over lunch one day a German publisher told me how the
Russian military had come to his plant and removed a full
barge load of very expensive technical books. He suspected
that the barge had never reached Russia, because a few years
later other Russian officials visited him and tried to buy
the very same books that had been carted off by their countrymen.

In 1945 and 1946 there was no interest on either side to
build up Germany. In March, 1946, the Allied Control Council agreed to restrict German industrial output to 55 per cent
of its 1936 level. Production in West Germany alone now
stands at 276 per cent of the 1936 level. Steel output was limited to seven million tons. Last year West Germany's mills
produced 34 million tons.

The Marshall Plan in 1947 put an end to reparations and
dismantling. Germany, as a key factor in European production, was allowed to step up its output. By this time the
British and Americans had linked their occupation zones into
what became known as Bizonia. The turn in American policy
toward Germany was signaled in a speech by Secretary of
State James Byrnes in Stuttgart in September, 1946. "We have
learned," he said, "that peace and well-being are indivisible
and that our peace and well-being cannot be purchased at the
price of the peace and well-being of any other country." Later
he went on: "The American people want to return the government of Germany to the German people. The American
people want to help the German people win their way back

to an honorable place among the free and peace-loving nations of the world."

This has continued to be United States policy toward Germany for the past fifteen years.

In the Eastern occupation zone the gun barrels were hardly cool when the Soviets began building a Communist state. The first Russian troops to enter Berlin brought with them a planeload of Germans in Soviet army uniforms: they were German Communists who had spent the war years in exile in Moscow. Now they came back to communize Germany. Their leader was Walter Ulbricht, spade-bearded present-day Communist Party boss in East Germany, who, with massive Soviet help, has imposed the Communist system on the Germans in the Soviet zone, but has yet to make it work.

Between 1945 and 1948, millions of refugees and expellees poured into the Western zone of occupation. In all, including those who fled earlier before the advancing Red Army, an estimated ten million arrived from Czechoslovakia and the former German eastern territories. Had it not been for the unbelievably rapid industrial build-up of West Germany, these refugees would have created a tremendous problem and provoked unrest. As it turned out, they have been absorbed into jobs, and West Germany still has the lowest unemployment rate in its history. It has imported laborers from Spain, Italy and Greece. Some German firms have been moving to Ireland where, besides tax benefits, there is plentiful labor.

Despairing of any co-operation from the Soviets in creating a unified or economically self-sufficient Germany, the British and Americans in Bizonia reformed the currency. Old reichsmarks were turned in, ten for one of the new Deutsche marks (which are still in circulation). But this blew off the lid. The Soviets walked out of both the Control Council and the Kommandatura, the inter-allied governing body for Greater Berlin. Soon the first attempt to push the Allies out of

Berlin began—the blockade. Although we still had a monopoly on the atomic bomb in those days, General Clay's proposal to send an armored convoy down the road to Berlin was rejected in Washington. We chose an airlift instead.

The Berlin blockade electrified Western Europe and had much to do with binding its nations together in NATO. It also marked the first time that the defeated Germans had a chance to identify themselves with one side or the other in the cold war. West Berliners stood fast. Even when offered a chance to buy plentiful food in the Communist sector of the city, they stuck to their meager airlift rations. The new postwar spirit of the West Berliner was forged in those trying days.

There was little that the West could do in its sector to counter the Russian squeeze on the city. Soviet communications lines that ran through West Berlin were closed off. One day the Americans caught a load of personal furniture belonging to Soviet Marshal Sokolovsky while being trucked through the city. It was confiscated and the Americans gleefully told the Marshal that he could have it after the blockade was lifted.

Another blockade would not allow the West even these minor satisfactions. Since 1948, the Soviets and East Germans have strengthened their position by routing their phone lines around West Berlin, and building an entirely new rail line and canal around the city.

Part of the Soviet strategy against West Berlin has been what Mayor Willi Brandt calls "salami tactics," shaving off a bit here and a bit there. Sadly, the West has not always stood firm against them. Prior to the blockade, British and American emergency stations existed on the single autobahn between Berlin and the West. They were maintained to take care of motorists who ran into trouble on the long drive. During the blockade the Soviets dismantled these stations. They also closed down our communications repeater stations in their zone. Our roving road patrols were re-established in 1949, but a while later when the Soviets objected to them, our command merely protested and gave in. We also let them take down our signposts along the autobahn.

The Soviet blockade was a failure, but it intensified the split of Germany and Berlin. In East Germany the puppet government began building up an army under the guise of a police force. In 1959, on the so-called third anniversary of the Volksarmee, I was permitted to visit an East German artillery regiment. I noted that my young officer escort was wearing a ten-year badge. "How come?" I asked. "I thought the army was only three years old?" "Oh," he replied ingenuously, "for seven years we were called a police force."

In West Germany, the Federal Republic was founded and on September 20, 1949, Konrad Adenauer was chosen by the Bundestag to be Chancellor—by one vote, assumed to be his own. The so-called German Democratic Republic was set up in East Germany that same year.

The next milestone in the German story was the uprising of June 17, 1953, a date observed each year by West Germans as Unity Day. Torchlight parades are held and bonfires blaze along the East-West border in sympathy for the seventeen million Germans still under Communist rule.

Stalin had just died, but the Soviets lacked no decisiveness when the revolt broke out. Construction workers building East Berlin's "Miracle Mile"—Stalin Allee—a bit of Moscow in the heart of old Berlin, laid down their tools and marched on the Government to protest against an increase in work norms. By next day strikes had spread all over the country and Moscow's puppet, Walter Ulbricht, and his government were tottering. The Soviets moved quickly. Tanks rumbled into the streets. In places youths threw stones at them, yielding some memorable pictures, but it was all over within hours.

This was the first of the East European uprisings. It belied Lenin's scornful appraisal of the Germans as too inflexible to revolt. If sent to storm a railway station, he predicted, they would first dutifully buy their visitors' tickets to get on the platform. On a modest scale it was a preview of what came later in Hungary. It showed two things: First, that when their basic interests were threatened, the Russians would not stop to debate legality. Second, that beyond radio exhortations the insurgents got no help at all from the West.

The real split of Germany now developed quickly. The Iron Curtain, 600 miles long, went up, from the Baltic to the Austrian border. Previously there had been a reasonably easy flow of Germans from one part of the country to the other. Now barbed wire was strung, a 30-foot-wide "death strip" was plowed, and wooden watchtowers were erected at strategic locations for machinegun fire along the border. This Iron Curtain has been a sobering sight. Each summer, numbers of American tourists have taken a look at it, strayed too far and ended up in jail in East Germany or Czechoslovakia.

It was after the blockade that the Western powers issued their first tripartite declaration on Berlin, promising to "maintain armed forces within the territory of Berlin" as long as their responsibilities required, and furthermore to "treat any attack against Berlin from any quarter as an attack upon their forces and themselves."

Even now, only a minority of Americans realizes that by this and subsequent statements we have promised to defend Berlin as we would our own coastlines. It is a grave promise to a city, 110 miles behind the Iron Curtain, that is admittedly militarily indefensible. But the United States, since the last war, has committed itself to defend a lot of foreign real estate throughout the world. We should not forget that there are more people living in West Berlin than in the whole kingdom of Laos. These West Berliners are a highly intelligent, highly skilled people who know the difference between democracy and Communism. Theirs is the most intelligent anti-Communism I have ever known. For them Communism is no vague theoretical system. Any day they can simply cross the street and see the life of their fellow Berliners in the East. This walk through the Brandenburg Gate should be a recommended trip for every American. Nowhere in the world can democracy and Communism be seen functioning so close together, and to such an advantage for democracy.

The sunny Summit conference at Geneva in 1955 produced a communiqué stating that "settlement of the German question and the reunification of Germany by means of free elections shall be carried out in conformity with the national interest of the German people and the interest of European security." The statement obviously meant different things to different people. In October, when the Foreign Ministers met to carry out this task, Mr. Molotov was insisting that free elections could be had only on the basis of agreement between the two German states themselves. This meeting, as the others before it, produced only disagreements. Then followed the "Dear Ike–Dear Nikolai" letters between President Eisenhower and Premier Bulganin, which also got nowhere and tapered off with the outbreak of the Hungarian Revolution. In subsequent years the West has failed to make enough of this Russian refusal to permit free elections in East Germany. Soviet inability to win over the East German masses is one of its greatest weaknesses.

In 1955, the Bonn Republic was granted its sovereignty. Later the same year the Soviets signed an agreement with the East German government purporting also to give it the status of a sovereign state, except for some reservations about the occupation status of Berlin. Since then the Western allies have been fending off a continuing series of efforts by the Soviets to win international recognition for their puppet government. The Soviets now hand back all Western protests with the notification that they should be presented, not to them, but the "sovereign Government of the German

Democratic Republic." Control of all German traffic at the border check points was also given to the East Germans; the Soviets now handle only allied military movements.

This was the situation when Premier Khrushchev dropped his bombshell in a speech at the Lenin Sports Stadium in Moscow. He followed up the speech with a note to the Western Governments on November 27, 1958, proposing withdrawal of all occupation forces from Berlin and the creation of a "free city" in West Berlin (not, however, in East Berlin which the Russians insist is the capital of sovereign East Germany). He gave the West six months to work this out with him, adding ominously that "if the above-mentioned period is not utilized to reach an adequate agreement, the Soviet Union will then carry out the planned measure through an agreement with the DDR [East Germany]."

The West shot back that it would not negotiate under threat, but it kept the diplomatic channels open and prepared for the worst (although not as energetically as many Americans felt was necessary).

The West got its strongest support from the West Berliners themselves. They rejected the Khrushchev plan almost unanimously. In local elections of December, 1958, the Communist Party (legal in Berlin although it has long been banned in West Germany) made the free-city proposal the main campaign issue. Each day en route to my office I drove under a big Communist campaign slogan hanging from the platform of the elevated railway (which the Communists control throughout all Berlin), reading: VOTE COMMUNIST AND DRIVE THE WESTERN POWERS FROM BERLIN. When the ballots were counted, the Communists got only 1.9 per cent of the vote, less than ever before, and not enough to put a single man in office.

Early in 1959, the Soviets proposed a German peace conference and Summit talks on Berlin and Germany. This was whittled down to a Four Power Foreign Ministers meeting that opened at Geneva on May 11, only a couple of weeks before the expiration of Khrushchev's six months' time limit, and, ironically, the death of Secretary of State John Foster Dulles. Again there was a deadlock. It was then, when fears mounted that Khrushchev would move against Berlin, that President Eisenhower relented and invited the Soviet leader to the United States. Although Khrushchev had failed to split NATO (one suspected aim of his offensive) he had managed to use the city as a lever to get his long-sought invitation to the White House. A year later he also got his Summit meeting at Paris.

It was during the Camp David talks that Khrushchev elicited from President Eisenhower the admission that the Berlin situation was "abnormal." This was something that no "normal" person could deny. The present situation is certainly anachronistic, as any occupation must be after it has lasted for a number of years. But to term Berlin "abnormal" implies that something must be done about it soon. It ignores the basic fact that it is the Soviets who have blocked reunification of Germany and created the "abnormal" situation. It overlooks another "abnormal" condition: West Berliners, after sixteen years of occupation, have been begging the Western occupiers to stay on lest something worse move in on them from beyond the city limits. Berlin's alert, forceful Mayor Willy Brandt pointedly has insisted that West Berlin, rather than being "abnormal," has really been the only "normal" city behind the Iron Curtain; it is a place where people can live free lives and express their wishes in free, open elections; it is a bright, prosperous city in sharp contrast to the drab, depressing existence that is the norm in Communist capitals.

We should never forget that the Berlin crisis is an artificial one stirred up by Moscow. It is not a disease, as Mr. Khrushchev has contended, but only a symptom of the real sickness of Europe—which is divided Germany. Mr. Khrushchev has the initiative and he can push to the brink any time he wants. This is the unpleasant reality of Berlin.

In the Jessup-Malik agreements of 1949, which ended the Berlin blockade, we got from the Soviets confirmation that all travel rights in effect prior to the blockade would be valid. One of the problems now is that no single person remembers the past agreements on which the Berlin occupation has continued to function. Only a very few were in writing. Most were verbal agreements made between field commanders, kept alive only by practice. That is why, although air travel is quicker and more comfortable, the American ambassador once a month runs his special train through the Soviet zone to Berlin. That is why American soldiers adamantly refuse to permit Russian sentries to inspect the interiors of their vehicles at the check point. That is why West Berliners were so upset recently when an American air-line strike cut the number of flights from West Germany to Berlin. Next time, they say, the Soviets will tell us that we do not need so many flights, because in 1961 we got along for many days on a smaller number. There is, and will continue to be, constant probing of our position in and around Berlin.

Berlin and the Iron Curtain in Germany are neither Laos, Cuba nor the Congo. Here American soldiers stand face to face with the Soviets. The crack striking forces of both nations are committed in Germany and both have their tactical rockets and nuclear warheads with them. In last winter's NATO war games in Bavaria the umpires counted more than a score of simulated nuclear demolitions and shellbursts within the first hours. Nobody expects the real thing, if it comes, to be any less violent.

In Berlin, the Western commandants have been more alert for demonstrations, disorders and riots stirred up within the city by agitators coming from the East, than for an overt attack by the Soviets or the East Germans. Thousands could pour in simply by stepping aboard the subways and elevated trains. Significantly, the main training effort of the Berlin allied garrison is in anti-riot tactics.

One might ask how the West Berliners themselves stand this constant strain. During the past few years living among them, I have asked it myself. They are certainly a remarkable people to have lived through the war and bombings, emerged from the ashes, survived the blockade and continued to live happy, productive lives under the relentless pressure from the East. To get out of the city and into the countryside for a weekend's diversion, they must drive 110 miles west and pass through two Communist check points. One Easter I witnessed a line of Berlin cars four miles long, waiting to clear a control point. The delay was seven hours, and this time the East Germans were trying to be co-operative and had put on extra clerical help. Yet despite the hardships, Berlin is home, and many will never leave it whatever happens. There is also such a thing as becoming inured to constant crisis. In the tense spring of 1959, West Berlin was much more placid than any other capital in Europe. West Berliners also have been proud of the renown they have won in the world. In a way they have been trying to live up to their reputation.

Morale, however, can be a fragile thing. It is important for us to see that their courage is not permitted to sag. Berliners study carefully every word, every pronouncement from Washington, including the irresponsible comments by American politicians. Adlai Stevenson is not popular in West Berlin because of remarks reported by a French journalist that made him appear to vacillate on Berlin. It did not matter that Mr. Stevenson later claimed to have been misquoted.

During the Berlin Blockade, General Clay was asked what he thought about bringing American families out to safety. He replied that it would be disastrous to the morale of West Berliners. During the most recent crisis, voices were again

raised in America urging the evacuation of dependents. Had
these been heeded, the will of the West Berliners to resist
would have collapsed. I received phone calls from German
friends during the dark days asking if I were planning to
evacuate my wife and four children. When I replied that we
would stay on, their voices changed to tones of relief. Sometimes it almost seemed easier to convince the Soviets of our
determination on Berlin than the Berliners themselves. At
any rate, one of the swiftest ways of undermining ourselves
in West Berlin would be to give the Berliners any cause to
suspect that we were going to slip out some day and leave
them at the mercy of the Communists.

Short of the reunification of all Germany, it is virtually
impossible to foresee a Berlin solution that could be acceptable to the East, the West, and the Berliners themselves.
At Geneva in 1959, the Soviets called for a temporary agreement to maintain the status quo in Berlin for a period of
eighteen months, while the two states of East and West Germany tried to work out some sort of unification or confedera-
tion. According to the Soviets, if a solution were not found in
eighteen months the occupation of Berlin would come to an
end and with it the rights of the Allied troops to be there.
Failing this, Mr. Khrushchev said, he would sign a peace
treaty with East Germany alone, and then Soviet and Warsaw
Pact military forces would help East Germany to defend its
sovereignty.

German reunification, not only on Soviet terms but on anybody's terms, is a controversial subject. U. S. government
policy is to insist that we desire it. It is, however, something
less enthusiastically sought by our Allies in Europe. On this
point they and Mr. Khrushchev agree.

The prospect of seventy million Germans again united in
the heart of Europe is enough to give both East and West

cause to reflect, even though neutrality were made the price of German reunification.

Few present-day West Germans would be anxious to make any great sacrifice to achieve reunification, but it is a mistake to delude ourselves that the majority of Germans do not want to see their nation pieced together again. The fact that there was no German nation prior to 1871 and Bismarck, makes German nationalism no less aggressive. A divided Germany is a potential for future trouble. One in every four West Germans is a refugee or expellee from the East. Germans will tell you indignantly in private conversation that what the Poles and Czechs did to them in 1945 and 1946 matched the worst of the Nazi atrocities. At present, however, in West Germany, in spite of the charges of irredentism coming from the Communist bloc, there is no surging movement to take back the homelands in the East.

The refugees have been absorbed into the pulsing economy. Some are too old and tired to want to go back, others are too young to remember what it was like in Pomerania, Silesia and the Sudetenland. A political party based on refugee support failed to win even a seat in the last national election. It has now joined forces with a right-wing party for a fresh attempt. Some German extremists continue to play the *lebensraum* theme at the frequent mass rallies of expellee organizations. Two things could make their appeals dangerous. One would be a depression, making life in West Germany difficult. The other could be appearance of a demagogue to stir up national pride and enthusiasm to recover lost territories. The two might come simultaneously. They did once before.

There is another element of instability in the German picture that is difficult to assess. After a decade and a half, Communism has failed to take root in East Germany. True, it has a Communist regime, but Walter Ulbricht and his followers are maintained in power by the presence of the Red Army, an estimated 300,000 to 350,000 man force. This attempt to impose Communism from above on an advanced, highly industrialized Western society such as exists in East Germany certainly must be frustrating to Moscow. Refugees continue to spill across the border to the West at the rate of several hundred daily, surely one of the greatest, sustained mass migrations in history. Close to three million have left since the official count was begun back in 1950. Half of those fleeing are under twenty-five years of age. Concerned about an eventual population void in East Germany that might be filled by Poles or Russians, the West German Government has urged East Germans to stick it out as long as they can. Refugee benefits are withheld from those who cannot prove they left under duress. But still they come.

Three-quarters of the refugees flee through Berlin, the biggest loophole. To thrive, Communism needs sterile conditions, free from outside contaminating ideas. As long as West Berlin remains free, the solidification of the system in East Germany can never be complete. This is understood by both Mr. Ulbricht and Mr. Khrushchev.

Even some of the Party's own functionaries find West Berlin an attraction. They come over from East Berlin to shop, to buy those little things unavailable in their own Workers' and Farmers' State. One day, as an object lesson to other wrongdoers, the East Germany Communist Party newspaper printed the following story with a straight face: A worker named August, from an East German factory, slipped into West Berlin to shop. He bought a suit and instructed the salesgirl to wrap it in a plain package. With the suit under his arm, August boarded a train for home. Suddenly he saw a pair of Volkspolizei coming through the train conducting a spot check. Were they to look in the package it would be obvious what he had been doing and he would be arrested. August thought fast. He took his package to the men's room and locked the door. Slipping hastily out of his old suitcoat, he tossed it out the window. The pants followed. August opened his package. He put on the new jacket and then his heart sank. He discovered to his horror that the girl at the store had forgotten to pack the pants.

Not all East German stories are so humorous. Life has improved in East Germany slightly over the years, but it is still grim. Given a free vote the people there would wholeheartedly toss out the present Government. The danger is that if things go on as they are, they will lose heart. On this the Soviets count heavily. These people, living gray lives east of the Elbe, have known nothing but totalitarianism for almost thirty years. From Nazism they went directly under Communism. The future for them does not look bright.

Germany is the real key to Soviet foreign policy. In spite of their sallies into the Congo, Cuba and Laos, geography and national interest combine to make Germany the prime Soviet target. Twice in this century Russia has turned back attacks from the Germans. The Russians fear the Germans, respect their skill and intelligence, and covet their industrial machine.

There are many reasons why Soviet Russia will not acquiesce in any settlement depriving her of the hold she has on East Germany. Militarily it gives her a base in the very heart of Europe. Were she to pull her troops out it would mean withdrawing them all the way across Poland and back to the homeland. This would leave her with a doubtful buffer on her most sensitive border. Mr. Khrushchev does not trust the West Germans, but he does not trust the East Germans, either.

Moreover, in spite of incredible bureaucratic bumbling, the East German economy is now strong. East Germany is Russia's biggest trade partner, ahead even of Communist China. The Soviet plastic program leans heavily on the East German chemical industry. East Germany is now an important mem-

ber of COMECON, the Communist bloc division of labor
system, and its output directly affects the economies of all the
other satellite countries.

In West Germany, President Kennedy has a different nation
to deal with than President Eisenhower had at the start of
his term. In 1952, West Germany had not even been granted
full sovereignty. Now she is again a power in Europe and in a
position to demand a voice in European affairs consistent with
her new status.

West Germany's development is an incredible success story.
Given a boost by three and a half billion dollars' worth of
U. S. aid, the West German economy has skyrocketed. The
story is evident in every business report. Steel production in
1959 was 29.4 million tons. In 1960 it was 34.1 million. Exports for 1960 were just under twelve billion dollars, giving
her a healthy, favorable trade balance of 1.3 billion dollars.
The production index, based on the year 1936 as 100, stood at
276 at the end of 1960. At the close of 1960 her holdings of
gold, foreign currency and other foreign effects amounted to
eight billion dollars, and even after the upward valuation of
the D-mark they continued to creep ahead.

The Soviets have used the East Germans and the Czechs to
spearhead their economic programs in the underdeveloped
areas. West Germans can and should play a big part in helping
the West. But the money will not flow from Bonn automatically or easily. It will take annual prodding by Washington
to keep it coming.

The trend of the West German economy is back to cartels
and centralization. Two of the most important industrialists
are convicted war criminals. Frederick Flick is the czar of the
automobile business, controlling the huge BMW and Mer-
cedes Benz plants. Alfred Krupp von Bohlen und Halbach
again heads the sprawling Krupp empire as sole owner. The
turnover for the Krupp plants in 1960 was more than a

billion dollars, an increase of 16 per cent in one year. Krupp does business with the East Germans, with other satellites and with Russia. He has just completed three synthetic fiber plants in Stalinogorsk, Novkuibishevsk and Kursk. Krupp's bustling, ambitious right-hand man, Berthold Beitz, is a frequent visitor to Poland and in 1961 worked openly to establish diplomatic contacts between Bonn and Warsaw, a mission reminiscent of the political roles played by former German economic giants.

Although Krupp had been ordered by the Allies to divest himself of his coal and steel holdings, he managed to obtain reprieves year by year. One excuse he gives is that no buyer has appeared for the plants. The fact is that no German would dare bid on them. Another factor behind West Germany's rapid industrial expansion is the trade unions. Their demands have been modest and they have been long-suffering. They have accepted low wages while industry built up plants and working capital for the "good of the country."

In April, 1957, the first West German draftee reluctantly entered service. Four years later, in April, 1961, armed strength stood at 300,000 with the promised goal of 350,000 expected to be reached by 1963. With France's army split by the April, 1961, insurrection and still involved in Algeria, the West German armed forces have become by far the strongest on the continent, next to the Soviets. The United States has five crack divisions stationed in Germany. There are many Europeans who want to see those troops remain, not only as part of the NATO shield against Russia, but to keep an eye on the Germans as well. Historians may wonder whether it was really necessary for the U. S. to push so hard for German rearmament in the mid-fifties. These were years before the Soviets had rockets, and when our own strategic airpower was unchallenged. There is not a general in the West German army who did not serve Hitler. The thought of these

men having nuclear arms is terrifying to more people than the
Poles and Czechs.

How long the West Germans can be denied nuclear weapons is debatable. With their ground force contribution already the largest in NATO it is difficult to explain to them
why their soldiers should be denied arms as modern and
destructive as those belonging to the Americans, British or
French. Under the Western European Union treaty that gave
West Germany its sovereignty, the Germans renounced the
manufacture of atomic, biological or chemical warfare
weapons. But there is nothing that says they could not get
them from others. It is also no longer a question of German
industry not being capable of producing such equipment. The
world was startled last year when it discovered that a West
German physics professor at Bonn University, Dr. Wilhelm
Groth, had developed a uranium refining gas centrifuge that
operated cheaply enough to put the ingredients of an atomic
bomb within any nation's reach.

Some day, in seeking atomic independence, the Germans
may cite the example of the French and their stubborn
insistence to push ahead to a separate nuclear capability
regardless of the cost or effect on world opinion. President
de Gaulle might be the first to complain if the Germans took
seriously his statement that "It is intolerable for a great state
to leave its destiny up to the decisions and actions of another
state, however friendly it may be."

Politically, a working democracy has been established in
West Germany. The question is: How firm are its roots? The
test has yet to come. In the years after Konrad Adenauer
ceases to be chancellor, we shall be able to judge better
whether the transition from a tragic past is real and permanent.

Since 1949, "Der Alte" has ruled Germany with a firm hand.
He has been the father image, counseling Germans, scolding

them, prodding them. He has put together in his Christian Democratic Union a political party of Catholics and Protestants—and made it work for the first time in German history.

Winston Churchill has called Adenauer the greatest German since Bismarck. State Department officials would agree, for they themselves could not have picked a finer man, from our standpoint, to lead Germany out of the defeat and guide her as she stumbled to regain her footing. She is now back on her feet. This is evident in the returned confidence and consequent officiousness of German officials. Foreign diplomats complain that much of the familiar arrogance is creeping back again. Germans are no longer the supine, obliging, defeated enemy of the immediate postwar years. Dueling clubs are again active. Former Nazis, hundreds of them, can be found in public office.

Konrad Adenauer will be remembered as a great European. Almost as though he did not trust his people on their own, he worked doggedly to integrate them politically and economically with the rest of Europe. He countenanced no hostile remark against France by anyone in his administration. His position has been to bind West Germany firmly to the West, while there was still time. Once I asked him what he believed was the most important decision of his administration. He thought a moment, crinkled his parchmentlike face and replied that it was almost the first one, made back in 1949: "Our decision to stand with the West."

Until Der Alte has departed there is not much to fear. A number of persons counted him out prematurely. But he has never let the British forget that after World War II they fired him as the mayor of Cologne on grounds of inefficiency.

Certainly John F. Kennedy never expected to have to receive him at the White House in April, 1961, when he wrote in October, 1957: "American policy has let itself be lashed too tightly to a single German government and party. Whatever the elections show, the age of Adenauer is over." Whoever the next chancellor may be, we have no assurance that he will tie his policy as tightly to the Atlantic alliance as has Adenauer. The great nightmare of Western politicians is the specter of a future deal between the West Germans and the Soviets. It cannot, of course, be completely ruled out.

But the point that President Kennedy was making in his comment on Mr. Adenauer was that there were other forces in West Germany which were anxious to turn over a new leaf.

In Germany our postwar policy has avoided many of the mistakes of the past. Instead of a vindictive peace we have substituted generosity and reason. In the long run this may make the difference. It has been a case of government policy advancing far ahead of the sentiments of the people. Without our knowing it Americans and Germans, bitter enemies of a relatively short time ago, have become allies, daily more dependent on one another.

One day in Berlin an American friend of mine in an automobile which prominently displayed U. S. Army license plates started across an intersection against the light. The traffic cop on duty angrily blew his whistle and waved him back. After the light had changed, the policeman motioned my friend to advance. Expecting a ticket, or at least a verbal dressing down, the American was startled when the policeman waved him on, saluted, gave him a big grin and said, *"Wir brauchen Sie doch."* (We still need you.)

They need us and we need them. Whether this new-found relationship will prosper and thrive is a question vital to every German and every American.

The Western camp cannot afford division. Berlin poses for the United States the greatest dilemma in its history. The ordeal ahead, for us and for Western Europe, will be long and perilous. Soviet actions will test to the fullest our nerve, will power, intelligence and determination. To survive, Europe and the United States must stand united as never before. Together, their power, if wisely applied, is more than enough to meet the Soviet challenge. But if they are divided, or show lack of determination, there is a grave danger of a Soviet miscalculation and a stumbling into war over Berlin.

—JOHN RICH

JOHN RICH, NBC News Correspondent in Berlin until March, 1961, lived two hundred yards from the Soviet zone while covering the divided city. Previously he had come into direct contact with the Communists as a reporter through assignments to two other divided countries, Korea and Indo-China. Born in Maine, he was graduated from Bowdoin in 1939 and promptly entered newspaper work as a reporter for newspapers in Augusta and Portland. During the Second World War, he attended a Navy Japanese language school which led to postwar assignment in the Far East for the International News Service. He joined the NBC News staff in December, 1950, to help cover the Korean war. In September, 1954, he received a Council on Foreign Relations resident fellowship in New York. Rejoining the NBC News staff the following year, he covered the revolution that overthrew Juan Perón in Argentina and later was named NBC News chief in Germany. He now is bureau chief in Paris.

# 5.

## ITALY:

## *"Two Countries"*

SOON after the war," recalled a reporter friend who works for the *Corriere della Sera,* "the courtyard of our publishing plant in Milan was full of bicycles owned by members of the staff. Several years later Lambretta and Vespa motorscooters took the place of the bicycles. Now we are building an underground garage to accommodate all the *Seicento* [small Fiat] cars owned by people working on the newspaper. The growth from bicycles to motorscooters to cars is the story of Italy's recovery from the war."

Like any generality, the Italian reporter's is only partly true. Milan is in Italy's prosperous North where living standards and income are enormously greater than in the South. The *Corriere della Sera* is Italy's best newspaper, not only in its editorial content, but in wages paid to its staff. Furthermore, a great many Italians have neither Fiat cars, Vespa scooters nor bicycles. Some do not own a pair of shoes.

The fact is, though, that Italy has made a remarkable recovery since the end of the war. Nineteen forty-five found Italy near moral and financial bankruptcy. The catastrophic collapse of Mussolini's Fascism, in which so many Italians believed, disillusioned an entire generation. The country suffered extensive damage to buildings, to its architectural treasures, its transportation and communications facilities. Industrial capacity, too, was hard hit, but well-organized partisan defensive action saved many factories of the industrial North from even greater damage in the final days of the German evacuation. Inflation was rampant. The cost-of-living index, with 100 as the base figure for 1938, rose by January 1946 to 2,781 and almost doubled within two years after that. Furthermore, the loss of Italy's colonies in Africa meant the return of thousands of Italians to a land which could not feed or employ its resident population.

Italy, always divided by regional loyalties and jealousies, now was further cleft by distrust between factions that fought a civil war in the last months of World War II. More Italians were killed in the eighteen months from Italy's surrender (September 3, 1943) until the Italian peninsula was rid of Nazi troops than in all the preceding months of battle. This war by the partisans against Germans and against those Italians who remained loyal to Mussolini was terribly costly in human life.

A fact which has greatly influenced Italy's postwar history is that many (and perhaps most) of the partisans who took up arms against Mussolini and against the Nazis in their bitterly fought retreat up the Italian peninsula were Communists. Whatever else may be said to deprecate them, Italy's Communists did have the strength of conviction and the courage to risk their lives against the Germans. (The Communists also had the cynicism to accept in their ranks large numbers of active and unscrupulous Fascists who saw in the Communist Party an asylum from retribution for their past actions. As their part of the bargain the Communists obtained an experienced cadre which had been running many of the country's activities for the Fascists and would now be ready to do so for the Communists.)

A truth to be constantly borne in mind in understanding the Italian situation then and now is that at the end of the war the Communists were respectable and respected by many Italians. Criticism in retrospect can be heard against the United States for including Communists in town and city governments at the war's end. As an occupying power, the United States had considerable option in choosing those who would participate in power. After its surrender in 1943, Italy joined the Allied side, declaring war on Germany, and this required America to take Italian opinion into account in the selection of pre-election officials. Even if it had been the American desire at that time (which it was not) to exclude Communists, it would have been difficult to do so.

The fall of Fascism left a considerable political vacuum in Italy. It is fruitless to argue whether or not all or most or any Italians were Fascists. For many, that was all there was—Fascism. Those of other political opinion had to operate underground. A forty-three-year-old Italian schoolteacher who grew up during the twenty years of Fascism expressed it this way to me:

"I was twenty-four and a second lieutenant when I was captured by the French in North Africa. Up to that time, more or less, we were Fascists. Not because we were convinced Fascists, but because we were raised in that doctrine and we didn't care too much. You know—at that age you are more interested in girls than in politics. But the fact is that as soon as we entered school at six years of age we started being soaked with Fascist doctrine. Even without realizing it—soon you *are* a Fascist. I spent fifteen years of my education in Fascist schools. Even at the university we were taught Fascist doctrines, we were told that Italy had a great destiny, that we inherited the glory of ancient Rome, that we were dominators of the Mediterranean Sea, that we were chained in the Mediterranean by England and so on.

"This was what we were taught for fifteen years, especially in liberal arts studies. Perhaps it was different for an engineer or a doctor, because there isn't a Fascist medicine or a Fascist engineering. But in philosophy, literature and history we were constantly influenced. Our teachers were all Fascists. In the University of Rome my main professor was Giovanni Gentile, the greatest philosopher of the Fascist Party. I attended his lessons for four years, three times a week, and you know—if you are taught three times a week on the basis of the theory of the superman, of the Latin hero, and so on, the typical idealism of Giovanni Gentile, of course you become— maybe not a Fascist—but an influenced man. At that time the Fascist Party was a matter of fact for us. When we heard our parents or people of our parents' generation speaking of the pre-Fascist period we hardly believed them, we almost thought of something prehistoric, because for us political life was just Fascism."

The vacuum left by the fall of Fascism was not easily filled by other Italian institutions. The Catholic Church, in a land whose population is more than 99 per cent Catholic, had lost prestige under Fascism. The church was not without the taint of collaboration with Mussolini. Leading church figures threw the weight of their considerable influence behind Il Duce and his anti-democratic regime. A typical example was a speech in March, 1923, by the Archbishop of Messina on the occasion of assuming his new diocese. He declared, "I feel it my duty to send my greetings also to him who is leading Italy along the right road, to him who is imbuing the Nation with new vigor—I mean, to the Head of the Government." Whether or not this endorsement had papal blessing, Pope Pius XI himself spoke approvingly of the Fascists for reintroducing Christian teaching into the primary schools, for ensuring the success of religious pilgrimages and, when an assassination plot on

Mussolini's life was nipped in the bud, the Pope publicly expressed his satisfaction. The most striking endorsement of Mussolini by Pope Pius XI was his statement on February 13, 1929, to faculty and students at the University of the Sacred Heart. The Pope said that the Fascist leader was "the man sent to us by Providence" who fortunately did not have the "preconceptions of liberalism."

A noted historian, A. C. Jemolo, Professor of Ecclesiastical Law at the University of Rome, has described the impact of these papal words: "In every quarter of the Catholic world the refrain was taken up, and Mussolini was hailed as the man who had restored not only social order, but religious and moral values." The Vatican's enthusiasm for Mussolini waned during the final years of Pius XI and under Pius XII as Mussolini's reckless adventures spread. The Vatican provided a haven for refugees from persecution and assisted them in escaping. Nevertheless, the end of the war found Italy's historical anticlerical sentiment on the increase and the Vatican's political potential diminished, at least temporarily.

Another foundation block of the Italian nation had crumbled during the war. The monarchy had fallen into disrepute through its questionable role during the Fascist regime. It was at the invitation of the King that Mussolini had taken over the Government on October 28, 1922. The King had accepted the title of Emperor from Mussolini after the disgraceful conquest of Abyssinia. Yet, after the war, King Vittorio Emanuele III tried to disassociate himself from responsibility, declaring that he, as the monarch, was not accountable for the actions of his ministers. Finally under pressure of public opinion the King resigned in favor of his son, forty-two-year-old Umberto II. Umberto reigned for only 34 days. In what must rank as one of the most politically inept tactics of the era, Umberto, instead of seeking popular sympathy, tried to shift responsibility for Fascism onto the Italian people. Umberto declared in a newspaper interview that popular approval for Fascism had made it impossible for his father to oppose Mussolini's rise to power. This unwise attack only provided ammunition for those Italians who hoped to cleanse their consciences by shifting blame for military and moral disaster to the monarchy.

On June second and third, 1946, a national referendum was held to decide whether to retain the monarchy. The vote was close, and charges still are heard that the count was dishonestly manipulated against the monarchy. Twelve million Italians cast their votes in favor of abolishing the throne and establishing a republic. Ten million voted to retain the King. To be precise, the figures were 12,718,641 votes to 10,718,502. In southern Italy and on the islands of Sicily and Sardinia a big majority of votes were cast in favor of the King. It was a further manifestation of the deep cleavages that complicate Italian political life.

In this political vacuum left by the total collapse of Fascism, the abolition of the crown, and the partial discrediting of the Church, an elected assembly met to draw up a constitution. The document's lofty phrases promised more than has been achieved in practice. For example, the constitution guaranteed each Italian child eight years of education, but in many parts of Italy there are facilities for only five years or less. The constitution forbade the rebirth of the Fascist Party, but Italy has a small but frankly Fascist Party today under another name.

In April of 1948, the first parliamentary elections of the young Italian Republic were held. There was great fear that the Communists would come to power through the ballot box. They had acted swiftly to try to capture control of Italian co-operatives and labor unions (underground organization in which they had been active during Mussolini's rule). The Communists had formed many of their adherents into an underground army that threatened to seize power if they did not win at the polls. The Communists had acquired important allies in the Socialists led by Italy's respected anti-Fascist, Pietro Nenni.

In a blatant and highly successful example of interference in another nation's internal affairs, the United States acted decisively.

The United States Government under President Truman moved on a number of fronts. The first ships carrying food under the Marshall Plan arrived with the bags and crates clearly marked as gifts of the U.S.A.; there was great fanfare, including a speech by the American ambassador, and many photographs in the non-Communist press. A State Department announcement warned that Italians who were known to vote Communist would forfeit any chance of being admitted to the United States; it was the dream of at least every other Italian to emigrate to America. Gold taken from Italy by the Nazis was returned with appropriate publicity. Twenty-nine American merchant ships were given to Italy as an outright gift. Britain and France joined with the United States in proposing to Russia that the former Italian port of Trieste at the head of the Adriatic Sea be returned to Italy. Under the peace treaty with Italy, Trieste had been taken away from the Italians and made a "free city." All Italians, regardless of political attachment, were Italians first, and fervent nationalistic feelings had been stirred by the loss of Trieste. The U. S.-British-French proposal was designed to embarrass the Communists. Communist Yugoslavia also laid claims to Trieste, and if it could not belong to Yugoslavia, the Yugoslavs at least did not want it to belong to Italy. Russia could not very well agree to the American proposal without betraying her Yugoslav ally, and by failing to agree, Russia alienated large numbers of patriotic Italians who might have intended to vote Communist.

More important than these moves on the official level was a campaign organized on a people-to-people level. Encouraged by Washington, Americans of Italian descent sent an estimated ten million letters, post cards and radiograms to relatives and friends in every city and mountain hamlet in Italy, urging them not to vote Communist. To many Italian peasants in villages which are not even serviced by a road, the arrival of a letter from Rome is a notable event. A cablegram from America was like a thunderbolt command from heaven.

There were other forces brought into play against the Communist challenge at the polls. Many wealthy Italian families had dirtied their hands by dabbling in politics with the Fascists; at the end of the war they sought only political obscurity. Now they re-entered the Italian political scene with big donations in an effort to protect their privileged status by defeating the Communists. Estimates published at the time stated that anti-Communist parties spent seven dollars for placards, sound trucks and advertisements for every one dollar spent by the Communists.

The Communist challenge forced political mavericks and individualists, who abound in Italy, to join hands against the common danger. There were about 300 separate political parties along the length of the Italian peninsula. Many of these abandoned their individual campaigns to join forces with the Christian Democrats. They had only one thing in common—their fear of Communism coming to power.

Another factor that worked against the Communists was that women had been given the right to vote for the first time at the end of the war. The Church, which had been working relentlessly and successfully to restore its prestige in the five years since Italy's surrender, has its greatest political influence among women in Italy. The Catholic Church supported the Christian Democrats in the 1948 elections without reservation, although it was a frank violation of the Italian electoral law forbidding the Church to mix in politics. The Pope warned that Catholics who voted Communist would be denied absolution; that is, their sins would not be forgiven at confession and their entrance to heaven thus jeopardized eternally. Priests delivered sermons instructing their flocks to vote for the Christian Democrats. The slogan was circulated: STALIN WON'T KNOW HOW YOU VOTED, BUT GOD WILL. The Catholic Action organization was busy throughout Italy with energetic young men exhorting people to vote against the Communists, making door-to-door visits, passing out pamphlets, delivering speeches. On election day Catholic Action members (as did the Communists) got out the vote by carrying voters to the polls by bicycle and car.

Italy's 1948 election was a crucial event in postwar Europe. In retrospect most parties agree that it was American intervention which turned the tide. Others say that the election was lost by the Communists in the confessionals; that the Church succeeded in tapping the intrinsically deep religious heritage of many Italians. By picturing the Communists as the anti-Christs, by invoking Hell's fire and excommunication, the Church swung the pendulum. In some public schools during the hour a week set aside for religious instruction, priests told children that their families would be condemned to Hell if their parents voted Communist. Nuns in trucks distributed Christian Democratic pamphlets in some towns. In some backward, illiterate areas the symbol of the Christian Democratic Party—founded by a priest—was enough to ensure that a pious peasant would vote for it. The Party's symbol is a cross emblazoned on a shield. The monologue of a peasant woman in Sicily is recorded by the English writer, Gavin Maxwell, in his fine book *The Ten Pains of Death*.

"Who carried the cross? Was it not Jesus Christ—so who should we vote for? The cross bears us to heaven. Who does Padre Pietro tell us to vote for? Always for the cross, for God knows how to reward us. My mother, too, paralyzed as she is—they carry her to vote, and I go into the room where you vote, and I put the sign for her, on the shield with the cross. I am not double-faced with God, I do not betray him. Certainly all of us make mistakes, and even in this party there are men who make them, but God looks after them. High-ups promise us a lot of things, make us hope, deceive us, and then give us nothing—but that isn't to say that one shouldn't vote for God. There's many priests in the Christian Democratic Party, and there's the Pope himself, too, and how can these make mistakes?"

The Communists were turned back at the gates of power by many of the very methods and with the same energy that too often are considered exclusively Communist traits. It may be that the Communist threat had been overestimated in the first place. In any event, the ballot count gave the Christian Democrats an absolute majority with 307 seats in parliament; the Communist Party and its Nenni Socialist allies won 182. This was the high point of Christian Democratic strength. Alcide De Gasperi, a man of political experience and a former Vatican librarian (a post more important than the title connotes) was confirmed by parliament in May, 1948, as Prime Minister, a post he had held provisionally since December, 1945. De Gasperi governed with consummate skill, with great courage and high principle until August, 1953—shortly before his death. At first De Gasperi's cabinet included both the Communist leader Palmiro Togliatti and Socialist Pietro Nenni. In all, he governed over eight different coalition governments, often maintaining a precariously balanced Center coalition only by virtue of his great skill and towering personality. Much of De Gasperi's energies had to be directed into getting the country on its economic feet and crushing the Communist Party's militant maneuvers. There was little opportunity to undertake the vast social reforms urgently needed. Unfortunately, a leader of De Gasperi's caliber has not emerged since his death.

Since the crucial election of 1948, Italy's economic prosperity has grown steadily and, at the advent of the 1960's, even

spectacularly. It is remarkable that a country that has virtually
no coal or iron ore resources to speak of has become an
important steel producer. Italy has become a significant industrial nation. The names of Alfa Romeo and Ferrari and Ma-
serati are respected, and their designs have influenced Detroit.
Olivetti is known as the International Business Machines of
Europe, and its office equipment is exported beyond Europe's
frontiers, too. The Necchi sewing machine is giving competition to the long-established and world-wide Singer. Under the
leadership of Enrico Mattei, a dedicated if somewhat dictatorial and controversial figure, natural gas has been discovered on the Italian peninsula, bestowing on Italy for the
first time a domestic source of power other than hydroelectric
power. With reconstruction came a greater influx of tourists
than this country has ever known in its two thousand years as
a magnet to foreign travelers.

Articles have been written about the "miracle" of the
Italian recovery. The miracle is part mirage. The Italian
economy has been expanding at the rate of 6 per cent per
year, but this expansion is concentrated in the north, and, as
a matter of fact, in only three regions of the north—the Milan
area, Piedmont Province and the Po River Valley. Statistics
show that Italy's national income has doubled in the past ten
years, but this, too, is largely a monopoly of the north, and
concentrated in relatively few hands. Italy's unemployment
has dropped in recent years from 10 per cent to 6 per cent
of the labor force. However, besides the nearly 1,600,000
chronically unemployed workers, at least an equal number
are only partially employed or seasonally unemployed.

One needs only to visit the western part of Sicily, as I
have done, to appreciate that over-all statistics are meaningless. This is more Africa than Western Europe. Next to a
visit, Sicily can best be comprehended by reading one of the
books of Danilo Dolci (an architect from the north who traveled to Sicily to study the ruins of Greek temples and stayed

as a self-appointed missionary to try to raise living standards). In his book *Outlaws,* Dolci examined the cases of 350 men whose cumulative time in prison was 3,000 years, but whose cumulative time in school was only 650 years—less than two years each on the average. Describing Partinico, where he now lives, Dolci writes of this admittedly extreme example of indigence:

A day laborer's wage for a ten-hour day is now from 500 to 600 lire [80 to 95 cents]; but there is only work for about six months in a year. The employers frequently avoid paying either health or insurance contributions. . . .

Rubbish is deposited, especially in the back streets, in large heaps always covered with flies. In many households, excrement and waste water run out onto the streets. . . .

The post office is dirty and inadequate and has only three windows. There are often so many people waiting to be served that the police have to be called to control the crowd. . . .

There are no public baths or washhouses where women do their household washing. A tiny stream is used by the women of one quarter for this purpose. The water comes from the slaughter-house, where it is used to clean out the carcasses of the animals. . . .

The inequities in the Italian economy help to explain the single most important fact in Italy today. That fact is that the Communists are numerically as strong today (in fact, a bit stronger) than they were in Italy's major moment of crisis in 1948. Italy's Communist Party is the largest in Western Europe. Actually, it is the largest on this side of the Iron Curtain, numbering almost 2,000,000 members. Of 596 seats in Italy's Chamber of Deputies, 140 are occupied by Communists, and 84 by Nenni Socialists who usually vote with them, for a total of 224 seats. The Christian Democrats hold 273 seats and need the support of other parties for a governing majority; to their embarrassment, the Christian Democrats for a time accepted support of the Neo-Fascist Party.

Italy stands as a revealing rebuttal to the thesis that Com-

munism automatically withers when a country prospers. This
has not proven true in Italy, in part because a thin, top segment of the population has benefited disproportionately from
Italy's economic prosperity.

Communism's chronic grip on a significant portion of
Italian voters is the main problem confronting the future
of Italian democracy and hence must be President John F.
Kennedy's main concern in Italy. It is a phenomenon which
should be examined, analyzed and corrected if possible.

There are a number of reasons for Communism's persistent
strength beyond the main one of disequilibrium in the distribution of the fruits of prosperity. The reasons vary from
area to area as indeed does Communist numerical strength.
A map of the former states ruled over by the Pope would,
if laid over a map of Italy, coincide to a great extent with the
regions of greatest Communist strength. This is clear evidence of the role of anticlericalism in Italy's voting pattern.
Although Italy is predominantly Catholic, many practice
their religion, if at all, only in the rites of baptism, marriage
and death. Many passionately believe that the Church should
stay out of politics. They resent the efforts of the Church
to influence elections through pastoral letters, visits by priests
to homes, and guidance from the pulpit. Under Pope John
XXIII, overt interference by the Church has diminished.
This is partially an appreciation of the fact that the Church
was alienating potential Christian Democratic votes by too-
candid campaigning. It is in part, too, responsive to the wishes
of the other Center parties on which the Christian Democrats
must depend to maintain a majority in parliament. Should
any of these parties withdraw support from the Christian
Democrats on the issue of clerical mixing in politics, the
Christian Democrats might fall and default their leadership
to the left.

The Communists actually govern a number of Italian

cities, the largest being Bologna, a city of splendid towers that were built three centuries before Columbus' voyage. Bologna's population of almost half a million has consistently voted a predominantly Communist city council and mayor into office at every election since the end of the war. It is particularly surprising since Bologna was a center of Fascist strength in another era. Students of the Bolognese character (friendly, gullible, gregarious, lovers of good living and good if greasy food, and above all, a tendency toward extremes) attribute in part the electorate's swing from Fascism to Communism to the Bolognese violent, volatile nature.

Besides Bologna's anticlericalism, its penchant for extremes, and the fact that Communists quickly gained control of labor unions and co-operatives, it votes for Communists because they have run an efficient and relatively uncorrupt administration. Another reason for Communist strength in Bologna and other areas lies in inactivity and lack of sufficient accomplishment by the Christian Democratic governments in the capital, Rome.

It has been said by one historian that "the real genius of Italy consists in an infinite capacity for avoiding action in the face of history." Italian legislative bodies confirm this. Few meaningful laws have been passed (and fewer enforced) to correct social injustices that make Italy a country of class consciousness and class privilege. A land reform law has only partially corrected Italy's medieval system of agriculture; estates are either so large that absentee landlordism prevails, or parcels of land are so small that those working them cannot make a living. Italy's agriculture is largely primitive, inefficient and costly, partially because much of the mountainous country is unsuitable for mechanized farming. In the United States, one farmer feeds twenty-four people. In the Soviet Union, one farmer feeds five people. In Italy, one farmer feeds only three people. In many areas of Italy, the Bologna region among them, Communism's main strength comes not from industrial workers, but from farmers.

The durable strength of the Communists in Italy does not mean that Italians are pro-Russian. It does not even indicate that those who vote under the symbol of the hammer and sickle necessarily believe in Communism. Neither does it indicate that Italians are anti-American. As a matter of fact, in no other country of Western Europe, with the possible exception of Denmark, are Americans more warmly welcomed, liked and well treated. What is more, few people in the world are as individualistic, as resistant to regimentation, as are the Italians. Despite a history in which oppressive systems and leaders constantly recur, the Italian spirit craves respect for the individual's freedom.

A number of Italians who consistently vote Communist have told me that they do not want to see Italy *go* Communist. Why then do they vote Communist? The answer is peculiarly Italian, reflecting a lack of confidence in the nation's leaders, a skepticism and a suspicion of Government: "Only by having a strong Communist Party keeping a knife at their backs," a factory worker in Milan explained to me, "will the Christian Democrats move. The only advances achieved by industrial workers since the war have been achieved by Communist pressure kept on the Government."

The Communist Party has become more than the party of pressure. It is *the* party of protest. Almost alone of the ten political parties represented in parliament, the Communists, through their newspapers and speeches, consistently accuse, expose, chide and scold the authorities. Of a dozen daily newspapers in Rome, almost all of which are published by one or another political party, only *L'Unità,* the Communist Party organ, reported regularly on one typical series of strikes including shipyard workers in Trieste, tax office employees in Rome, and lead miners on the island of Sardinia.

The Communists have retained their grip partially by default—default on the part of the Christian Democrats to produce leaders. Since the death of former Premier Alcide De Gasperi, Italy has lacked inspired, forceful, effective leadership. The names of Fanfani, Segni, Scelba, Piccioni, Andreotti and Tambroni are scarcely known outside of Italy and are unlikely to electrify even fellow Italians.

The lack of leadership is a heritage of the Fascist period when development of leaders was stunted. Also, Italy's electoral system of proportional representation encourages every variety of political opinion to form a party, and it is thus difficult for any single party to achieve a parliamentary majority. This imposes on a prime minister the need to collaborate with, and concede to, other political parties in order to survive a parliamentary vote of confidence. Political programs are watered down to satisfy collaborating politicians. In fact, on at least one occasion an Italian premier (Fernando Tambroni in 1960) solemnly solicited votes by pledging, in effect, that he would do *nothing* if confirmed by the parliament. This carried to the ultimate absurdity the obligation of Italian premiers to satisfy a large spectrum of political opinion in order to stay in office. Under these conditions it is no wonder that Italy's young republic has had no fewer than ten premiers since its founding in 1948. In addition, De Gasperi ruled over eight successive coalitions.

Furthermore, the largest party (and the party which has controlled all governments since the end of the war) is really not a cohesive political entity. Christian Democrats have only three things in common: they are Catholic; they are anti-Communist; they want to stay in power. This is unpromising soil for sowing a harvest of political action.

It is not surprising that such a heterogeneous party should be divided within itself. There are influential members among the Christian Democratic Party leadership who favor association with the Neo-Fascists. There are those who

favor a much-discussed "opening to the left"—that is, coalition with the left-wing Socialists of Pietro Nenni. In
its brief history of postwar government, the Christian Democrats have been at times affiliated with the Communists and
at other times with the Fascists. A Christian Democratic premier's elbow room for action is restricted by the need to keep
the collaborating parties of the moment from defecting, by
the need to keep his own party from fragmenting, and by the
desire to retain the Vatican's approval.

There is little the United States can do at this point beyond
subtly and diplomatically making it known that it sympathizes
with the more liberal elements in Italian politics, in particular with the Center and Left of the Christian Democratic
Party, which favors reforms and social progress.

Strong American support should be manifested, too, for
non-Communist labor unions. Italian unions lack both money
and fundamental legislation similar to the Wagner Act
which would facilitate effective action (such as protracted
strikes) to improve labor's lot.

The United States is unfairly blamed for including the
Communists in postwar administrations; U. S. policy simply
recognized the context of affairs. The United States is unfairly
blamed for interfering in Italian domestic politics in the 1948
elections; it was justified in bringing its full wealth, power
and influence to bear to save Italy from Communist control.

United States policy, however, can be blamed in part for
the fact that the Communists have retained their immense
numerical strength in Italy. American aid to Italy since the
end of the war has totaled more than five billion dollars. That
aid should have carried with it an immeasurable quantity of
influence on Italy's leaders to oblige them to correct the causes
that motivate people to vote Communist.

In announcing his aid program for Latin America, President John F. Kennedy has made it abundantly clear that

basic economic and social reforms must take place to ensure that the poor as well as the rich benefit from the fruits of American aid. It is unfortunate that a similar requirement was not applied stringently enough to Italy. Surely, it should have been. The circumstances were such that the United States could have imposed almost any conditions it wished on its aid in the early days after World War II. Italy was a defeated, occupied country completely dependent on the humaneness and generosity of the United States for its food and well being. It was considered contrary to our philosophy to impose conditions on American aid that might be considered interference in the internal affairs of another nation. Nevertheless, the United States did intervene with notable success, as has been pointed out, in the elections of 1948. By not interfering effectively enough to see that our aid was applied in a sufficiently equitable manner, the United States has, in a sense, contributed to Communist strength in Italy.

The futility of aid without adequate action was recognized by President Kennedy when he declared in June, 1961: "We do not intend to go on indefinitely helping those who will not help themselves—those whose only claim to consideration is that they are alternatives to Communism—those who are unwilling to put into effect the reforms in administration, education, taxation and social justice without which our aid will be of very little value." Although the criticism implied in these words is overly strong when applied to Italy, the shoe does fit in some respects.

The Italian tax system, for example, is regressive, favoring the rich. Taxes are only halfheartedly collected. It is a game between taxpayer and tax collector. The taxpayer submits an income figure much lower than his actual income. The tax collector challenges it. They argue, and bargain, and settle on a mutually satisfactory sum that may bear no relation to the man's true income. The more prosperous the Italian, the more likely he is to benefit from the national game of tax evasion. The national legislature, with its Right and Center deputies representing largely business, landowning and professional classes, has never manifested sufficient principle to pass a truly equitable and effective tax law or to see to it that the laws on the books are enforced. The United States has exerted some pressures. At a luncheon some years ago attended by members of the Italian Government, aid administrator James D. Zellerbach (later ambassador) surprised his audience by picking up a piece of bread from the table and pointing out that, under Italy's complicated tax structure, there were several score of different taxes on it. The Italian leaders considered it in questionable taste for Mr. Zellerbach to criticize them in public, but in any event, nothing important was done to rectify the tax situation.

Inequities in the Italian social system are many. It is extremely difficult for a young person without means to receive more than five years of education in Italy, and college is usually limited to the wealthy or privileged. In Italian bureaucracy—tax offices, post offices, police stations—the foreign visitor or a person whose clothes and bearing indicate that he has social position are dealt with courteously, but the ordinary citizen often gets brusque treatment. Nepotism frequently is practiced in hiring. The class consciousness of the country is demonstrated by a reverence for titles. The constitution prescribes that "titles of nobility are not recognized." The monarchy is dead, but the titles of *principe* (prince), *marchesa* (marquise), and others, whether originating from the Vatican or from the former Italian throne, evoke an obedient reaction from Italians. A man who has any university degree usually insists on his prerogative to be addressed as *Dottore* (doctor). Even a high school trained bookkeeper is entitled to be known by the title of his profession, *Ragioniere* (bookkeeper), and he may well resent anyone who addresses him as ordinary *signore* (mister).

Now it will be difficult for the United States to influence

social and economic reforms. Italy is less dependent on the
United States, and hence less responsive to urgings that injustices be rectified by legislation as the price of American
aid. Moreover, with the passage of time and the development
of the struggle between the United States and Russia, America has become dependent on Italy.

America's dependence is in terms of military bases. The
United States has ground, air or sea forces situated in cities
with such evocative names as Verona, Vicenza, Leghorn,
Udine, Naples, Catania and Taranto. Near Taranto we have
our first missile platforms on the European continent. Italy
was the first ally to agree to the stationing of American missiles on its soil despite threatening words from Moscow that
such bases would make Italy a prime target for Soviet nuclear
missiles in a war. This is just one of many co-operative acts
on the part of Italy, the most co-operative member of the
American alliance. It is a paradox that Italy, the country
with the largest Communist Party in the Western community,
should be the most willing to do its share in the Western
alliance. Partly this is explained by the peculiarly unrevolu-
tionary Italian character of Italy's Communist Party. Partly
it is due to the recognition by Communist leaders of Italian
affection for the United States (where more than 4,500,000
persons born in Italy or of Italian parentage live). Partly it is
attributable to a regard for the lira. Although a main theme
of Soviet foreign policy for many years has been the dismem-
berment of American overseas bases, Italy's Communists were
never able—and in fact, never really tried—to mount a demonstration of impressive numbers against the stationing of
American rockets on Italian soil. No mobs howling "Italia,
si; America, no" march the streets of Italy. The dollars ex-
pended by the United States in the construction, manning
and servicing of its bases go indiscriminately into Italian
Communist as well as Christian Democrat pockets. Even
Palmiro Togliatti, the cultivated and genial chairman of

Italy's Communist Party, recognizes that a reduction in bases means a reduction in income and an increase in unemployment. Italy's workers recognize this also, and Togliatti does not too fervently advocate dismantling the bases, because he would risk dismantling votes for his party.

A problem that confronts the Kennedy Administration as military bases become less imperative, as the result of economy considerations or technological development, is the impact dismantling will have on the economies of countries like Italy. Even a small diminution in national income has a magnified effect on unemployment.

One of Italy's principal ways of dealing with her chronic unemployment is by encouraging emigration. Although Italy's present birth rate is less than that of the United States, Italy is an overpopulated country. With an area about three-quarters the size of the state of California, Italy has four times as many people. Italy's population of fifty million lives on a peninsula and two major islands (Sicily and Sardinia), which are mainly mountainous and not arable. (It is said that before undertaking his campaign into Italy, Napoleon crumbled a sheet of paper in his hand to demonstrate the terrain to his officers.)

The priority the Italian Government attaches to emigration as a means of solving Italy's overpopulation and underemployment problems is demonstrated by the fact that Italy has two deputy foreign ministers. One deals exclusively with emigration matters. The second deals with the vast array of other matters that concern a foreign ministry.

It is something of a national disgrace for a nation to cope with a problem involving its people by trying to get rid of those people. It is defeatist, unnationalistic, and, in many cases, inhumane. But there it is. Italians who choose to emigrate to new lands usually list the United States as their first choice. Most must be satisfied, however, to go to Australia, Venezuela or Canada. The quota set by the United States at the present time is only 5,666 Italians each year. Including Italian wives and children of Americans who are exempt from quota limitations, a total of 9,353 Italians emigrated to the U. S. A. in 1960. There are many tens of thousands of Italians waiting for permission to emigrate to the United States. Some have been waiting for a decade or more. One of the decisions with which President Kennedy will be confronted in his relations with Italy is whether or not to propose to Congress to raise the quotas. The pressures and pleas from Italy will be constant. Admission of greater numbers of Italians annually would conform with American tradition and would contribute to a solution of Italy's economic problems. But in this era of population explosion a government's first duty is to its present citizens and future generations. Also, the United States finds itself in a new situation of hard-core unemployment caused not by recession but by technological progress. Under these conditions the Kennedy Administration must regretfully withstand Italian pressures for more generous immigration quotas, and open the door perhaps not more than a crack wider.

In speaking of American relations with Rome, there really are two countries involved. There is the Italian Government and there is the Vatican. The United States has had no formal diplomatic contact with the Pope except for a period during World War II when Franklin D. Roosevelt named Myron C. Taylor as "personal representative of the President to His Holiness Pope Pius XII." The American Embassy in Rome, on a personal basis, has usually maintained informal and unpublicized contact with the Holy See (a word derived from *sede,* meaning "seat" or "throne" of a bishop). The U. S. Embassy's contact has largely been at diplomatic parties and receptions. The principle of separation of church and state, American wariness toward a suspected papal predilection for interfering in a nation's affairs, the influence of some religious organizations and of the Masons and even the Ku Klux Klan, have all operated against the establishment of diplomatic relations with the Vatican.

Because he is America's first Catholic President, Mr. Kennedy naturally bends over backwards to demonstrate to critics that he is not influenced by the Pope. It may be that President Kennedy is bending over backwards too far and looking somewhat ridiculous as a result of this posture. For example, when W. Averell Harriman came to Europe on his first mission as the President's roving ambassador, he meticulously avoided an audience with the Pope. He was conspicuous by his absence from the Vatican. Almost without exception, and regardless of religious affiliation, government statesmen visiting Rome are received by the Pope. This is arranged by the visitor out of respect, tradition, curiosity or good politics back home, in the case of countries with important Catholic populations. Ambassador Harriman made it clear from the moment he stepped off the plane that he would have no time in his schedule for a trip across town to the Vatican. The fact is Mr. Harriman had plenty of time for a long news conference, a longer briefing session with American correspondents, a dinner with Italian business figures, conferences with relatively minor personalities in Italian political life. It became clear from Mr. Harriman's more private and franker utterances that he was avoiding the Vatican because of fear of political repercussions back home. It was felt by Mr. Harriman that the narrowness of President Kennedy's victory in the election was due to religious prejudice, especially in the Bible Belt of the Middle West. A visit to the Pope by a Kennedy representative so early in the new administration might only feed those bigotries, injure the President's popularity, and raise new and avoidable issues.

Whatever the merits of Averell Harriman's decision, the question of whether or not the United States should have diplomatic representation at the Vatican should be decided not on political expediency but on the basis of national self-interest. There are persuasive arguments in favor of the point of view that the United States should establish diplomatic relations with the Holy See.

About fifty nations have embassies or legations at the Holy See. Among them are countries with big Catholic populations such as France, Spain, Austria, Argentina and Portugal. But also Great Britain, Japan, India, Iran, Indonesia and Pakistan maintain representatives at the Vatican. The reasons which make it worthwhile for these countries to maintain diplomats at the Court of St. Peter's and the reasons which made it expedient for the United States to send Myron Taylor to the Vatican apply, too, in the case of the United States today.

The Vatican is a unique institution, an institution which has survived for nineteen centuries, an institution which is the spiritual center (to greater or lesser degree) for almost a half-billion people of every race and color. Through its bishops and diplomatic representatives stationed in foreign lands, and through visits paid to the Pope by representatives of every sort from many lands, the Vatican is in an advantageous position for gathering information and for evaluating trends and events. It can be argued that an American ambassador can obtain whatever information a papal nuncio (Vatican diplomat) has access to in any capital simply by personal contact with that nuncio. It is, after all, common for diplomats of friendly powers stationed in a capital to exchange information. However, this is not the same as being privy to information at the center, the Vatican, where the data is correlated with information from bishops and other sources, and evaluated.

The principal value of representation at the Holy See is to have a formal avenue of communications for explaining to the Pope and his organization American policies, ideas and objectives so that these can be taken into account by the Vatican in its pronouncements and actions.

The values of diplomatic representation at the Vatican can be overstated. Neither an ambassador at the Holy See nor a papal nuncio in Washington is likely to contribute much to America's grave international problems. But diplomatic recognition should not be based on prejudices, on approval of a state's morality or religion, or on domestic political emotions. The question of American representation at the Vatican should be settled by the simple yardstick of American self-interest. It will be particularly difficult for the Kennedy Administration to do this, because Mr. Kennedy is a Catholic. But it should be done.

The Italian peninsula and the island of Sicily jut down into the incredibly blue Mediterranean, reaching almost to the shores of Africa and splitting the Mediterranean nearly into halves. The ancient Romans called it *Mare Nostrum* ("Our Sea"), and indeed the Roman Empire included the entire shoreline of the Mediterranean. It is a great instructional thrill to travel in this area and find impressive evidence still remaining of the Roman civilization that enveloped the Mediterranean basin. At the eastern end of the sea the Romans established a capital at Constantinople (now Istanbul) to rule that part of their empire. There, as well as at the western terminus in Spain, can still be seen the remnants of the baths and the temples that the Romans built so well.

Mussolini aspired with a pomp that lacked power to reconstitute the glory of the days when Rome was truly the capital of the civilized world. He thought and taught that the Mediterranean was an "Italian lake."

The Italian desire for Mediterranean empire motivated the Government in September, 1911, to send an expeditionary force to annex Libya from the Arabs. One pretext for the war (besides the need to assert the Italian nation's virility) was that it would provide a place for Italy's surplus population. However, Italians resisted emigrating to that arid, hot region with a soil even less productive than the southern parts of Italy they were asked to leave. For every Italian who emigrated to Italy's African colonies of Libya, Somaliland (now Somalia), Abyssinia (now Ethiopia), and Eritrea, forty Italians went to the United States.

Even today, Italians consider themselves more Mediterranean than European. Italian officials have told me that they believe history and geographic position endow them with a special status to have their voices heard in the affairs of the region. This view is not always shared by other nations of the Mediterranean.

At the present time, Italy's Mediterranean "expansionism" finds expression largely in trade and particularly in the activities of *Ente Nazionale Idrocarburi,* the State Oil and Energy Monopoly. ENI (as it is usually referred to) is a state-operated enterprise that has obtained various oil rights—exploration, drilling, refining, distribution—in a number of countries. Around the Mediterranean these include Morocco, Tunisia, Libya, Egypt, Lebanon, Greece and Spain. ENI has also reached into the Sudan, Ethiopia, Somalia, Iran, Austria, Germany, Switzerland and Panama with its aggressive commercial empire. At the end of World War II, Enrico Mattei was commissioned by parliament to liquidate the remnants of Mussolini's profitless oil development corporation. Instead of liquidating the assets of the state company, Mattei convinced parliament that it could be profitable, and he has been accused of converting ENI into a "state within a state." Sometimes Mattei is called "a state *against* the state." Mattei's efficient, money-making organization controls so much money and so many jobs (and he himself has been so free of accusation of corruption) that he has been able to criticize and even influence the Government with relative impunity.

Under Ambassador Clare Boothe Luce the United States defended American oil interests by trying to restrict Mattei's expansion of ENI's activities into regions which previously had been the exclusive preserve of American and British companies. This served only to anger this influential Italian Mattei, and the Kennedy Administration would do well to remain aloof from the oil companies' competitive squabbles.

The United States cannot remain unperturbed, however, by Mattei's commercial dealings with the Soviet Union. Mattei went to Moscow in 1960 to sign a trade agreement under which Russia sends Italy crude oil in return for steel tubing, synthetic rubber and oil pipeline equipment. In the context of over-all Italian trade with the U.S.S.R., the Mattei deal is of a significant magnitude. All Italian trade with Russia in 1960 amounted to two hundred million dollars. Mattei's oil pact is for this same sum over a four-year period, and it, of course, is limited to one segment of the Italian economy. The influence that Mattei's action may have on future Italian trading patterns is a cause for concern.

Italy's claim that she has special knowledge of, and interest in, the Mediterranean must be respected even if not taken too seriously. It is not important whether or not the Italians really *have* prerogatives in the area. What is important to U. S.-Italian relations is that the Italians *think* they do. The U. S. A. must respect the *bella figura* ("good face" or "prestige") of a second-rank nation that reminisces constantly of its past glories. *Bella figura* to the Italian is what "saving face" is to the Japanese, plus pride, honor and vanity. It is a very real ingredient of the Italian character.

By supporting Italian membership on United Nations commissions concerned with the Mediterranean regions, by seeking Italian counsel in Mediterranean and African problems, and by listening to Italian views, the United States Government will contribute at no monetary cost at all to an Italian national need.

Italy's principal international dispute is not in the Mediterranean, but along her northern frontier, near the 12,459-foot-high Alpine Brenner Pass. The dispute is with Austria over a region that the Austrians call the South Tyrol and the Italians call Alto Adige. The origins of the dispute date back to April 26, 1915, when Italy agreed to enter World War I on the side of England, France and Russia against the Austro-Hungarian Empire. A treaty signed in London (and kept secret for a long time) promised that when victory was achieved Italy would get (along with other coveted territory) an area of Austria that lay within Italy's natural frontier of high Alpine ridges.

The population of the region was predominantly South Tyrolese, German speaking, loyal to Vienna. Annexed to Italy, this population resisted assimilation and has been a source of trouble to Rome ever since. During the period of the Rome-Berlin Axis, about half of the German-speaking population chose, under the terms of a Hitler-Mussolini agreement, to migrate to Austria, receiving reimbursement from Italy for their homes and land. With the Third Reich defeated, many of them came back at the end of World War II, claiming their property on the ground that the Hitler-Mussolini pact was invalid. Italy acceded to this argument, restoring their property and Italian citizenship. In addition, the German-speaking people have the right to use their own language in schools, newspapers, courts, and in all private and official acts. Street signs in cities of the area—Bolzano, Merano, Trento—are in two languages, German and Italian.

The Italian Government has, to the profound dissatisfaction of the German-speaking population, encouraged migration from other regions of Italy (principally from the south) to the Alto Adige region in order to dilute the German-speaking majority. In addition, in a brazen case of gerrymander, the Italian Government has combined the Alto Adige Province (with its predominantly German-speaking population) with the Province of Trentino (with its heavily Italian population) into a single administration. Naturally, this serves further to attenuate the influence of the malcontent portion of the population and to place them at a disadvantage with the Italian majority.

Figures tell the story of the Italian maneuver. In 1919 only 3 per cent of the population of the Alto Adige was Italian. The rest was German-speaking South Tyrolese. Now, following migration into the region, Italians have swelled their numbers to 34 per cent of the Alto Adige population. With the merging of Alto Adige with Trentino the Italians are in the majority, constituting 68 per cent. There are about 516,000 Italians living in the Trentino-Alto Adige Province and 220,000 South Tyrolese, all of them concentrated in the Alto Adige (South Tyrol) part.

The result has been an outcry from the Austrian Government (at the instigation of South Tyrolese nationalists and their relatives in Austria) that the German-speaking minority is being mistreated, discriminated against in housing and schooling, and denied their treaty rights. The Austrians claim that the ethnic and cultural characteristics of the Austrian minority are not being preserved. The promised parity for Italian and German languages in public life, complain the Austrians, has not been implemented. Another grievance is that proportionate employment of the two nationalities in public office is not enforced, and more than 90 per cent of the Civil Service posts are held by Italians who also receive preference in housing.

The matter has been brought up at the United Nations. The Austrians want a genuine autonomy for the South Tyrolese to safeguard their national entity. More extremist-minded South Tyrolese want reunion with Austria. At the United Nations the U. S. A. voted with Italy. Not only was the United States obliged to back its active ally on this matter (against a friendly, anti-Russian, but officially neutral Austria), but the balance of rights of the complicated case seem to be on Italy's side. Candid conversations with Austrians convey the impression that Vienna is acting reflexively in this matter under minority pressure, but without real conviction.

The problem does not end there, though. Militant members of the German-speaking population intermittently bomb housing construction projects because the apartments are intended for new Italian inhabitants, and blow up Italian state railroad tracks, bridges and power lines.

In the spring of 1961, a particularly persistent series of dynamite explosions halted trains, destroyed electric transmission towers, interrupted production in factories, and caused deaths. Troops were transferred quickly from other sections of Italy. A curfew was established during hours of darkness when it was forbidden to approach hydroelectric installations (dynamite charges were discovered at several dams which could have flooded inhabited areas), bridges, railways, and other state property. Persons who failed to respond to soldiers' challenges in the night were fired upon, and, in some cases, killed. Volleys echoed against the mountain slopes. The number of extremists engaged in sabotage is probably small, but their effectiveness is enhanced by material help they apparently receive from within Austria.

The Italian and Austrian Foreign Ministers have made no headway in bilateral talks recommended by the United Nations. The matter is certain to come before the world body again. The Kennedy Administration has precedent as well as the merits of the matter on its side if it continues to vote with Italy in this dispute.

Italy has a way of enrapturing the foreigner. This has been true in all ages. Fulsome phrases have extolled the endearing qualities of Italy's sun and scenery, its art and atmosphere, its people and poverty (which insensitive travelers sometimes find folkloristic or quaint).

It was Percy Bysshe Shelley who exclaimed, "Thou Paradise

of exiles, Italy." Lord Byron was equally rapturous: "O Rome! my country! city of the soul!" And it was Robert Browning who became the most ecstatic in declaring:

> Open my heart, and you will see
> Graved inside of it, "Italy."

This attachment takes monetary form, too. Italian emigrants send about half a billion dollars back to relatives in their homeland each year. Most of this comes from the United States—a considerable sum, especially when America's balance of payments shows a dollar deficit.

Italy lures 20,000,000 tourists annually. This is a total equal to 40 per cent of the Italian population. In proportion, it is as if 72,000,000 foreign tourists were to visit the United States each year. Americans are rather far down the list. The greatest number of tourists to Italy comes from West Germany, followed by Switzerland, France, Austria and England.

This magic magnetism of Italy means that sentiment rather than sense prevails sometimes in our thinking about Italy. It is easy to think of Italy as a land of romantic, gay people rather than a former Fascist ally of Hitler. The tourist sees the *canelloni* but not the Communism. Lacking a de Gaulle to verbalize grievances and aspirations, Italy's problems seldom find expression in newspapers or newscasts. Italy is taken for granted as a firm member of the Western alliance. But Italy should not be taken for granted. Wisdom, sensitivity and constant attention must be applied by any American administration in its relations with Italy. Like Italy's topography itself, from which dramatically rise Europe's most active volcanoes, the nation's political, economic and social conditions are capable of unanticipated eruptions. The prudent traveler in Italian affairs must be mindful of the hazards of Mount Etna and Vesuvius as well as of their beauties.

—IRVING R. LEVINE

IRVING R. LEVINE is NBC News Correspondent for the Mediterranean, based in Rome. Before assignment to Italy in 1959, he had been the first American newsman permitted to broadcast on a regular basis from Moscow since the end of World War II. He accomplished this by appealing personally to Soviet Premier Khrushchev for permission to cover the Soviet Union. A native of Pawtucket, R. I., he is a graduate of Brown University and the Columbia University Graduate School of Journalism. After working for the International News Service from 1947 to 1950, he joined the NBC News task force covering the Korean war. Subsequent NBC assignments included Hong Kong, Formosa, Indo-China and Siam. In September, 1952, he returned to Columbia as a Council on Foreign Relations Fellow. He left for Moscow in the summer of 1955. He has written for the leading magazines as well as two books on the lighter side of things in the Soviet Union. He is a member of Phi Beta Kappa.

# 6.

## RUSSIA:

### *"Real Peace Is Impossible"*

MR. KHRUSHCHEV," said the Senator, "is no fool—and the American people know that. He is shrewd, he is tough, he is vigorous, well informed and confident."

The Senator was John Kennedy. He went on to say, "The Khrushchev whom I met, in his session with the Foreign Relations Committee, was a tough-minded, articulate, hard-reasoning spokesman for a system in which he was thoroughly versed and in which he thoroughly believed. He was not the prisoner of any ancient dogma or limited vision, and he was not putting on any act; he was not engaging in any idle boasts, when he talked of the inevitable triumph of the Communist system, of their eventual superiority in production, education, scientific achievement and world influence."

Mr. Kennedy made that speech at the University of Rochester in October, 1959. Fifteen months later the production, education, scientific achievement and world influence of the United States became his primary responsibility. As we have seen, the new President entered the White House under no illusions about the stature of the Man in the Kremlin. In the first months of his administration, as he grappled with crises in Laos and Cuba, struggled with Soviet intransigence in the United Nations and at Geneva, learned that the first man in orbital flight was a card-carrying Communist, Mr. Kennedy had more than ample opportunity to judge the shrewdness, toughness, vigor and confidence of Nikita Khrushchev and his Communist system.

Mr. Kennedy had warned in January that the news was to get worse before it got better. Mr. Khrushchev confirmed this thesis in his meeting with the President at Vienna in June. With what amounted to diplomatic arrogance, the Russians at Vienna told the President that the great issues which divide and endanger the world were negotiable only on Soviet terms.

To many Americans, experiencing the spring cleaning of the mind that accompanies a new administration in Washington, the main question was: how did we get into this fix? A lot of people in the United States remembered when the Russians were on *our* side. Russo-American amity lasted for four years, during the Second World War. For the last sixteen years the Russians have been our enemies in the cold war: and the end of this conflict is not in sight.

When John Kennedy took his seat in the 80th Congress in January, 1947, the cold war was nearly two years old. Two months later, Nikita Khrushchev was named Chairman of the Council of Ministers of the Ukrainian Soviet Socialist Republic. Kennedy was twenty-nine: Khrushchev was fifty-two. Both men had served in the war with distinction. Neither man had had anything to do with the origins of the cold war they were both to inherit.

It is easy today to look back on the years of wartime alliance and see clearly the ineluctable forces of ideology and *real-*

*politik* that shaped the conflict to follow. But at the time the object was, as Winston Churchill put it, to "tear the guts out of the German Army"; and the main part of that task, as Churchill said, had been accomplished by the Russians. Toward the end of the war people in high places and low believed that, once the Germans were beaten, the Soviets would join in creating a stable and honorable European peace.

What Russia did after the war, of course, was to protect the security of her borders by the military and political seizure of buffer states from the Baltic to the Adriatic. Before Yugoslavia bolted in 1948, the Communist zone had been extended to ten and a half countries and a hundred million people. These postwar gains increased Soviet industrial strength by an estimated 30 per cent, and increased the number of people living under Communism by 50 per cent. Russia's annexation of the Baltic States became a permanent reality. The eastern provinces of Poland, which the Russians had stolen in their 1939 partnership with Hitler, were retained by the Soviets and, to compensate the Poles, their western frontier was moved 300 miles into German territory. Thirteen million Germans were evacuated from their homeland. And the Western powers seemed powerless to interfere.

When the leaders of the wartime alliance met at Yalta in February, 1945, there was no surface indication of the trouble that was to follow. Yet two weeks later, Soviet political officers pressured King Michael of Romania to install a pro-Communist government—a government which the United States never recognized. In the weeks that followed, the Russians ignored the promise Stalin had made at Yalta to bring anti-Communist Poles into the postwar government of Poland.

Harry Truman replaced Franklin Roosevelt at the Potsdam conference in July, 1945, and when the results of the Labour Party's victory in the British elections were tallied, Clement

Attlee replaced Winston Churchill. Marshal Stalin remained, however. The Soviets demanded trusteeship of Italy's African territories; control of the Dardanelles; pieces of Turkey; control over the Caspian and northern Iran; an extension of Soviet influence in the Middle East; partial control of occupied Japan; a hand in the development of the Ruhr; and a giant American loan. These things they did not get. They did obtain some reparations and they completed arrangements for a veto in the United Nations and a three-seat share in that fledgling organization. Potsdam had its moments of Western ineptness, but it did resist, in the main, the biggest Soviet demands.

At Potsdam there was no showdown on the basic, fundamental and still unresolved question of Germany. The Russian Army stood all across Europe, filling the vacuum left by the retreating Germans. No one really believed that the Russians would pull back. And it seems that fatigue and preoccupation with other problems (Truman still faced the Japanese in the Pacific, Clement Attlee faced the building of a Labour administration in Britain) rather than innocence brought about the fatally vague language embodied in the Potsdam documents. These papers comprised the first real confrontation of opposing ideologies expressed in identical terms: both sides agreed on "democracy" and "free elections"; both sides had different things in mind, and both sides knew it. When the conference adjourned, both sides went to work setting up regimes of their own kind in the areas they controlled.

The United States had been strengthened in the Potsdam negotiations by the announcement that the first American atomic bomb was tested successfully at Los Alamos as the conference opened. But the fact that Marshal Stalin—if he had not known beforehand—was told of the achievement at Potsdam probably strengthened the Soviet resolve to consolidate gains in Eastern Europe as quickly as possible. For the

balance of military power had shifted conclusively to the
United States, where it was to remain for many years. According
to James Byrnes, who attended the conference as Secretary
of State, Stalin showed no surprise when he was told of the
successful American test. Governor Byrnes later wrote that
Stalin's only comment was "that he was glad to hear of it
and hoped we would use it" against Japan. This contrasts
vividly with subsequent Soviet propaganda condemning the
United States for the use of the weapon.

After Potsdam, the Grand Alliance began its long, steady
decline into the rigors of the cold war. The Potsdam
conferees agreed to the American suggestion that a Council of
Foreign Ministers be formed to deal with the unresolved
questions. As the months and years passed, the split between
East and West became wider and wider. And the consolidation
of Soviet influence in Europe and the world continued apace.

Eight months later, Winston Churchill said in a speech at
Fulton, Missouri, "From Stettin in the Baltic to Trieste in the
Adriatic, an iron curtain has descended across the continent."
Marshal Stalin's answer came eight days later in a newspaper
interview: he called Churchill a "warmonger" and compared
him with Hitler. But the curtain had dropped over Albania,
Romania, the Carpatho-Ukraine and East Prussia in 1945;
Poland, Hungary and Bulgaria went under formally in 1947;
Czechoslovakia fell in 1948; and Communist control over East
Germany, which had existed all along, was formally announced in 1949.

These early years of the cold war were characterized by the
nearly instantaneous withdrawal of American military power
from Europe. When the war ended, the Americans in Central
Europe numbered 3,500,000 men: 68 divisions, 149 air groups.
A little more than a year later, the United States had 2 divisions
in Europe, about 200 military aircraft, and 6 battalions
in ready reserve at home. The Soviets had 40 divisions on the

line ready for combat, 100 more on reserve. Although no one thought much about it then, the only military means the Western alliance had at that time was the potential of massive retaliation through the American atomic bomb. By 1947, we were taking the final pieces out of what had once been the world's strongest military apparatus, and preparing for a complete return to normal peacetime life.

At the same time, Europe was going under for what appeared to be the third time. The Western Europeans were bankrupt and nearly starving, with no foreign exchange, sadistically bad weather, ruined crops and growing Communist parties. In February of 1947, Britain announced she could no longer maintain troops in Greece and Turkey, which meant a tremendously increased danger of Communist penetration of those countries. President Truman and his brand-new Secretary of State, George Marshall, thereupon took the first formal steps to bring the United States into a position of full leadership of the Western alliance. The 400 million dollars spent in Greece and Turkey brought the United States back into the world and face to face with the Russians.

The Truman Doctrine in Greece and Turkey was followed by the Marshall Plan in Western Europe and by the public declaration that the policy of the United States was henceforth to "contain" the expansion of the Soviet Union. As conceived in 1947 by George Kennan, then chief of the State Department's Policy Planning Staff, "containment" meant that ". . . the main element of any United States policy for Europe must be that of a long-term, patient but firm and vigilant containment of Russian expansive tendencies . . . by the adroit and vigilant application of counterforce at a series of constantly shifting geographical and political points."

The Russians had been invited to participate in the Marshall Plan and Soviet Foreign Minister Vyacheslav Molotov headed a large Russian delegation to the first planning conference in Paris in June, 1947. It is interesting to note that the Soviet attitude toward the Marshall Plan bears a striking resemblance to the subsequent Soviet attitude toward disarmament and inspection and controls. In 1947, the Soviets wanted the American aid, but could not bring themselves to accept economic integration with other European countries—and the American supervision of that aid. Molotov said such supervision would be interference in Soviet internal affairs.

The same attitude of brooding suspicion has characterized other conferences on various aspects of disarmament. In March, 1946, the United States proposed to the United Nations the Baruch Plan for control of nuclear weapons. As proposed by Bernard Baruch, the American representative on the UN Atomic Energy Commission, the plan called for an International Atomic Development Authority with complete control over all the basic materials and the processes of atomic energy. The Authority, under the American proposal, was to have had full inspection rights in all member countries to insure that atomic energy would not be used for military purposes. Once the inspection apparatus of the Authority was in motion, the United States would agree to destroy its stock of atomic weapons, the only nuclear arsenal in existence at that time. The Soviets rejected the idea of any inspection of Russian industry, and, although the Baruch Plan was overwhelmingly endorsed by the United Nations, a Soviet veto killed the plan. Three-and-a-half years later the Russians exploded their first atom bomb.

The allocation of high priorities to a nuclear development program in the terrible postwar years is another indication of the Soviet system's ability to move quickly in chosen areas. When the war ended, at least 7 million Russians were dead, another 25 million were homeless, and nearly half the material wealth of the Soviet Union had been spent or destroyed in the war. Stalin began rebuilding Russia's heavy industrial machine with the same disregard for human rights and comfort which he had shown before the war. In this period, however, he was aided by the forced appropriation of an estimated $800,000,000 worth of machinery from Manchuria (taken as a result of one week's war against Japan), by the wholesale carting off of the industrial equipment of East Germany, by massive reparations from Germany, Hungary and Romania, and by trade pacts shamelessly weighted in Russian favor with the rest of the occupied satellites. The rioting in Eastern Europe in 1953 was a testimony to years of extreme Soviet plundering of the satellite economies.

By the time the Soviets blockaded Berlin in 1948, the full outlines of the cold war in Europe were clearly drawn. The successful Allied airlift to Berlin, and the ultimate Soviet defeat pointed up the impossibility of agreement on Germany. The airlift ended in the spring of 1949. The blockade had failed, and with it Russia's foremost attempt to forestall the political unity and economic emergence of West Germany. In August, in the zones of French, British and American occupation, West Germany's first postwar elections were held. In October, the East German regime was established. In November, the West German regime of Dr. Konrad Adenauer was recognized by the Western Big Three. Nineteen forty-nine was the year in which Germany was formally cut in half.

Nineteen forty-nine also saw the formation of the North Atlantic Treaty Alliance and the Communist "Council for Mutual Economic Assistance," more commonly known as the Molotov Plan—the Communist answer to the European Recovery Program.

On the other side of the world in April of 1949, the Chinese Nationalist capital at Nanking fell to the Chinese Communists, Chiang Kai-shek's force lost Shanghai in May, and by the end of the year the Generalissimo, with the remnants of his army, had taken refuge on Formosa. Another permanent crisis-point in the cold war was thereby fitted into place. In

French Indo-China the long war which was to result in the partition of Vietnam had passed its halfway mark.

An event even more important than the fall of China took place in September, 1949, when the Soviet Union detonated its first atomic weapon. The nuclear weapons gap at that moment seemed to be a little more than four years. Four months later, President Truman approved production plans for the hydrogen bomb. The first such American bomb, which was probably not a deliverable weapon, was exploded in the Pacific in May, 1951; two years and three months later the Soviets exploded their first thermonuclear device. The gap was narrowing, and the nature of the gap was to have far-reaching consequences. As popular theory puts it, the American concentration on smaller nuclear warheads allowed the United States to place a lower priority on the development of rockets powerful enough to deliver heavier payloads. The Soviets, on the other hand, with less sophisticated and heavier apparatus, were forced into a program of constructing much more powerful booster rockets. The massive Russian boosters have not been needed in war, but their peacetime value in science and propaganda was first demonstrated by Yuri Gagarin.

The military and economic entrenchment of the years from 1945 to 1949 shaped the pattern of troubles to follow. In these years, from the difficulties and bad tempers at Potsdam to Chiang Kai-shek's flight to Formosa, from the detonation of the first American atomic bomb at Los Alamos to the explosion of the first Communist bomb somewhere in the Soviet Union, from the meeting of Russian and American soldiers at the Elbe River to the formation of the NATO alliance, the outlines of the conflict were drawn. The West learned that the Communists could not be pushed out of Eastern Europe, and that Russia could maintain political and economic control of a hundred million people along her frontiers and at the same time fix her attention on her enormous internal resources.

Both East and West learned in this period that there could be no settlement of the question of Germany favorable to either side. East and West realized and acknowledged the fact that the division of Europe was a fixed reality: that the curtain *was* iron. The Communists learned that the West had unexpected resiliency and determination as demonstrated by the beginnings of European economic recovery started under the Marshall Plan, Truman's aid to Greece and Turkey, and the tenacious miracle of the Berlin airlift. The lessons of the late 1940's were applied by both sides to the next battleground, Korea.

If the outline of the cold war had been molded before Korea, that conflict showed that East and West had learned some of the rules of the new game. The Korean war was a bloody and dangerous fight, but it was strictly limited to the Korean Peninsula by the antagonists. Chiang Kai-shek was not unleashed, Japan suffered no major bombing. The threat of nuclear annihilation was not realized.

All through the 1950's the two camps refrained from major military operations in the other's territory. The British, French and Israelis were not stopped in Suez by the threat of Communist volunteers. The agony of Hungary, the riots in East Germany and Czechoslovakia and Poland that took place in this decade were repressed by the Soviets without interference from the Western Allies. The United States may have thought long and hard about it, but in the end it did not intervene in Indo-China to help the French. The belief that major conflicts must be avoided at all costs grew in these years, along with the skill to live in moderate dignity with such a belief. What did take place was major rearmament.

The United States defense budget had ambled along, in the years before Korea, at an annual average rate of about 14 billion dollars. In 1951 it stood at 77 billion. Greece and

Turkey joined NATO that year, the ANZUS Treaty was
signed by the United States, Australia and New Zealand, and
the Americans tested the first H-bomb. In 1952, the NATO
Conference approved a unified force in Europe of 50 divisions
and 4,000 airplanes. In 1953, the Soviets tested their first
H-bomb. In 1954, following the division of Vietnam, the
SEATO alliance was formed, with a prophetic protocol on
Laos. In 1955, the Soviets gathered the military forces of the
satellites into the Warsaw Pact. In 1955, the Baghdad Pact
came into being. Two years later the Eisenhower Doctrine
was declared. In 1957, the Russians announced a successful
flight of an intercontinental ballistics missile; the Americans
followed a year later.

Many of these actions were taken by the West under the
unique stewardship of John Foster Dulles. Mr. Dulles did not
begin the policy of containment, but he carried it to its fullest
flowering. Containment, it must be remembered, began as the
building of a foundation from which negotiations could be
carried on with the Russians. It was not designed as a policy
in itself, but rather as a means of building strength in the
West while the expansion of Communism was held in check.
The theory was that the Russians would deal only with
strength, and the line of treaty frontiers that began to ring
the Communist bloc, from Japan, through Formosa, Southeast Asia, Pakistan, through Turkey and Greece and on across
Europe and Scandinavia, were expressions of that theory.
So were the sums voted by Congress for military and political
support of governments in these cold-war border areas whose
anti-Communism (and anti-neutralism) could be relied upon.
Mr. Dulles' own definition that neutralism was immoral was
part of this policy. His unfulfilled promises about "rolling
back" the Iron Curtain, his warnings to allies that, unless they
followed Washington, there would have to be "an agonizing
reappraisal," his endless travels, his "brink of war" statement,

may all be open to broad interpretation and much criticism, but they were clearly the actions of a man who believed that if you could isolate and bottle up the Communists and show them your strength, they would listen to reason.

Indeed, Mr. Dulles went further. He believed, in the summer of 1955, that the Soviet economy "was on the point of collapsing"; he said in 1956, speaking of the liberalization of Eastern Europe that was to lead to the uprisings in Poland and Hungary, "The great goal of our policy [is] a Russia which is governed by people responsive to the wishes of the Russian people, who had given up their worldwide ambitions to rule, and who conform to the principles as are embodied in the United Nations Charter." Mr. Dulles believed, in short, that the posting of Allied strength around the borders of Communism would bring an ultimate change—for the better—in the Communist world, and the end of our troubles with it.

The trouble was that containment became a policy in itself, not a prelude to policy. It did not work. The Communists spent the time rebuilding. Too many of the West's Allies were governments out of touch with the people. Too many changes were taking place in the parts of the world inhabited by black, brown and yellow people. The British were dismantling their colonial empire, and other people wanted out, as well. Too many opportunities were open to the Communists in the undeveloped world. In many places our Allies were powerless to halt the trend; in some places they were, and are, liabilities. While we stiffened the spine of the anti-Communist alliance, too many changes were going on behind our backs. A few months after the cordial Summit conference at Geneva in 1955, the Soviets jumped the curtain and concluded an arms deal with Egypt. Containment was not working, and the changes within Russia precluded neither the collapse of her economy nor a change in her manners.

The death of Stalin, in March, 1953, brought many changes,

to be sure. It did, however, catch the Americans off balance. In his book on the Eisenhower Administration, Robert J. Donovan describes the state of things on the day following the death of Marshal Stalin:

On March 6 the dictator's death was discussed briefly in the cabinet. Lodge said that Soviet officials in the U.N. seemed nervous. He urged a cautious attitude on the part of the United States. The President said that since 1946 officials at the State Department and the Psychological Strategy Board had been speculating on what would happen when the Soviet Government changed hands. But now that it had occurred, he complained, he had looked in vain for any plans or studies that might have been worked out in advance so the Government would be ready to react.

What the Western powers did after the death of Stalin was largely what they had done before he died: remained linked around the borders of the Soviet Union and Communist China, without thinking too much about the political erosion taking place behind them in the rice paddies, jungles and savannas of the undeveloped world. Negotiations during this period produced no great changes, and the two East-West summit conferences that have taken place since the death of Stalin accomplished nothing. During this post-Stalin period, the *status quo* was restored in Korea, half of Indo-China fell to the Communists, Tibet was lost and Mr. Khrushchev issued his long-range ultimatum on Berlin.

Since the death of Stalin, Mr. Khrushchev and his colleagues have found time to keep busy abroad while dealing with knotty problems at home. The Khrushchev era began with a struggle for power in the upper branches of the Soviet hierarchical tree. The liberalizations of the early Khrushchev years were intended to both dignify and speed up the satellites; they resulted in the East European uprisings. Mr. Khrushchev's farm policies, in which he often appears as a determined architect surrounded by inept builders, have not yet brought him any lasting reward. Indeed, agriculture remains his most serious and most annoying domestic problem. He staked heavily on the potential result of his trip to America, and opened himself to the charge of consorting with capitalists when he returned to Russia and described Dwight Eisenhower as "my friend." His anger over the U-2 incident and his subsequent rage over Washington's treatment of the matter are understandable in this context. Yet, since he assumed full power in 1958, Nikita Khrushchev has been firmly in control.

The society he runs has been a shade more liberal, more productive, and much better armed than that of the Stalin era. The Stalinist use of police terror is gone, even if the police powers—and the police—are still around. There has been more freedom to speak and criticize, although in 1961 the authorities published a warning that Mr. Khrushchev had given to the intellectuals a year earlier: stick to the party line. More money has been made available and a few more things to buy with it, although the Soviet consumer market is still shaken by sudden uncontrolled shortages. Censorship of bourgeois correspondents has ended, which is a sign of maturity, although the press treatment of Commander Alan Shepard's flight in May, 1961, and its comparison with Yuri Gagarin was anything but mature.

In 1959, the Soviet volume of housing construction was half that of the United States. The Russians have been devoting only a third of their over-all construction program to housing for people, and there has been some evidence that they have been just keeping up with the growth of population. No one knows the precise statistics, including possibly the Russians themselves, but the housing problem in the Soviet Union remains, by our standards, terribly severe. The main allocation of capital investment in Russia has gone to industry. The Soviet Gross National Product has been growing, as the American electorate learned in 1960, at a rate of about 7 per cent a year, while the American economy has been slumbering along at a 3 per cent annual increase. In the early 1960's the total annual capital investment in the USSR is expected to equal that of the United States. If things continue at their present levels, the annual expansion of Soviet industrial capital will soon be much greater than the American rate.

There are several reasons for this situation. The American economy has not been utilizing its full industrial potential, for one thing. Another reason lies in the fact that the Soviet Union in 1961 is in a stage of capital investment, of building an industrial machine, that the United States went through many years ago. Some economists have pointed out that the highest rates of growth in the capitalist countries took place when the employers and the state were able to direct a very high percentage of profits back into capital investment, while at the same time keeping wages and costs under strict control. That may have been capitalism, but it is a valid description of the conditions in Russia and the reasons for Soviet growth.

In agriculture, the Russians have not been doing as well. In the simplest terms, about half the people in the Soviet Union have been kept busy feeding the other half. Production has been high in some areas, but productivity of individual farm workers has been at an extremely low level. The Soviets may catch up to the over-all American level in some agricultural products, but they will do so only through the utilization of four times as many people. Mr. Khrushchev knows this and has devoted more and more of his time to what appears to be a burning personal crusade to raise the production level of the average Russian peasant. Stalin had more trouble with the peasants than with any other group, and he never really solved the problem. From available statistics, neither has Mr. Khrushchev. And Soviet planners know they cannot build a truly modern, flexible industrial state unless they get more food from fewer workers on the farms. Politics can still be a risky occupation in the Soviet Union, and these days a man's rise and fall are often measured in bushels of grain and gallons of milk.

Nevertheless, there is no lack of confidence in Russia. The world as Mr. Khrushchev sees it involves an antique capitalist system which will decay within the next generation or two even if the Communists fail to help it along. He believes that capitalism will be replaced by Socialism, and in these twin concepts he is a true believer. He will not, however, stand by and wait for it to happen. As he said early in 1961, "Communists are revolutionaries and it would be a bad thing if they failed to spot new arising opportunities, to find new ways and means leading most surely to the set goal."

One of the approved Soviet methods of reaching the set goal is through support of what the Communists call "Wars of National Liberation." In the Communist vocabulary of the 1960's there are three kinds of war. Two are bad. World wars, say the Russians, will simply destroy us all. World wars are to be avoided. So are "local wars," which have the subheading "small-scale imperialist wars." Here is what Mr. Khrushchev says about conflicts of this type: ". . . a small-scale imperialist war, no matter who among the imperialists starts it, may develop into a world thermonuclear rocket war. We must therefore fight against such wars."

The third kind of war, which *is* allowed, is the "War of National Liberation"; an example given by the Soviet Premier is the Communist-supported guerrilla warfare against the government of South Vietnam. "What should our attitude be toward such uprisings?" asked Mr. Khrushchev. "It should be most favorable. These uprisings must not be identified with wars between states or with local wars, because the insurgent people fight for their right to self-determination, for their social and independent national development; these uprisings are directed against decayed reactionary regimes, against the colonialists. Communists support such wars fully and without reservations, and march in the van of the peoples fighting for liberation."

While Mr. Khrushchev was saying this to an audience at the Academy of Social Sciences and Institute of Marxism-Leninism, four-engined Russian IL-18s with Russian markings were airlifting supplies to the Pathet Lao rebels in the jungles of Laos. The twenty-odd planeloads a day that the Soviets put into Laos over a period of several months were a clear indication that Mr. Khrushchev meant what he said.

Many theories have been advanced about the Chinese influence on the Russians in this context. Some say the Russians became involved in the Laotian airlift to prove that the Moscow party was still the vanguard of the revolutionary movement. Others believe that the Chinese, who are known to support policies more belligerent than the Russians, deliberately involved the Russians in the dangerous situation in Laos. Last year, documents in the hands of western Communists indicated that the Russians and the Chinese fought bitterly over the correct approach to war as an instrument of world Communism. The dispute is believed to have reached its peak at the conference of Communist and workers parties at Moscow in November, 1960. However, there is no real evidence as to the actual relations between Moscow and Peking, although most Western experts agree that no love is lost between the two capitals. What is most tantalizing to Western observers is that relations between Moscow and Peiping may constitute the most important chapter of postwar Communism; and yet very, very little is known about the state of those relations.

The Chinese have, however, at least on paper, joined the Russians in an endorsement of peaceful coexistence. Soviet theorists have indicated that a plank on peaceful coexistence may be inserted into the new Soviet constitution, scheduled to appear late in 1961. Coexistence is certainly a central theme for Mr. Khrushchev, and this is what he said about it in his speech at the Academy of Social Sciences and Institute of Marxism-Leninism:

"The policy of peaceful coexistence promotes the growth of the forces of progress, of the forces fighting for Socialism, it facilitates the activities of the Communist parties and other progressive organizations of the working class in the capitalist countries, makes it easier for the peoples to combat aggressive war blocs and foreign military bases, and contributes to the success of the national-liberation movement. The policy of peaceful coexistence is thus, as far as its social content is concerned, a form of intense economic, political and ideological struggle between the proletariat and the aggressive forces of imperialism in the world scene."

There is more to Mr. Khrushchev's belief in peaceful coexistence than its use as a means of furthering Communist aims. He realizes the dangers of a thermonuclear war as well as the leaders of the West, and he can be expected to act as vigorously as they do to avoid annihilation. There are those who believe that a more realistic basis for peaceful coexistence would be an agreement, tacit or otherwise, to stay away from the major danger points between East and West, leaving the undeveloped territories as economic, ideological and, if necessary, guerrilla battlegrounds.

Yet it seems more and more difficult to avoid escalation into major crises in areas where there is a confrontation of Soviet and Western interest, prestige and ideology. And during the first few months of the Kennedy Administration, the likelihood of any rational and distinterested international administration of these recurring troubles diminished.

The reason for this was what came to be known in the West—if not in the Soviet Union—as the "Troika" concept. "Troika" was the Soviet insistence that the administration of all international organizations be shared with equal veto power between the West, the uncommitted and the Communists. The Russians admitted that their demand for a veto stemmed directly from diplomatic defeats they had suffered at the hands of disinterested international civil servants —notably Dag Hammarskjöld in the Congo situation. They told the West privately—that "Troika" was valuable, for it gave the West a weapon against what one day would become an even more powerful bloc of uncommitted nations in the UN. However, as of 1961, the Russians wanted it for their own protection—and they are unlikely to abandon it as a concept or trade it as a bargaining counter.

When "Troika" is linked with Soviet policies on wars of "national liberation," with the Soviet definiton of peaceful coexistence, with the difficulties of controlling nuclear tests, with Soviet intransigence on disarmament, and with the Kremlin's attitude on Berlin and Germany, the picture is gloomy indeed. And it must be remembered that the Soviet Union has not made one major concession, not one major move toward an easing of tension since its sudden agreement in 1955, a few months before the Geneva Summit conference of that year, to an Austrian peace treaty.

These are the problems that face us. They are not made more soluble by a number of follies and faults on the part of many Americans.

It is folly to expect that if Mr. Khrushchev is replaced, it will be by what Joseph Alsop has called "a more monstrous monster." Mr. Khrushchev is a good organization man, and if he departs, he will be replaced first by a team and then by one other single powerful organization man. Since his organization represents a country in the full flush of internal development, Mr. Khrushchev can be counted on to do his best to avoid the nuclear conflict advocated by some of his Chinese allies. But it is folly to believe that Soviet policy will automatically turn harder if he is not around to direct it. The Russians feel they are doing well with things as they are.

It is folly also to believe overmuch in the possibility of the Chinese and the Russians publicly falling out. The evidence suggests that this might one day happen, but harping on the theme, or, worse still, planning on it, will only drive them closer together.

It is a fault, and possibly a fundamental one, of Americans to think of dealings with the Russians in the terms of everyday language. An example: in the future colonization of, say, the moon, an American and a Russian may be discussing the political complexion of the lunar community. The American will say that his country wants to see a democratic, freely elected government with a broad base of popular support. The Russian will respond that his government insists on the full democratization of the electorate, full freedom in elections and the broadest possible support from the working class for the new government. Both men will mean what they say, and neither man, if past performance means anything, will say precisely and explicitly and fully what he means. It is a melancholy probability that once the split has developed in Moon City, both sides will be calling each other rebels.

It is a fault of people everywhere to believe that to negotiate at the Summit is a virtue, that not to negotiate there is a sin. The difference is that in some Western countries the pressure of popular opinion, or the necessity of winning the next election, will force a politician to the Summit. Such journeys, made in the best possible faith, are dangerous escapades. In the history of postwar Summit meetings, involving the prestige and talents of our chiefs of government, has the West tallied one major gain? Chatting amiably in front of photographers on a Geneva lawn may be pleasant; but unless it is preceded by hard bargaining and followed by some chance of major agreement, it is without virtue.

Finally, the most serious and understandable fault of all:

Americans believe that war is followed by peace. This once was true, but it is true no longer. It is naïve, and the many years of cold war that followed the six years of World War II prove it. The belief that peace follows war has been at the root of many of our postwar difficulties. It has allowed us to think that defense could be put on the expense account, and that freedom was deductible. It has caused us to fatten up mentally while other people did the hard thinking. We were able to maintain a major Army overseas, to pay high taxes for outlandishly expensive defense weapons, to contribute to the rebuilding of Europe and the inflation of many an underdeveloped economy without realizing that we were ourselves involved. Money will not win the cold war. Production will not keep the Communists quiet. The Americans are capable of achieving any goal, if they want it badly enough. Our trouble has been that we wanted something else —peace—and real peace is impossible in the world.

Here is how the Communists put it: "Comrades, it is a magnificent time we live in! Communism has become the invincible force of our epoch. The further successes of Communism depend to a tremendous extent on our will, our unity, our foresight and determination. By their struggle, by their work, the Communists, the working class, will attain the great goals of Communism on earth."

Said by Nikita Khrushchev, shrewd, tough, vigorous, confident. Mr. Khrushchev does not think of it as peacetime.

—JOHN CHANCELLOR

JOHN CHANCELLOR until July, 1961, was NBC News Moscow Correspondent. He brought to his assignment the searching curiosity of a police reporter and the severe intellectual discipline of the thorough student. Born in Chicago, he grew up there and took on a mass of hard jobs as a river boatman, hospital orderly and carpenter's assistant. Before entering the University of Illinois to study history and philosophy he served a tour of Army service. He joined the Chicago *Sun-Times* in 1948 and NBC News two years later, soon proving himself a masterful all-around newsman. After a series of domestic assignments, he went overseas to Vienna in May, 1958. This was followed by a stint in the London office before being sent to Moscow to head the NBC News bureau in the Soviet capital. His travels abroad have taken him to most parts of Europe, to Afghanistan, North Africa, Lebanon and Jordan. He now is host of the "Today" program.

# 7.

## AFRO-ASIA:

## *"Freedom, Fragmentation and Ferment"*

THERE is a ferry called Congolia No. 9 that plies the Congo River between Leopoldville and Brazzaville and that I commend to President Kennedy.

Not that he would find Congolia No. 9 outstanding in any way. The smallest Presidential family yacht is a more impressive vessel. But to me Congolia No. 9 symbolizes a little of the heady art of the impossible that makes emergent Africa and Asia such enigmas to us.

Congolia No. 9 is small, white, scuffed, weary and redolent as only a common carrier in Africa can be. Its steel lower deck is thronged with strapping, barefoot African women in loud prints, jabbering furiously as they balance crockery on their heads and babies in each arm. Directly above on the sun-scorched first-class deck sit the few whites who still make the daily crossing: lean, dour, tight-lipped men in bush shirts and women in faded cottons—a tolerated minority in the continent they once ruled.

Congolia No. 9 and its sister ferries are the sole public transportation across the Congo. They operate only in daylight and then turn back at the first sign of one of those tropical thunderstorms that blow up so quickly over the Lower Congo. A few thousand yards downriver are the roaring rapids that seal Leopoldville off from the Atlantic and turn its face to Africa.

There is supposed to be a rescue ship always standing by in the river if Congolia No. 9 should foul its propeller in the octopuslike water hyacinths that float endlessly down the Congo. I never saw a rescue ship, but then—as the Africans would point out—I should be glad I did not need to.

After many trips I should say it takes twenty minutes for Congolia No. 9 to cross the Congo but about 200 years for the passengers on the lower deck to climb to the top.

The transcendent facts on the continents of Africa and Asia today are discord and diversity. Everywhere there are barriers of language, religion, custom, tribe, nationality and economic interest. In Afro-Asia everything is local. What appears on the map as one country is really a congregation of feuding provinces. What appears as one province is in fact a hodgepodge of warring tribes.

Nigeria's Ibos and Yorubas despise one another and are despised in turn by the Moslem northerners. In the Congo, Balubas and Luluas are age-old enemies but the Balubas themselves are split into two factions, each claiming to be an autonomous state. In the Punjab, Hindi-speaking Punjabis battle Punjabi-speaking Sikhs. Bombay state has already bifurcated and may be subdivided again. On the Trucial Coast of Arabia most sheikhdoms are too poor to afford a post office but too jealous to yield a whit of "sovereignty." Laos has no railroad but more than enough tribal feuds to spark World War III. The so-called Afro-Asian world is in fact a myriad little worlds, often in collision, always in tumult.

Such a definition of Afro-Asia clearly excludes Russia and China despite the nationality problem in both countries. It also excludes Japan, which is politically, economically, and even psychologically much nearer Europe and the United States than any of the former Asian or African colonies. Nor does what I have to say about Afro-Asia apply to the Republic of South Africa, a white fossil precariously preserved on a black continent, or to such vestiges of white imperialism as Portuguese and Spanish Africa.

What remains is still bewilderingly heterogeneous, but there are common characteristics. Of these the most obvious is independence. Since 1945, forty-five new nations have been born and at least a half dozen others are about to be delivered. Nothing like it has ever happened before. Independence has exploded even more violently than population in most of the Afro-Asian world. The search for flags, anthems, emblems, coats-of-arms and government letterheads has assumed frantic urgency. Fortunate indeed is the Afro-Asian country that has visa forms and official portraits to match its current regime.

Like the products of most explosions, the new nations of Africa and Asia have covered the earth with fragments. President Nkrumah of Ghana accuses the West of Balkanizing Africa. India blames partition on the British. The Arabs blame their disunity on everyone but themselves. The fact is that the Afro-Asian world, through its multiple particularisms, has Balkanized itself to an extent that would make the most callous imperialist recoil in dismay. Centrifugal forces are supreme.

Given an opportunity in 1955 to choose independence or union with Egypt, the Sudan voted overwhelmingly for independence despite the evident advantages of unity of the Nile valley. Newly independent Kurwait resists annexation by Iraq. Senegal seceded from the Mali Federation after only four and a half months. Impoverished Mauretania refuses to accept Moroccan suzerainty despite the logic of economics. The Himalayan principalities of Bhutan and Sikkim fight shy of both India and China. Khampa tribesmen in Tibet and Naga "hostiles" in eastern Assam each carry on a hopeless struggle for independence.

Most unity moves in the Afro-Asian world have been still-born. After more than three years of unity on paper, the United Arab Republic has yet to issue a common currency for use in Egypt and Syria. The Ghana-Guinea "union" is almost exclusively a matter of words. Somalia, one of the poorest of the new nations, may the sole exception. It incorporates former Italian and British Somaliland.

Political fragmentation is both a cause and symptom of the breakdown of the old social and economic order all the way from Dakar to the Pacific. In the Arab world and parts of Southeast Asia, feudalism is disintegrating. In sub-Sahara Africa, tribalism is on the decline.

The beef is tougher in Cairo today because the big herds have disappeared with the breakup of the huge estates whose owners used to rule Egypt through the Wafd party. Life is harder for the sons of the same families who find no foreign exchange to educate or disport themselves abroad. Northern Iraq's feudal overlords drowned in their own blood in a Mosul cellar in March, 1959, when Communist vigilantes murdered all the old families on the excuse that they had supported an abortive coup against Abdel Karim Kassem.

The revolution in India and Pakistan has been less sanguinary but perhaps more far-reaching. Princely rulers have succumbed to the persuasion of the purse and stepped aside to make way for the new order. Land reform and government-sponsored co-operatives are slowly undermining the Zamindars and other powerful feudatories.

The revolution in ideas is often more sweeping than the transformation of economic patterns. A Westernized Indian diplomat boasts that his mother no longer objects to riding on a train with Untouchables in the next carriage. Restive

Indian young people wriggle free of the patriarchal village but still place matrimonial advertisements in Delhi newspapers in their parents' names rather than their own. For many Indian girls of good family it is now acceptable to find work in Europe but still not, of course, in India.

The anomalies are even more striking in Black Africa. The transistor and the witch doctor are competing for the Bantu mind. Tribalism is under attack from all sides. Ambitious autocrats like Nkrumah and Guinea's Sekou Touré undermine tribalism by setting up nationwide political machines. The Sudan fights it by teaching a common Arabic language to all children. A social worker in Leopoldville's African *cité* teaches an African woman how to sew and finds a part-time job for a vagrant youth from the interior. Tribalism has receded again.

The greatest enemy of tribalism is probably the bicycle. Next in importance are the book, the white collar and the office desk, all more eagerly sought after in Africa today than the magic protection of the most powerful tribal chief.

Ironically, tribalism has suffered most in the land where white men make its preservation an article of faith. Prime Minister Hendrik Verwoerd's pious insistence on "Bantustans" to enshrine the black man's traditional way of life has not prevented Johannesburg and the grim Rand mining towns from attracting the largest, most rootless detribalized proletariat in Africa to the squalid locations and barrackslike miners' compounds.

The disintegration of the old social and economic framework in Africa and Asia creates the need for new forms. The revolution is in search of a sequel. The quest has produced many slogans—free Arabism, African personality, Panchayati Raj and basic democracy—but few results. The most far-reaching political revolution in history is in danger of being nullified by Afro-Asia's failure to carry the concomitant social revolution to a fruitful conclusion.

Whatever happens, the search for new social institutions and ideas is not, in my view, likely to end up in the Kremlin, on Main Street, U.S.A., or inside the Great Wall of China. Like most people, Africans and Asians prefer to fail by their own efforts than succeed by effacing themselves in the service of an alien system. Foreigners have ruled most of Africa and Asia for so long that imported doctrines meet almost automatic resistance among the newly independent of these continents. No system could be more alien and uncongenial to the soft human clay of Africa and large parts of Asia than the nineteenth-century European doctrine of Communism as interpreted by its present Slavic and Chinese exponents.

The so-called simple people of Africa and Asia are less easily duped than Pentagon psychological warfare experts believe. In fact, suspicion is so widespread that it conditions every social relationship east and south of Suez. A Negro-American agronomist told me he always insisted that Indian villagers themselves spend every penny of American improvement loans. He would be accused of cheating if he bought so much as a shovel with village funds. How much more difficult to overcome the villagers' distrust of a draconian and impersonal collectivism exported from Moscow or Peking! Force and deceit may, of course, win acceptance, but insofar as Africans and Asians can exercise free choice, I think we might regard the specter of Communism in the former colonial countries a bit more dispassionately.

Freedom, fragmentation and ferment can thus be said to be the leitmotifs of the former colonial world. There is another one. Since 1955, a new and potentially epochal awareness of its own collective power has dawned on Afro-Asia. For the first time in modern history the non-whites of the world are conscious of the strength of their combined wills. Afro-Asian consciousness is still groping, fitful and contradictory. But its emergence as a new element in world politics cannot be ignored or discounted.

The idea of Afro-Asian solidarity found tangible expression for the first time after World War II at a Communist-sponsored meeting of African and Asian representatives in New Delhi in April, 1955. That meeting was overshadowed by the now famous conference at Bandung later the same month attended by more than twenty African and Asian countries, including Communist China. African and Asian leaders met one another at Bandung for the first time. Nasser emerged on the world stage and was deeply influenced by Prime Minister Nehru and Premier Chou En-lai. Chou himself introduced Communist China to more or less polite international society. Nehru and President Sukarno of Indonesia strove to enhance their reputations as apostles of Asian non-alignment.

At the same time an embryonic Afro-Asian bloc had been developing at the United Nations.

Since Bandung, Africa and Asia have been speaking oftener and more stridently, albeit in different voices, in world councils. The Afro-Asian bloc has become the largest single concentration of voting power in the UN General Assembly.

The first so-called Afro-Asian People's Solidarity Conference met in Cairo from December 26, 1957, to January 1, 1958, and was sucessfully converted by the Soviet and Chinese delegations into an anti-Western propaganda forum. The Afro-Asian Solidarity Council established in Cairo as a result of the conference plays an insignificant role in the area despite Soviet and Chinese financing. Subsequent Afro-Asian youth and women's conferences and a second Afro-Asian "people's" conference in Cairo have been so patently Communist-inspired that they have been ignored by most African and Asian leaders of any standing.

Accra has been another focal point of efforts to forge regional solidarity. The first conference of independent African states held on Dr. Nkrumah's initiative was attended by representatives of eight African governments in April, 1958. In December of the same year the Ghanaian leader opened an All-African People's Conference in which delegates from twenty-five countries, including the Belgian Congo, took part. This meeting produced an Accra Secretariat that has thus far escaped Communist domination. The Accra organization concentrates on subversion in South Africa, Rhodesia, Portuguese Africa and wherever else Nkrumah feels his influence can be profitably exerted. The obvious rivalry between Nasser and Nkrumah should not encourage the complacent notion that the neutralist camp is hopelessly at odds with itself. Cooperation for agreed and often destructive aims is a fact.

African and Asian members of the Commonwealth surprised themselves in March, 1961, when they succeeded in making South Africa withdraw from that traditionally white-dominated association. The Commonwealth's non-white members have graduated from second-class membership to controlling power.

Afro-Asian consciousness means they hope to wipe out dark corners ruled by white men in Africa or Asia. Nothing done by Europeans can long escape the critical scrutiny of the self-appointed inheritors of the white man's burden. Angola, Spanish Sahara, Southwest Africa, Goa and even tiny colonial specks like the Cocos Islands are probed and prodded by the Afro-Asian bloc in the UN or in more direct fashion through subversion.

I remember visiting a new and almost empty primary school in Abu Dhabi on the Trucial Coast of Arabia. When I asked why there were so few pupils, someone said, "The sheikh doesn't want his people getting ideas." The sheikh's peace will be short-lived.

It would be unfortunate if collective action by the Afro-Asian countries should arouse panicky Western fears of a new "yellow," "black," or "brown peril." Unless Afro-Asia succumbs to Moscow or Peking, we need hardly fear the area's military potential. Only if African or Asian armies come to possess nuclear weapons could they endanger us by their unaided efforts. That eventuality must be firmly resisted.

Under present conditions the solidarity movement reflects the Afro-Asians' realization of their own military weakness in an age of nuclear-equipped missiles. Many African and Asian leaders are convinced that only by exerting their collective diplomatic and political weight can they even partially offset their military and economic deficiencies.

Nor should we exaggerate the true extent of Afro-Asian "solidarity." On the Congo question African governments have been as bitterly divided as UN African troops and Congolese in the streets of Leopoldville. As one Ghanaian soldier told me, "If only the Congolese were white, we could really hate them." Despite the handicap of common color, the Ghanaians have done a respectable job of disliking their Congolese brothers.

In its communications the Afro-Asian world is still a series of appendages to Europe. East-west air service is still almost unknown in Africa. All air routes lead to Europe. To go from New Delhi to Leopoldville you pass through Brussels or Rome. A cable from Lagos to Nairobi passes through London. Intraregional trade is microscopic.

Afro-Asians communicate through European languages, read about one another in European or American newspapers, and often find more in common with their former European rulers than with fellow Afro-Asians. An educated Egyptian and an educated Iraqi will converse in English because neither knows the other's Arabic vernacular. I remember hearing an indignant Nigerian policeman of the UN force telling a French-speaking Congolese, "You are apparently speaking some foreign language. I speak English." I can still hear a Nigerian sergeant telling me after he had moved into barracks occupied by Moroccan troops in Leopoldville, "We're used to dealing with proper black chaps and proper white men. But we don't know what to make of these Moroccans."

When trouble broke out in Leopoldville's African quarter, friendly Congolese warned UN Tunisian technicians to get out fast. "But we're like you. We're Africans," the Tunisians protested. "Oh, no, you're not," was the firm reply.

However severe its practical limitations, the Afro-Asian movement is a fact of growing importance that the United States has been slow to grasp. We have been unduly suspicious of the motives behind the movement and unduly skeptical of our own ability to influence its development. The United States first advised Turkey to boycott the Bandung conference, then urgently insisted that the Turks attend as a pro-Western "counterpoise."

We have often forgotten that most representative Afro-Asian assemblies have exerted a moderating influence on the extremist leaders of both continents. Nehru is a more effective restraint on Nasser than any Western leader. Sekou Touré would heed Houphouët-Boigny (President of the Ivory Coast) long before he would listen to Charles de Gaulle.

The Soviet Union and Communist China recognized the potentialities of Afro-Asian regionalism from the beginning. Moscow realized that a Guinean and an Indonesian have little in common except their colonial past and their impoverished present. The Chinese have been able to exploit the additional element of common anti-white sentiment.

Until 1955, the Soviet Union and Communist China treated the former colonies of Africa and Asia with undisguised contempt. Such leaders as Gandhi, Nehru, Nasser and Haile Selassie were dismissed as imperialist strawmen. The independence of the new states was belittled. What overtures Moscow did make were so crudely propagandistic and accompanied by such blatant subversion by local Communist parties that no non-Communist African or Asian leader could find any basis for co-operation with the Soviets or the Chinese.

In 1955, the situation changed dramatically. The Chinese spoke in dulcet tones at Bandung while the Russians applauded the conference from the sidelines. In June of that year the newly pre-eminent Khrushchev invited Nehru to the Soviet Union for the most prolonged and lavish reception accorded until that time to a non-Communist visitor. In September the now famous Czech arms deal with Nasser was announced to a disbelieving world. For the first time the Soviet bloc was furnishing military assistance to a "bourgeois" ruler in one of the former colonial states. Later the same year Khrushchev and Bulganin set the new style of Soviet diplomacy with a freewheeling tour of India, Burma and Afghanistan, dispensing aid and anti-Western propaganda in copious measure.

The West alternated between dismissing these developments as mere propaganda gestures or seeing them as the prelude to a massive Soviet take-over in Afro-Asia. Neither the complacency nor the dread has proved justified. It is now acknowledged that the Russians' short-term objectives in Africa and Asia have been the elimination of Western influence and the cultivation of neutralism among local leaders.

In both aims the Russians have been surprisingly successful. By aligning themselves with Arab nationalism, they have helped eliminate France from the entire Middle East with the exception of Israel. British influence has all but vanished in Egypt and Syria and has declined sharply in Iraq. Britain has lost her huge Suez Canal zone base as well as the RAF bases in Iraq. In Africa, Guinea and the new Mali Republic have severed most ties with France and now rely increasingly on the East bloc. Morocco is buying Soviet arms. Ghana is establishing closer links with the Sino-Soviet bloc. Despite Chinese encroachments on India's northern border, Moscow has maintained Nehru's friendship and succeeded in limiting Western influence in New Delhi. In Indo-china, more forceful methods have rendered the whole area of doubtful value to the West.

Such achievements are not simply Moscow's handiwork. They are the outgrowth of complex historical forces at work in Africa and Asia. But in view of Russia's low estate in Afro-Asia as late as 1955 and the West's almost unchallenged supremacy until that time, it is remarkable that Moscow's prestige and influence have risen so rapidly. Although Communist-bloc economic aid now goes to some thirteen non-Communist Afro-Asian countries, the amount is negligible in comparison to the huge American outlays. But the propaganda return has been high.

The Russians and Chinese have now established themselves as permanent fixtures in the Afro-Asian landscape. It is idle to talk about keeping them out. The problem facing the Kennedy Administration and the West is to limit East-bloc penetration of Afro-Asia, not exclude it.

Although the United States starts with a comparatively clean slate in Africa and Asia, our image is often distorted by association with European colonizing powers. American policy in the area takes on the sickly hues of a moribund imperialism. In Iran, for example, much of the resentment once directed against Britain and Russia, historic intruders in the country, now focuses on the United States despite fundamentally different American aims and methods.

An American vote for a UN inquiry in Angola does not dissociate the United States from Portugal in the minds of politically conscious Angolans. Still less does it erase the memory in Indian minds of Secretary Dulles' espousal of Portugal's claim that Goa is an integral part of the metropole. Although American motives are generally trusted in Africa, it is not surprising that most educated Africans believe the United States has more in common with its white European allies than with the new states of Africa.

Filling the gap left by declining European power in Afro-Asia might have been less difficult had the United States not relied so heavily on military assistance agreements of the kind associated with European imperialism.

The intricate network of bilateral and multilateral treaties sponsored largely by the late John Foster Dulles to ensure Afro-Asian security has cost us heavily in money and prestige without enhancing regional security. On the contrary, Iraq's membership in the Baghdad Pact (now the Central Treaty Organization since Baghdad dropped out) stigmatized the late Nuri as-Said's regime as a Western puppet in Arab eyes and undoubtedly contributed to its bloody downfall on July 14, 1958. On that day America's downfall in Iraq was second only to the regime's.

Nor did the Baghdad Pact save Syria from near subjugation to Communism. Quite the reverse. The threat of Turkish and Iraqi intervention in Syria enabled Syrian Communists in 1956 and 1957 to cast themselves in the role of patriotic defenders of the fatherland. It was Gamal Abdel Nasser, the bête noire of the Baghdad Pact and reputed tool of Moscow, who rescued Syria from Communism in February, 1958, by uniting the country with Egypt in answer to the insistent appeals of anti-Communist Syrian army officers.

The Eisenhower Doctrine of aid to Middle Eastern regimes menaced by Communism proved even more counterproductive than the Baghdad Pact. The Doctrine, enunciated with fanfare in January, 1957, died some time the following year but has never been officially interred.

King Saud was temporarily forced out of power in Saudi Arabia after he had antagonized even his own supporters by "endorsing" the Eisenhower Doctrine and accepting the role of counterweight to Nasser unwisely conceived for him by Mr. Dulles early in 1957.

In Lebanon, former President Camille Chamoun sealed his own political doom and plunged his country into civil

war in the spring of 1958 after abandoning traditional
Lebanese neutrality for the doubtful benefits of the Eisenhower policy. Even after United States Marines had landed
in Lebanon, the very forces who had most bitterly opposed
the Doctrine emerged on top.

In the Sudan, the pro-Western regime that espoused the
Eisenhower Doctrine disappeared in November, 1958, albeit
largely because of domestic corruption. Morocco, another
early Doctrine adherent, has now veered sharply to the left
and won a promise that United States air bases in the country
will be relinquished. King Mohammed V's death is likely to
accentuate Morocco's drift toward Nasser-style neutralism.

American policy expressed in CENTO or the Eisenhower
Doctrine is clearly not the only, or even the main, reason for
the growth of neutralism with a pro-Soviet tinge in the
Middle East and North Africa. It is now apparent, however,
that the elaborate network of Middle Eastern security commitments fostered by Mr. Dulles was designed to meet the
threat of overt Soviet attack against the countries of the
region, which became unlikely after Stalin's death in 1953
and inconceivable after the Soviet rapprochement with Nasser
and Nehru in 1955. It was this kind of threat to Greece and
Turkey that the Truman Doctrine of March, 1947, had
successfully overcome.

The Southeast Asia Treaty Organization has proved even
more unsuited to the actual security needs of the area it covers
than CENTO and the Eisenhower Doctrine in the Middle
East. The only Asian countries in SEATO are Thailand, the
Philippines and Pakistan. The alliance has been unable to
stem Communist subversion in Laos or South Vietnam. By
arousing Nehru's suspicions it has retarded Indo-Pakistani
reconciliation.

There are signs the Sino-Soviet offensive is now shifting to
Africa. By now no one suggests Africa can be insulated from
Communist encroachments by herding reluctant African

states into Western-sponsored defense pacts. In Africa a text-book may prove a more lethal anti-Communist weapon than the finest rifle.

The change in the character of the Communist challenge in Africa and Asia was appreciated by the Africans and Asians when the West was still thinking in terms of armed Soviet attack. The Afro-Asians' understanding produced instinctive and remarkably effective reactions in almost every one of the new countries. Afro-Asian nationalism has proved more resistant to Communist tactics than most Western observers predicted. Hungary, Kerala and Tibet helped disabuse many of the gullible in Africa and Asia. Communist excesses have strengthened the hand of powerful conservative forces in most Afro-Asian societies. These include landowners, peasant proprietors, army officers, religious leaders and the growing business and professional communities.

Iran's Tudeh (Communist) Party threw away almost certain victory in August, 1953, when party zealots antagonized the powerful Iranian officer corps by pulling down statues of the late Reza Shah as part of an avowed campaign to put Iran in the Soviet orbit. Iraqi Communists soon lost their mass following after the 1958 revolution by dragging their opponents through the streets of Baghdad and committing other atrocities. Indian Communists are suffering the political consequences of their fiasco in Kerala and their refusal to condemn Chinese Communist aggression on India's northern border. Communist guerrilla tactics in Malaya and the Philippines have strengthened pro-Western regimes in both countries.

In most of the Afro-Asian world local Communist parties are small, ill-disciplined, faction-ridden and divorced from the main stream of national life. The ineptitude of local Communists is compounded by the East bloc's unfamiliarity with conditions in most parts of the former colonial world.

Contrary to popular American belief, few Soviet or Chinese diplomats speak the languages of Africa and Asia. Even fewer East bloc technicians know anything but their own tongue. The language barrier proved almost insuperable when Russian engineers replaced Westerners at the Iraqi government oil refinery in 1958. Similar difficulties have arisen with East-bloc technicians in India, Yemen, Ghana, Guinea and the Congo.

Soon after the Congo became independent in June, 1960, Moscow sent a sizable shipment of wheat as a gift to the Congolese people, little knowing that the tribes of Central Africa eat hardly any wheat flour and that there is not a single flour mill in the Congo. The Soviet wheat had to be shipped to Casablanca for milling and returned to an ungrateful Congo.

In Egypt the Russians supplied wheat which was unsuitable for making flat Arab bread, and crude oil with such a high salt content that it quickly corroded Egypt's catalytic crackers. In Yemen the Chinese Communists brought hundreds of Chinese laborers to work on road-building projects despite high unemployment in that backward realm.

The Russians and Chinese are handicapped in Afro-Asia even more severely than the West. But they often work harder to overcome their shortcomings. The East bloc has a knack for picking spectacular aid of high propaganda value, such as the Bhilai steel mill in India. A line of credit is opened with appropriate publicity and then each time project agreements are approved, using the promised funds, the Soviet Union gets another round of applause.

American aid is too often diluted in a cloudy alphabet soup of competing agencies. The Export-Import Bank and the Development Loan Fund have contended for "choice" projects in India and other countries. CARE and the Catholic Welfare Organization squabbled ignominiously over who was to distribute U. S. farm surpluses in Egypt. The Egyptians solved the problem by ensuring that neither agency was given any credit for its work.

Like a well-heeled customer in a cafeteria, the United States samples almost everything offered it as an aid "project." At one time in India we were supporting more than one hundred different projects, including a study on "The Effect of Climatic Conditions on Productivity" which concluded wisely that heat reduces productivity. But for a long time not a single new factory or power plant could be labeled as exclusively American-financed.

Under prodding from our ambassador in New Delhi, John Kenneth Galbraith, the Kennedy Administration appears ready to take the plunge into assisting India's fourth state-owned steel mill. The Bokaro project would be an imposing monument, not only to American aid but to the passing of our traditional reluctance to underwrite government-owned industry abroad.

Unfortunately, however monument-conscious Washington is becoming, it is now clear that an ever larger portion of American foreign aid to countries like India will henceforth be absorbed in financing so-called "maintenance imports" and the provision of working capital to keep existing factories and facilities from grinding to a halt. As Turkey discovered during the last years of the Menderes regime, the price of sustaining progress is often higher and more difficult to pay than the initial outlays.

Nothing is more quickly and unceremoniously absorbed by import-starved Afro-Asian economies than replacement parts and other such maintenance-of-plant supplies. And since working capital from abroad is required wherever under-developed economies are working above handicraft level, the net effect is to accentuate the very dispersion of American aid that the Administration wants to overcome.

The buckshot approach causes us particular problems because Congress insists that separate and detailed agreements be negotiated to cover every project to which we contribute. This produces nightmares in countries like Laos and Liberia where the fine print is mostly unintelligible. The old Imam of Yemen became so suspicious of our project agreements at one point in the talks that he told the American aid mission to quit the country.

President Kennedy should consider the creation of a single agency to administer all forms of foreign economic aid, including outright grants, short- and long-term loans, sales of foodstuffs, local currency support and the exchange-of-persons program. We should also make up our mind now not to expect gratitude for our overpriced food surpluses. A hungry man does not read the label on his rice.

Japan and Western Europe could certainly bear a larger share of the aid burden. When the Congo was the hardest hit, West Germany canceled its modest guarantee program that ensured German suppliers against losses on sales to the Congo. Sometimes our own overeagerness to enter the field, as in Iraq before the revolution, offers other aid-giving countries (Britain in this case) an excuse for reducing their contribution.

Europe and Japan are the natural trading partners of most Afro-Asian countries. It is easier for them to assist economic development in these areas than for the United States to break new ground. Aid is most effective when it flows through well-worn channels of trade, although our obligation to continue aiding Afro-Asia is inescapable.

It is also inevitable that the Soviet Union will furnish increasing economic aid to Africa and Asia. Moscow hopes to win friends with its foreign loans, much as we do. If the Kennedy Administration were to reach an understanding with Moscow on more basic issues, I see no reason why there should not be some agreement on sharing the increasingly heavy burden of aid to the less developed countries. That charge already exceeds the capacity of any one country or group of countries. Whatever we do, the Russians and Chinese are bound to play an ever more important role in Afro-Asia.

Americans often assume that aid is the magic key to friendly relations with any African or Asian country. This attitude ignores the fact that Africans and Asians respect America for itself, not simply for the amount of aid it disgorges. I have never experienced more intense anti-Americanism than among Palestine Arab refugees who had been existing for more than a decade on American generosity. Conversely, I have never heard more outspoken pro-American feelings expressed than in Communist Romania, which has had no American aid in a generation. Our relations with European colonial powers are more important to American prestige in Afro-Asia than the amount of aid we give or withhold.

No infusion of aid could erase the impression left in India and other Asian countries by our role in the abortive invasion of Cuba in the spring of 1961. Politically sophisticated Indians, although they made the expected deprecating noises in public, were shocked not by the Administration's evident complicity in the affair but by the failure of a great power like the United States to carry through what most Asians would regard as a legitimate protective exercise. Asians and Africans are often a good deal more hardheaded politically than we give them credit for, or than we are ourselves. Few politicians in the underdeveloped world would seriously question the United States' right to do all in its power to ensure friendly governments on its borders. But in Afro-Asia, as perhaps in other parts of the world, there can be no virtue without success.

The U-2 fiasco in May, 1960, had a similarly disconcerting impact on sophisticated Asian opinion, not because it showed that the United States was conducting aerial espionage (which even the Indians also do) but because we were ignominiously caught in the act at the worst possible moment.

Second only to our obsession with aid is our distress at what we imagine is Afro-Asian reaction to America's own race problems. Anyone who knows the Bantu peoples of Africa must smile at the notion that these "carefree materialists," as one English reporter aptly describes them, are brooding that some American citizens whose ancestors originally came from Africa do not enjoy full equality under the American Constitution. The African is not given to worrying but if he does, it is about something nearer home than school segregation in Louisiana.

This is no excuse for racial inequality in the United States. But in the course of reporting assignments over several years in Ghana, the Congo, South Africa, Angola and other parts of Africa, I have never been asked by an African about American race relations. African whites, on the other hand, harp endlessly on the subject in hopes of embarrassing the United States.

Many black Africans do, however, resent the practice of assigning Negro American diplomats to Africa. Educated Africans are usually burdened with deep-seated feelings of inferiority. They take it as a sign of second-class status in America's eyes when an overwhelmingly white country sends members of its Negro minority to represent it in Africa. The leaders of the new African states are far more concerned about how America treats them than about how American treats its own Negroes. Any Negro American who assumes he understands contemporary Africa simply because his great-great-grandfather came from the Bight of Benin is doing Africa and America a disservice.

Pious clichés about "common aims" should never obscure the vast gulf that separates Americans of any race from Africans and Asians. That gulf is not narrowed by well-meaning but often clumsy efforts to promote "understanding" and a bogus camaraderie. Africans and Asians are expert in the detection of fraud, including hypocritical expressions of admiration. Few Indians, for example, were impressed by the issuance of a Gandhi commemorative stamp by the U. S. Post Office. I have worked many years in Moslem countries but have yet to meet a Moslem who cared that there is a mosque in Washington, D. C., that was opened by President Eisenhower. I am glad that King Saud's crippled son was treated at Walter Reed Army Medical Center but I hope no one in Washington expected anyone but the boy's father to feel grateful. America's still considerable prestige in Africa and Asia is based on what we are, not what our propagandists hope to make us appear.

The counterpart of trying to ingratiate ourselves with Afro-Asians is our tendency to believe our own propaganda about them. For too many years our ambassador in Cairo pictured Nasser in his reports to Washington as "the George Washington of Egypt." Our early dealings with Nkrumah were based on a naïve assessment of his attachment to democratic government. Our simple-minded faith in Nuri as-Said's omniscience blinded us to signs of the approaching Iraqi revolution in 1958. I cannot remember how many successive "strongmen" have won the Pentagon's misplaced admiration. A kindred susceptibility to generals without armies has cost us more than $300 million and much heartache in Laos. Overburdened and increasingly undemocratic Turkey was advertised as the "Texas of the Middle East" by our impressionable representatives in Ankara—until we were too deeply committed to back out.

Such lapses are rarely, in my opinion, the fault of our professional Foreign Service officers in Africa or Asia. Most of them impress me as able and devoted. Wrong advice most often comes from ambitious but inexperienced political ambassadors, from self-seeking military attachés or Central Intelligence Agency "spooks."

In Laos, for example, our military attachés and CIA agents operated in direct opposition to State Department policy.

In Egypt a CIA official told Nasser not to attach "too much importance" to the visit of George Allen, Assistant Secretary of State for Near Eastern and African Affairs, to Cairo after the Czech arms deal.

Such tactics should be forbidden by the Kennedy Administration. Foreign policy should be made by the State Department.

We should recognize there is nothing inherently beneficial to us in the overthrow of an old oligarchy by a new dictatorship. We would be foolish to oppose the inevitable passing of the old order but our assessment of what succeeds it should be based on realities, not wishful thinking or the endearments of the new regime.

In one sense our most serious barrier to understanding the Afro-Asians is the disparity between their words and ours and between their words and what they actually do. For the better part of the last thousand years most Afro-Asian countries have been vassals of someone. They have developed the extravagant mode of expression of the man who expects his words to come to naught. Verbal self-delusion persists.

A high Egyptian official announces plans for an automobile plant have been "implemented," meaning simply he hopes to see such a factory built some day. The Congo's foreign minister announces Congolese troops will attack the UN by 3 P.M. unless certain conditions are met. He knows the conditions will not be met and the troops will not stir. Nkrumah announces the formation of a Ghana-Guinea "union" that will not change life for a soul in Accra or Conakry. India's state of Uttar Pradesh reports 10,000 agricultural co-operatives formed in two weeks, which means only they exist on paper. Arab states threaten endlessly to "drive Israel into the sea," thereby unwittingly helping sell Israeli bonds in the United States but perturbing no one in the Middle East.

We ourselves are not free of the cult of meaningless words. By adopting such slogans as "Marshall Plan for Asia," "dynamic production drive" and "crash program," we forget that most movement in Afro-Asia is artificially induced and therefore slower and more painful than the explosive, self-sustaining thrust of the West and Japan. Communist bloc progress is also induced but on a scale and by methods unmatched in any of the non-Communist former colonies of Africa and Asia.

It is fashionable today to talk about Afro-Asia's "revolution of rising expectations." Such a revolution is probably taking place among urbanized Asians and Africans who have an opportunity to observe amenities enjoyed by the more affluent members of society. But Afro-Asia's real problem is not its ambitious urban minority but its earthbound rural majority which accepts too little rather than demands too much. The Asian peasant and the African tribesman are both disinclined to work more than is necessary for minimum subsistence. This situation may change with time but there is no denying it is almost universal today.

Indeed in many parts of Afro-Asia prosperity has outstripped expectations. Newly wealthy Turkish peasants in the Adana cotton bowl used refrigerators as furniture before they learned the white box's real use. African miners habitually return to their villages as soon as they have enough money to buy beer, salt, cloth and a few other necessities.

The oil-producing Sheikhdom of Kuwait showers the most lavish welfare-state benefits on its citizens but has yet to find a way to make all of them abandon the clapboard hovels they call home.

If Afro-Asians' expectations are rising it is for the removal of old abuses, such as landlordism and usury, rather than the provision of new amenities.

The danger is that our own expectations of progress in Africa and Asia are rising so much faster than those of the people concerned that we will eventually become discouraged and stop giving aid. Nothing could be more harmful. Development in Africa and Asia is the work of generations. It is a task to which we can and must contribute on a sustained basis. Much has already been accomplished and more can certainly be done. I am particularly hopeful about the contribution American educators and technicians can make in creating a new elite in Afro-Asia who can direct future development.

Our aid must be selective. Projects must have a completion date and a precise target expressed in terms understandable to the people of the country concerned. Aid that trails off into eternity only breeds recriminations and regrets. We should do more to help what India calls the "private sector." We should encourage American private capital to go where it is wanted and where it can earn a respectable profit in Afro-Asia.

Underwriting long-term economic progress in Africa and Asia must never entail our underwriting unsavory regimes or artificial frontiers. The United States must never commit itself so irrevocably to any African or Asian regime that we cannot profitably deal with its successor. Nor should we bind ourselves to preserve frontiers drawn by Winston Churchill or other former European colonial secretaries in the heyday of imperialism.

Jordan is an example of a country created for dynastic convenience without regard to economic, ethnic or geographical realities.

Neutralism or non-alignment is probably the dominant trend in Afro-Asia today. We were wrong to oppose it before 1956. We are equally mistaken if we think we can now endear ourselves to Afro-Asians by vocally championing neutralism. It is incongruous when the head of the most farflung military coalition in history warns leaders of the new African states, as President Eisenhower did in October, 1960, that, "You cannot afford to put money into costly armaments."

President Kennedy never should feel impelled to tell any African leader, as President Eisenhower did, that we do not wish him to join "any association, even though it may be a voluntary association for military defense against the threat that does exist in the world."

The United States cannot speak with one voice in Africa and another in Europe and Asia.

Simply dumping African or Asian problems into the lap of the United Nations on the pretext that we do not wish to act unilaterally solves nothing. After all, existence is unilateral. The Congo has shown the UN is subject to the self-seeking intrigues of its ninety-nine members. UN officials or troops are not necessarily impartial or disinterested when their own country's aims are affected. By abdicating our power to the UN, we simply let others decide the outcome of a particular situation. We can never escape the consequences of misjudgment, regardless of who was immediately responsible. Disuse of power may be its gravest misuse. There is no rote formula to spare us the necessity of independent policy formulation every time a crisis erupts in Africa or Asia, or anywhere else in the world.

Above all, we should never delude ourselves about the broader trends in the world. Underlying all else is the fact that the gap between per capita income and production in Afro-Asia and the industrialized countries is widening, not narrowing, despite all aid programs and the Afro-Asians' own efforts. This means the economic disparity between the first- and second-class passengers on old Congolia No. 9 is increasing. We should be naïve not to anticipate increasing jealousies and antagonisms arising from this fact. It is another of the harsh conditions imposed by nature and the past on the great work that lies ahead in Asia and Africa.

—WELLES HANGEN

WELLES HANGEN is NBC News India and Middle East Correspondent. He makes New Delhi his headquarters. At twenty-five, a Phi Beta Kappa graduate of Brown University, he became the youngest member of the NBC News overseas staff. He joined the organization in December, 1956, in Cairo. As the man responsible for the major portion of Middle East coverage, he has reported from Syria, Jordan, Iraq, Kuwait, Ghana, Morocco and Egypt. In 1960, he was sent to South Africa to report on racial strife and then to the Congo to cover events in the dissension-ridden new republic. A native New Yorker, he worked for the New York *Herald Tribune* and *The New York Times* at various overseas posts prior to becoming associated with NBC News. Assignments for these newspapers took him to the United Nations, Paris, Bonn, Ankara and Moscow.

# 8.

## JAPAN:
## *"Switzerland of Asia"*

A N American correspondent who happens to be in the
presence of a sophisticated, talkative Japanese gentleman
finds himself embarking on a rare and startling excursion:
penetrating the inner core and outer space of the Japanese
mind.

Japanese have devoted a considerable part of the past three
thousand years training their minds to deceive their tongues.
They have succeeded better than most peoples. In our own
times, through war and defeat, and a decade and a half of
monumental reconstruction and individual remodeling,
Japan's ancient and number one defense has remained intact.
Through all the rigors of cataclysmic change in recent years,
Japan's number one problem has come unsullied to the
American people, President Kennedy and the Decade of the
Sixties: How can the Japanese communicate candidly with the
outside world?

Those from the outside (the precise Japanese definition for all non-Japanese) suffer from the same hardship. The inquisitive foreigner feels tempted to resort to truth serums or other restraint-easing drugs. But they are hard to administer to a subject who has developed circumlocution to a fine art.

After numerous safaris into the intellectual jungles of Nippon hunting the really big game of frankness, the genuine thoughts of an intelligent Japanese who has examined his country and the world around it and reached a few conclusions, are indeed a rare catch. The knowledgeable Japanese gentleman dissolves into a composite figure of assorted sizes, shapes and manners, but whether short, stout, thin, gay, somber, with or without hisses, he invariably follows the same pattern. He falls into a mixed euphoria, brooding and exulting over the evils and benefits visited upon Japan by the United States. And rightfully so.

All the problems facing the United States in Japan and with Japan flow only partly from Japanese character, history and geography. More immediately and visibly they are problems fastened on Japan by the Occupation. These come to light in any imaginary conversation with a composite Japanese, such as this.

*"All our troubles come because you defeated us."*

*It is almost a fair statement. It is decidedly a paradox in the complex Japanese character. Their individual stoicism is almost always accompanied by national whining about "orphan of Asia, small poor country with nothing but mountains." Since this is a truth session, the articulate, composite Japanese gentleman grudgingly adds the fillip of fairness. "I suppose I should say that many of our good things come from you, also."*

*And the Japanese gentleman is primed now to tick off the catalog of United States naïveté, generosity and general misdirection as well as the items Japan intends to ignore and accept.* "*You Americans are responsible. Permit me to say again, you Americans are responsible. So if you are disappointed in what we have become or where we are going, it is because you forget so easily. Do you remember that General MacArthur said Japan should become the 'Switzerland of Asia'? Ah, I thought so. You have forgotten that. We do not say it aloud but most of us thought then and we think today that to be a Switzerland means a nation has no international commitments. General MacArthur gave us a divorce from international responsibility. We are delighted. The irritations come between us because you want to marry us to international troubles.*"

Our truth-talking gentleman nestling on a *tatami*, nibbling on raw fish, wiggling his toes while he reflects on the insulated past and uncertain destiny of a remarkable people, could not have reached more quickly the concealed treasure in the Japanese vault. In 1945, when General MacArthur imagined that the mountains of Nippon were Swiss Alps because they too were snow covered, he bestowed upon the Japanese people the one ukase of the Occupation they bought without question or equivocation.

It seems to have escaped latter-day architects of U. S. policy that no action or statement of the entire Occupation was more wholeheartedly accepted in abject defeat or is more fervently held now in pristine equality. It appeared to be a natural recipe for rehabilitation when the General handed it to a defeated, prostrate and disillusioned Japan. It is less natural that the world should change and few Japanese minds change with it.

The "Switzerland of Asia" concept has become a bill of divorcement. It is cherished by a booming Japan, now fat with foreign currency reserves, pursuing a goal of doubling its national income in ten years and with a good chance of achieving it; even now its people engage in a furious scramble for American-style creature comforts, luxuries and leisure. The

Japanese people see a cornucopia of twentieth-century riches moving toward them like lava from a volcano and they are rushing out to meet the stream. Their dash seems so American, despite the flash of gay-colored kimonos and the intensity of small, serious sons of Nippon; but the Americanism of the race is an optical illusion, if the U. S. is seeking full-time partners in the fight for survival. In all their hurry to be modern and comfortable, the Japanese are not heedless of reality. They remember that Japan has been priced out of modern weaponry, and they are glad of it.

Ambassadors and other well-meaning observers tend to indulge in eccentric convolutions to explain Japanese departures from what are considered American norms of democratic conduct or manliness in participating in challenges. The ensuing tongue-clucking ("the demonstrations were organized by the Communists" or "we need to understand better the unhappiness of the Japanese intellectual") is intended to signify that Japan merely indulged in a momentary lapse or is enjoying a moment's hesitation before getting back on the ball and beam.

Considering where Japan has been in this century and its present perch on the downhill half of the turbulent twentieth, Japan's collaboration with the United States and co-operation with American policy in the Far East could be hailed as the "reform" of our former enemy. Some might be tempted to see it as proof of the "lovableness" of our current friend. What has happened, in fact, is a tribute to the unique self-discipline of the Japanese people. It is also proof-positive that when the Japanese people are removed from tyranny they display marvelous adaptability, flexibility and an extraordinarily keen sense of reaching the haven where they think their self-interest lurks.

Japan has had its stages of redemption. It has gone from absolute defeat to supine waiting under the Occupation, followed by rapid transition from inferiority to present-day equality.

In that time, three principles, engraved on Japanese hearts and fixed in Japanese minds, have dominated this country's national and international behavior and, if the Japanese people have their way, will shape Japan's destiny. American policy which ignores the grip the three principles have on Japan will be inviting profound disillusionment:

1. *Antimilitarism.* Japanese easily win laurels as the most pacifist-minded people in the world. They do not even honor their national flag or national anthem.

2. *Pro-business.* The impact Japan once tried to make on the world with military conquest it seeks to do now with commercial success.

3. *Noninvolvement.* The "more equal" Japan becomes the more authority it will have to give tangible expression to "We are the Switzerland of Asia," and attempt to maintain its divorce from international responsibility.

Of course, there have been deviations from these three lodestars of Japanese desires, particularly in the matter of noninvolvement. But all occurred before Japan had gained full sovereignty or almost full equality and unequaled prosperity, save one. That deviation was the unwelcome (and destined to be ineffective) passage of the revised U. S.-Japan Security Treaty on June 19, 1960.

*"You took away our images and thereby you laid the basis for terrorism and evil times. The Emperor. Ah yes, as you say, the little man on the big white horse. I do not protest too much that you brought him down from heaven. Frankly speaking—all right, frankly speaking?—the Emperor should not be considered divine. But for us he was a unifying faith, the core of a code of ethics."*

No man in Japan was happier than Emperor Hirohito to come tumbling down from the rarefied atmosphere where he communed only with the Sun Goddess and his aggressive generals and admirals. Japan's defeat was Hirohito's liberation. Removing the halo of divinity (and authority) helped to ease the agonizing guilt he felt as the instrument of Japan's catastrophe and the tragedies that Japan had inflicted on the world.

As a "divine being" the Emperor was the sum total of veneration. He was a faith to cling to during the turbulence of the times—first power madness, then wholesale confusion, then numbing hopelessness. He gave cohesion to a national Japanese mental state which had become a headless horseman racing through a storm-filled night. With or without the American nudge, though, the Emperor's authority was destined for dilution. With defeat, respect for all indigenous symbols of power and authority virtually collapsed. Death and destruction had come from betrayal by buddhas, shinto priests, gods, generals, admirals, politicians, police, bosses, intellectuals, parents. That in this wholesale rejection of all symbols of power and respect, Emperor Hirohito has suffered as little as he did is evidence of how much the Japanese really needed him as a continuing symbol.

While the Japanese highly respect but no longer worship the Emperor, they have yet to determine whether to retain him, tarnish his position even more, or eventually abolish the Imperial House. Ironically, the Imperial House got a new lease on life by being sensationally un-Imperial. Crown Prince Akihito was sensible enough to ignore the antiquated, frightened Imperial House advisers and marry an uncommonly fine, intelligent and charming commoner, Michiko Shoda. As a further insurance the Crown Prince and the Crown Princess, with touching and sometimes pitiful eagerness, copy the activities, codes and performances of British Royalty.

Most Japanese appear quietly content that the postwar constitution barred the Imperial Family from exercising political power. But unavoidably the Emperor exercises political influence. All Japanese consider the Emperor a symbol of opposition to Communism; as such he is an automatic friend of the United States and the West.

That provides adequate incentive for the pro-Communist and left-wing groups, which oppose most aspects of U. S. policy, to seek further to downgrade the Emperor. Since the Japan Socialist Party, the Japan Communist Party, the largest labor unions, teachers, writers, professors and intellectuals in great numbers wish to remove impediments to their aims, the Emperor, simply by being Emperor, stands in constant danger.

The condition excites right-wing, ultranationalist groups, which call themselves anti-Communist and pro-American, to scheme and dream not merely for the protection of the Emperor but for his restoration to a prewar position of divinity or infallibility. With him they imagine Japan can re-enter the glory road to power and speed down the highway toward Empire. As the struggle between left and right sharpens over the role for the Emperor, the United States will be drawn in. Inevitably, the United States will be reviled as a scapegoat or praised as the savior of the Imperial House. It seems inescapable that the Imperial House, which was the symbol of Japanese militarism to one generation of Americans, will become the symbol of the cold war in Japan to another generation.

*"At the time of the street demonstrations in the spring of 1960, I do not understand why the American people were shocked by the behavior of our university students. Or some of them. Or by the trade union people. Or some of them. Have you forgotten also that General MacArthur opened the jails in Japan and let out all the Communists so they could take over the labor unions and the educational system in Japan?"*

As we sowed in Japan, so do we reap.

The clearest way to record an incontrovertible verdict is to state it in its simplest form: Never in the sordid history of man's inhumanity to man has one country been more genuine in its motives and more generous in its actions than the United States has been toward Japan in the sixteen years from 1945 to 1961. While memories may be either bitter or sweet they are almost unanimously short. And American propagandists in Japan have been so engrossed in underscoring the evils of the Communists that they have failed to underline that the Japanese have been the beneficiaries of an American concern for the welfare of another nation unparalleled in international history.

The objectives of the Occupation were models of simplicity, honor, magnanimity and self-interest. They were to assist in the installation of democratic reforms so that the Japanese people might enjoy the blessings of peace with justice and freedom. The method employed was to assist Japan's economic rehabilitation and recovery, to make the nation economically viable, so that the Japanese people could prosper and enjoy a better life. Nobody who survived World War II, whether victor or vanquished, could have asked for a better deal than that, not even in the wildest opium-pipe dreams.

And those splendid objectives were pursued with such generosity and good will and effectiveness that even the natural ingratitude of human beings, and certainly of nations, might have been held in abeyance for a period of reasonable and respectable duration.

The Japanese nation and people flunked their first serious test. They proved that not only were memories short and gratitude thin, but they demonstrated that the courage to uphold democratic principles was remarkably flabby in Japan. When Uncle Sam needed a friend in Japan, no one of substance, from big business offices in Tokyo's Marunouchi section to the rice roots in rural prefectures, from the northernmost island of Hokkaido to the southern tip of Kyushu, spoke up with the exception of an ex-war criminal who happened to be Prime Minister and one English-language newspaper in Tokyo.

But the minds of Japanese had been carefully prepared to flunk the test in just the way Japan did.

In the perilous, rioting days of May and June, 1960, in those anti-American, anti-Eisenhower, anti-democracy, anti-Kishi disorders; in the pro-neutrality, pro-defenselessness, pro-anarchy, pro-Communist demonstrations, the industrious Red teachers of Japan never halted their preparations for the Future Day. One Japanese grade school teacher had his young students write a "penmanship" lesson over and over, day after rioting day: *All the Japanese people are very angry at the reactionary Kishi Government which is trying to make Japan a colony of U. S. imperialism.*

The teacher who gave out that "lesson in objective teaching" was one of the 500,000 members of Nikkyoso, the Japan Teachers Union. Nurtured by the Occupation, it now embraces—perhaps suffocates would be the better word—80 per cent of the elementary schoolteachers. Education Minister Masuo Araki attempted to discharge the teacher who gave out that "penmanship" lesson. The Union easily balked him. At the time, Araki pointed out that Nikkyoso was spearheaded by 3,000 card-carrying Communists (probably an underestimate) and charged that it "is perverting education by daily brainwashing of the pupils as future bearers of revolution in Japan."

Since that particular future had been in the making since 1945, its first contingent of bearers emerged from Japan's universities in 1960–61. This was the first crop of young men and women who had had their entire education in the postwar period. These were the products of the reformed, liberated, *vague nouvelle* system, denuded of all militarism with much of the Prussianism scrubbed out. From first grade through university they had been largely supervised by left-wing, Marxist-inclined, indubitably fuzzy-minded intellectuals. They began moving into the main stream of Japanese business, political, professional, intellectual and artistic life at the same time that a progress-filled chapter in U. S.-Japan relations was coming to an end.

Were all these young men and women, schooled since defeat, brain-washed into becoming bearers of revolution and harbingers of disorder? Some were, and they performed their first act of revolutionary faith in May and June of 1960. Obviously many were not, or were not quite prepared to be at that moment. They remained aloof. Some did so because they disagreed with the objectives of the disorders or because they were indifferent to political issues, or because they were more eager to safeguard their chances for material gains in a country where materialism has become almost a state religion.

Political passivity among university graduating classes seems to be considerable and it is worth noting. But the political future of Japan will be shaped by the political activists. They have tasted blood, demonstrated strength and gained authority. And from now on the mob leaders will be those who gained all their education in the postwar period.

Mobs, like bombings, never become familiar or comfortable. The more I experience both, the less endurable they become. I would not even suggest that a Japanese mob is any less insane than an American mob. Personal emotions aside, the savagery of frenzied Japanese whirling crazily around the Parliament Building shouting "Kill Kishi! Kill Eisenhower! Kill! Kill!" was not a sound that should quickly be forgotten. It was a sound of the sixties in Japan. It was a spine-chilling and ear-splitting result of postwar education in Japan, where teachers and intellectuals, and even reporters on Japanese newspapers, competed at the ramparts with students for high marks in anarchy.

To forget who and what inspired the May and June 1960

riots, and who participated in them, is to ignore the possibility of future disorders and the forces that will control Japanese policy.

And far behind the barricades, well removed from the chanting, snake-dancing youngsters weaving in a ritualistic, orgiastic ceremony, were the supply depots. The presidents of some of Japan's leading universities issued flaming words of encouragement to the demonstrators to tear apart the flimsy fabric of Japan's parliamentary democracy.

Virtually no one in Japanese academic circles stood up boldly for the preservation of a governmental system in its gravest postwar peril. Not a single businessman stepped forward in the darkest hour to offer his bared chest in sacrifice, if need be, to help preserve what had brought him immense profits. Decency was deserted by all those who peddle the printed word to the 100 per cent literate Japanese public.

The 1960 riots are best remembered because they kept President Eisenhower out of Japan. However, U. S. policy makers should remember that when Japan stumbled into its worst postwar degradation before the free world, when mobs snatched at the tattered hem of representative government, so few voices were raised in defense of the U. S.-Japan Security Treaty.

In journalism, there was *The Japan Times* with its 50,000 circulation, mainly among foreigners. The other voice was that of Prime Minister Nobusuke Kishi, member of Tojo's cabinet of aggression, ex-war criminal, alumnus of Sugamo prison, eventually stabbed and ultimately toppled for fighting to keep Japan on the side of the West.

There were signs that contrary to the Eisenhower years of self-hypnotism, the objectives of the United States and Japan had not been the same. The United States had been hunting military partners and Japan had been squirming to avoid the trap. For fifteen years the Japanese had been nodding their heads in agreement while Uncle Sam talked, but precious little had percolated and even less had coursed to their hearts.

A decade and a half of remarkable association, during which more than three and a half billion dollars of aid and assistance had been poured in and over two million dollars had been spent annually on an information program in Japan, ended the moment Eisenhower had to tear up his ticket to Japan. It was apparent that the United States had to start again to find a means of communicating with the Japanese people.

"A broken dialogue" was the description given those riots by Edwin O. Reischauer, the Japanese-born Harvard professor, long before it dawned on him or anyone else that he might be assigned to repair the fragmented communications.

Ambassador Reischauer arrived on the Tokyo scene in a unique role. He was the product of a notion that U. S. envoys should get closer to the people of a country even at the cost of irritating those in charge of the government. A refreshing notion, it was so unrealistic as perhaps to succeed in Japan. His handicaps were quite as lofty as his assets. Born in Japan, speaking and writing and reading Japanese, married to the granddaughter of a Japanese prime minister, a genuine authority on Japan, possessing a deep love of the country of his birth and its people, he seemed the perfect new-style ambassador. Yet contained in every asset were seeds of disaster.

Reischauer's wide contacts with Japanese intellectuals were full of contradiction. As a Harvard professor, his exposition of the American viewpoint was given the most courteous attention, and sometimes accepted. As a U. S. ambassador, making the same points to the same Japanese professors and teachers, he ran the constant risk of being condemned as an "official propagandist and apologist."

The Reischauers were preceded by gracious remarks. "How nice," said highborn Japanese, "to have a Japanese woman as mistress of the American Embassy residence" when they meant the opposite, since they disapprove of mixed marriages.

"An American ambassador who speaks Japanese," said high and low Japanese, "is a compliment to us." But a cartoon appearing at the time he was appointed more closely represented the attitude of Japanese bureaucracy. *He speaks Japanese,* the caption read; *he knows too much.*

Since the Japanese live, eat, breathe, dream and constantly scheme on trade matters, there was more to the "new look" in American diplomacy toward Japan than Reischauer's ability to enlighten the Japanese intellectual. His predecessor, Douglas MacArthur II, was fond of saying and quite accurately that he spent "at least" 70 per cent of his time on trade matters. "Perhaps," said MacArthur in his swan song remarks, "I should have paid more attention to the intellectuals in Japan."

Japanese intellectuals, like those of India before the Chinese Communists attacked Tibet and the Indian border areas, place a tax on a Westerner's patience almost beyond sustained endurance. Japanese professors, teachers, artists, writers, editors, cosmopolites, the opinion spreaders who dominate the newspapers and magazines, are committed to nonresponsibility and noninvolvement.

It has evolved into a religion for most of them that the ideal security for Japan is to be found in invalidating the security arrangement with the United States. They aim to present to the world, and especially to Soviet Russia and Communist China, a Japan devoid of all military protection, naked of all but virtue. On a broader scale, the Japanese intellectual—like the Indian intellectual until he did his absolute flip-flop—was ready to hand over vast areas of the world to Communism.

While Japanese-speaking Ambassador Reischauer could draw Japanese intellectuals into the Embassy atmosphere with an air of "please do not feel that you are an outcast here," his task of going beyond that was formidable. It was estimated that about 15 per cent of Japanese intellectuals were hard-core Marxist types. Another 15 per cent were described as having some understanding of and even sympathy for Western philosophies and concepts of individual freedom. About 70 per cent of Japanese intellectuals (Reischauer told the Senate Foreign Relations Committee that a Japanese intellectual is anyone who graduated from a university and does not work for the government) were said to be so fuzzy-minded, baffled and emotional that they could hardly distinguish between sukiyaki and Irish stew. Thus, most Japanese who have been exposed to higher education appeared wide open to what seemed to them to be dynamic. To many observers it had always been doubtful that democracy would be dynamic to the Japanese nature. Reischauer did not share that notion when he arrived.

As I waited for Ambassador Reischauer to arrive at the same airport where James Hagerty was mobbed and where President Eisenhower was supposed to land, I saw small chance for the conversion of Japan's "thinking people." The teachers of Japan were not going to be converted to the alleged virtues of a military alliance with the United States or even to a democratic concept of society just because an ambassador spoke their language.

Conversation between Japan and the United States would continue to be fascinating, enriching and rewarding when confined to trade, prosperity, economics, tourism, architecture, painting, sports, kabuki, flower arranging and sister cities. The dialogue would become stumbling, incoherent and then incomprehensible when Americans began talking to Japanese about ideals, the preservation of the free world and the dignity of all individuals.

*"You lose face with us because you expect from us what you have no right to expect. When the United Nations wanted troops for the Congo, Japan could afford to laugh*

*in the face of Mr. Hammarskjöld. You Americans gave us a
constitution. Gave? You forced upon us a constitution which
denied Japan military force and power. Those are the symbols
of national manliness. Very well, we have made a virtue of
the denial. So it is nice for us. We have membership in the
United Nations, without obligations. Financial, of course.
We pay our way. But what is money? What physical duty
need we perform? I will answer. None. Thanks to the United
States."*

A disturbed and conscience-stricken Japanese official returned to Tokyo from New York in February, 1961, for consul-
tations. Dr. Koto Matsudaira, Japan's thin-faced, quiet-spoken,
competent and shame-faced ambassador to the United Nations
was weary and embarrassed. On behalf of Japan and on every
challenging occasion, Dr. Matsudaira had been dodging from
responsibility into Japan's storm-cellar refuge.

Article Nine of the made-in-America constitution compelled Japan to "forever renounce war as a sovereign right
of the nation and the threat or use of force as a means of
settling international disputes." And the second paragraph
of the same article pointed out that Japan would "never"
maintain land, sea and air forces.

Ambassador Matsudaira's lengthy residence among Westerners may have infected him with heretical ideas. At any
rate he returned to Tokyo in that frame of mind. He had
come to question the virtue of the exquisite and refined
Japanese skill in having one's cake and eating it, too. While
all spectators of the human comedy could admire the gas-
tronomical feat and even envy it, some few Japanese wondered whether it was ethical or even good table manners.
Among the unbelievers was Dr. Matsudaira.

When the United Nations called upon Japan to send
uniformed men to Lebanon in 1958, Japan flatly refused.
In 1960, when Hammarskjöld sought Asian and African
forces to serve in the Congo on a mission of peace, Japan

looked the other way. Matsudaira felt shamed by the fact that fifteen nations responded to Hammarskjöld's initial invitation to send troops to the Congo. And not one of those countries considered that it had assumed any "belligerent" status by contributing to the UN force.

With a courage born of shame, Ambassador Matsudaira stood up in Tokyo and said that Japan, at the very least, should send some observers to the Congo to fulfill a small fraction of her responsibility to the United Nations. The roof fell on the hapless ambassador. He was compelled to apologize in private to officials of Prime Minister Hayato Ikeda's government. He was compelled to grovel and retract in public.

The Japanese were determined to see in Lebanon and the Congo only what they wanted to. They were then able to ignore an acceptable contradiction. While the constitution did indeed ban armed forces, Japan has Self-Defense Forces of land, sea and air units. True, the Self-Defense Forces have been held in such low public esteem that the ground forces could not secure a full strength of 180,000 men. Japanese courts have upheld the Self-Defense Force as not violating the constitution. But it is hard to believe that a Japanese government in the foreseeable future would dare outrage public opinion by sending Japanese troops in uniform abroad on any assignment.

It is a source of much comfort to the Japanese to be able to hold two contradictory ideas or positions on the same matter at the same time without being aware of any contradiction. Neither Japanese officials nor the public, with inconsequential exceptions, are disturbed by the provision in the United Nations charter requiring all members to "give every assistance" on a UN action, including the use of armed forces. While Japan agreed to respect the charter, it entered the UN, as they say in court, with mental reservations. Switzerland's permanent neutrality has contravened the UN charter and its requirement that members take collective action against an aggressor, but Japan has tried to make clear, without daring to mumble the words, that Japan has accepted its obligations in the UN with the attitude of Switzerland.

Sometimes the noble sentiment is voiced in Japan that "Japan cannot always expect to stand aside in cases of grave international difficulty." It echoes across the temple roofs and floats above the manicured countryside searching for someone to hear or heed it.

*"You are anxious to know whether you can count on Japan. Count on us for what? To use the naval and air bases you have here? In a dangerous situation, in an emergency? Surely you are not serious."*

The test of a treaty has always been found not in the quality of the paper bearing its words but on the sincerity of the contracting parties and their capability in fulfilling the terms. On that basis the future of the U. S.-Japan Security Treaty is as dim as our Japanese friend on the *tatami* suggests. Japan's desire and capability to implement the treaty are open to grave and continuing doubts.

Shortly after the antisecurity treaty riots in 1960, the USS *Grayback,* a submarine, entered the U. S. Naval base at Yokusuka, near Tokyo. The *Grayback* was capable of carrying Regulus II missiles. When the Japanese protested the introduction of nuclear weapons into Japan, the Pentagon explained that the *Grayback* was not carrying nuclear warheads. Japanese officials remained dissatisfied with the explanation, or had to say so in order to pacify the Japanese people.

Implementation of the U. S.-Japan Security Treaty—in other words, doing what one has a right to do under that agreement—would not be contingent on the good will or sincerity of the Japanese Government. It would be controlled by passivity of the Japanese public and the opposition of the Japan Socialist Party and the viciousness of pro-Communist and Communist-financed street mobs. The political climate in Japan denies a Polaris submarine or a U-2 access to U. S. bases in Japan; not even the Japanese expect the U. S. would use its bases here in case of another war in Korea. The bases are not even barns in case of a rainstorm; they are for minor repairs in times of tranquillity and for servicemen's rest and recreation.

The future of the current, revised U. S.-Japan Security Treaty—the core of military relations between the two countries—cannot be estimated by the performance record of its predecessor. The 1951 treaty was imposed by a victorious United States (fighting a war at that time in Korea from invaluable bases in Japan) on a conquered and still not sovereign country. It gave Japan virtually no rights, no voice in the equipment (meaning atomic weapons) brought into Japan or in the movement of U. S. forces on Japanese soil or off it.

Japan was shackled with a military tie-up that kept it and its people firmly in bondage. That was not materially altered even after Japan recovered its sovereignty in the 1952 peace treaty. But sovereignty on paper did change the Japanese frame of mind. In the Diet, the treaty was denounced with increasing frequency as unequal and unilateral. That it certainly was. "While the defeated cannot be choosers," Japanese officials were saying, "we are not defeated any more." In a manner of speaking, no; but that treaty was living proof of nonsovereignty.

Shortly after Ambassador MacArthur arrived in 1957, the Socialists, seeking an issue in the burgeoning prosperity, moved to capitalize on nationalism, then a toddling infant still learning to walk. They began agitating for revision of the treaty to bring respect to Japanese honor and independence.

It was a case of the issue and the man arriving under the cherry blossoms at the same time. MacArthur was sympathetic to revision for he arrived imbued with the feeling that his role in Tokyo was a logical succession to that of his military uncle. The nephew would be the architect of Japan's transition from a position of inferiority to one of equality. It had to come anyhow, MacArthur reasoned, and if equality were secured at a speed Japan preferred and could absorb, it would produce a net gain for the U. S. in future friendship and co-operation.

It was a point of view, as tenable as any other and more supportable than most. Ambassador MacArthur moved energetically in many different directions to make the Japanese feel ten feet tall.

The Socialist Party agitation for treaty revision was mildly shared by the ruling Liberal-Democratic Party and it was heard with the friendliest consideration in Washington. The whole affair had one flaw, a major one. The Japanese Socialists, working then as now in harmony with Moscow and Peiping, had their eyes and minds on much more than mere revision. They aimed for abrogation of the treaty, expulsion of U. S. forces, elimination of U. S. bases and adoption of a neutral role for Japan.

As the responsible party in power, the Liberal-Democrats were lackadaisical, indecisive, inconclusive. The government of Prime Minister Kishi was uninspired. The absence of passion for treaty revision among the Japanese politicians was shared by a vastly indifferent public. It took fifteen months and twenty-two meetings for Foreign Minister Aiichiro Fujiyama and Ambassador MacArthur to agree on the terms. It was an inordinate length of time for agreement on a matter of this kind to be resolved between two friendly nations.

The difficulties were not in the two personalities directly involved. MacArthur, a hard driver, and Fujiyama, a pleasant man, got on well together; and besides, MacArthur's strategy was to allow the Japanese to set the pace of the negotiations. The sand in the grease was the one facet of Japanese character seldom mentioned, usually ignored, but essential to an understanding of Japanese behavior. Our friend sitting on the *tatami* and voicing his views brought it up at the very beginning of our encounter.

The Japanese abhor responsibility. As individuals they cringe in terror before it. As a nation they shrink from it. That is the clue and perhaps the main one to the big, round "why" of the 1960 anti-treaty riots. It was the mental state which made university students receptive to Communist money, Socialist slogans and bottled frenzy.

When helpless Japan was saddled with the 1951 military alliance, Japan had to accept U. S. forces on its soil. The Japanese neither assumed responsibility nor suffered the burden of decision. But 1960 was entirely different. Japan was sovereign. It had initiated the talks for revision of the treaty. It had come to terms with the United States. The treaty it apparently wanted was going through the parliamentary processes preliminary to passage. It was all up to Japan. Japan could elect to have a treaty with the United States. Japan could elect to abandon such a treaty. As the "moment of truth" bore down upon them the Japanese people looked upon the event with the rapidly widening eyes of astonishment and incredulity; they and their Government were deliberately and voluntarily choosing to side with the free world and to engage in military collusion with the United States.

*"If you Americans did not have bases here then there would be no reason for Russia and China to threaten us. The bases really do not provide us with security. They are an open invitation for Communist attack. The American military does not protect Japan. It puts Japan in jeopardy. I believe this and I am not a Socialist. Even many of your so-called best friends in Japan think this way about the American bases, even though they do not say so to your face."*

When Francis Powers and his U-2 came down in the Soviet Union, the Russian reaction won many new Japanese converts to absolute neutrality. There was only one Russian reaction that the Japanese found worth noticing but it was most impressive. Moscow radio announced that the Soviet Union had missiles on the launching pads directed at Japan and ready to be released if any more "espionage planes" took off. Since there were two "Black Jets," as Japanese newspapers called them, in Japan, the Japanese people visibly quivered and quaked. And Ambassador MacArthur allowed the Japanese mobs to score another clean-cut victory.

Denouncing U. S. "imperialism," Socialists and Zengakuren students marched on the Atsugi Air Base, where the high-flying jets had been based, and demanded that they be removed from Japan. The next day the Japanese Government announced that the jets had indeed been removed. It gave the Japanese public the impression that the demonstrators had won their objective, had saved Japan from a possible rain of missiles. Not until twenty-four hours later did the U. S. Embassy say that the U-2s had been sent back to the United States several weeks before, long before the demonstrations against their presence in Japan.

The revised U. S.-Japan Security Treaty gained automatic passage on June 19, 1960, as the clock ticked midnight and mobs howled outside the official residence of Prime Minister Kishi, screaming for his or anybody's blood. Failure of the mob to turn Kishi into a craven creature who would quit to save his neck was the turning point in the fight. If Kishi had resigned before midnight of June 19, the legislative process for automatic passage would have been halted and treaty revision would have fallen in flight. It was dawn of the 20th before Kishi dared to leave the official residence and go to his own home, a hero to almost no one in Japan.

Whatever Kishi's fate might turn out to be, the revised security treaty was on the books. And U. S. officials in Japan and in Washington said, "We have won." On November 20, 1960, the election victory of another pro-Western prime minister, Hayato Ikeda, was hailed as evidence that relations between Tokyo and Washington were "better than normal." Behind this American self-delusion, Japan in 1961 moved toward neutralism at a gallop. Japan smiled and bowed and apologized. It sent Crown Prince Akihito and Crown Princess Michiko to the U. S. for that purpose. Students traipsed to America to do their *mea culpas*. In statements and editorials Japan put on the face of penitence and reassurance. But in practical terms Japan kept edging away from involvement in "American quarrels."

It became more evident to Japanese and Americans alike that Japan would not mix in any brawl if the initiative to remain aloof could rest with Japan. The usefulness of U. S. bases remained at the mercy of mobs, since police authority remained weak. Police powers could not be elevated to those held by law officers in any so-called law-abiding democracy because the Japanese public, having drunk the bitter brew of prewar police tyranny, refused to support any politician who had the desire to do so. Very few even had the desire.

Between easily organized street mobs, flabby government leaders and hamstrung police, both democracy and the Security Treaty remained in constant peril.

Those Japanese who yearned for defense were caught in the same dilemma. They had almost no hope that Japan could resolve its missile problem. Without daring to breathe the horrible word *nuclear,* a few Japanese Self-Defense officers have tried to point out that one of the simplest modern weapons of self-protection were guided missiles. They were indispensable even in a highly limited defense action against air attack, because AA guns would be as effective as BB guns against a jet.

Yet let anyone mention "ground-to-air missiles" or "air-to-air missiles" for warding off an attacker in the skies and leftist

newspapers, unions and Socialists immediately yelp that
Japan is being hurled back into her military past. So it has
been in Japan, so it will continue to be.

*"What is the reason for this phobia you Americans have
for bases? The United States will have to give up its bases
in Japan in a few years. It would be better for that to happen
when there is no pressing need—not when you think you
are in great need to use them and instead are forced to
retreat from Japan under threat."*
In other words, say the so-called friends of the United
States in Japan, you had better get out while the getting is
good. (And the same Socialist unions stage strikes at the
bases when the U. S. military says fifty workers are no longer
needed, or a hundred workers will be separated from their
jobs three months hence.)
"Now that Americans have ICBM missiles and Polaris
submarines, you do not really need bases." That is getting
to be the number one contention among increasingly nervous, or frightened, or dismayed U. S. allies in Asia. And if
there is any satisfaction to be dredged out of the arms race
toward mutual destruction, it might be found in the scientific advances which provide long-range weapons when
American acceptability on foreign soil is turning frosty.
But military experts emphasize that the more acute danger
is in the outbreak of the limited war in Asia. That postulates
the need for bases in the area. The Japanese trend toward
neutrality, toward disassociating the country from a military
future with the United States, weakens U. S. capacity to keep
the Far East out of Communist hands. It settles down to an
equation. The fewer the number of bases which the U. S.
has in the Far East, the more impossible it would be for
the U. S. to fight a limited war. Therefore, the more firmly
the U. S. becomes committed to fighting a nuclear war.
To defend South Korea now without the use of bases in

Japan and Japan's collaboration would make it mandatory for the U. S. to direct its major attacks at the source of the aggression, Peking or Moscow, or both, with weapons capable of leapfrogging over a Japan that decided "to sit this one out." My own view is that Japan would indeed sit out a future Communist attack on South Korea.

Japan is a classic example of a country that commits itself to nothing while Americans pretend they have a deal. I was in Singapore in the months before December 7, 1941, and as the time approached for the simultaneous Japanese attack on Pearl Harbor, Manila and Singapore, the delusions and wishful thinking from allegedly responsible people were almost enough to give death to reason.

Something of this same sort was loosed on the American public by the Eisenhower Administration after "we got the revised U. S.-Japan Security Treaty on the books." The fact of the matter is that the moment the United States won "this monumental victory" the U. S. military planners had to revise drastically their plans for defending the Far East. The revision had to be headed: How to defend without using bases in Japan.

The treaty contained a small paragraph usually glossed over in all discussions. It required the United States to consult Japan on the deployment of U. S. forces and weapons in and out of Japan. So far, a normal provision. Though it was not expressly stated in the treaty, the provision for "consultation" meant approval. And approval meant Japan's right to veto. This cardinal point was understood by both governments. This was the built-in assurance that the Switzerland of Asia wanted. The United States policy makers, President Eisenhower, Secretaries of State Dulles and Herter, and Ambassador MacArthur were happy to provide the escape hatch so that Japan could "include itself out" of any imbroglio.

The military ties that bound the U. S. and Japan could

come under the heading: How to Pretend You Have a Treaty
So You Can Sleep Nights.

Ambassador Reischauer came to Japan carrying these same
delusions. On April 19, 1961, he arrived in Tokyo, but on
April 11 he had appeared at a news conference in Washington.

**Q.** Do you have any comment on the prospect of revision
of the Mutual Security Pact between the United States and
Japan?
**A.** Well, I think we have just gotten through making a
new treaty between the United States and Japan. I might
say that I am somewhat distressed that everybody always
refers to it as a "Security Pact." If I remember correctly, it
isn't called that, but the "Treaty of Mutual Co-operation and
Security," or something of that sort. And from my point of
view the whole concept of mutual co-operation ought to be
the very important aspect of it. Of course, security is part of
the co-operation.

Ambassador Reischauer failed to note the supreme irony
of a mutual co-operation treaty that is not a treaty of mutual
co-operation. Of the forty-four treaties of mutual security
and assistance on the U. S. books, only one lacks mutuality,
the arrangement with Japan. The United States is committed
to Japan's defense. Japan need not budge to help the U. S.
in case of attack.

This monumental exception came about because the U. S.
approach to Japan in the Eisenhower-Dulles-Herter-Mac-
Arthur II era was to give Japan anything it wanted (within
elastic reason) and to reserve the fewest possible rights for
the U. S.

("Careful, careful," cried Japanese officialdom, "you had
better agree or you will push us toward Communism.") The
U. S. military in Japan was aghast and indignant over "the

sellout" of every U. S. right under the revised Security Treaty. U. S. businessmen in Japan privately said Ambassador Mac-Arthur "never" took their side in a dispute with Japanese businessmen.

When Ambassador MacArthur departed Japan in March, 1961, bound for his new post as envoy to Belgium, former Prime Minister Kishi was among those who went to the Yokohama pier to see him off.

"Don't say good-by," said MacArthur to Kishi. "We shall see each other again."

"You were so generous to Japan," replied Kishi, "that I often wondered if you were not a Japanese ambassador."

*"You want to know whether you can count on us to stand with you against the Communists? We are not sure any more where you stand. We are a conservative people, a non-Communist people, but we are drifting without a rudder for we have been torn from our traditional moorings. If you carry the map of Asia in your head you know we are a few miles from Soviet Russia, a few minutes by jet from Communist China, and one missile second away from both. As you Americans would express it, we must mend our fences with our two biggest neighbors. Both of them happen to be Communist."*

On occasion Japanese place a tape measure around their allegedly gargantuan guilt complex for the Manchurian grab, the Nanking rape and the Shanghai massacre and wonder if it is not time that "we begin showing how sorry we are." Japan's largest and most influential newspaper, the left-wing *Asahi*, said in early March, 1961, that for Japan "a solution of the China problem [*Asahi* meant diplomatic relations and full association with Peking] is not a matter merely of common sense, necessity or peace. It is a problem of ethics for the Japanese people. We believe it will afford an opportunity to make amends for the grave mistakes of which Japan was guilty before and during the war."

The Chinese, who have unforgettable reasons for knowing the Japanese as well as the Japanese pretend they know the Chinese, have shown no evidence of being impressed by the unnatural spectacle of Japan wearing sackcloth and ashes. Rather than assuaging guilt, Japan has more pertinent and persuasive reasons for "normalizing and regularizing" relations with mainland China.

And what does Red China seek from Japan? In frank moments Chinese Communist officials are known to say that the paramount aim of the Peking Government is to expel the United States from Asia and the Western Pacific and to add Japan's tremendous industrial power to that of China. But few Japanese seem to be aware that their country is made for conquest, in Peking's hungry but patient eyes. One who does, Taizo Ishizaka, head of the great Toshiba Electric Company, fears that the day Japan recognized Communist China might be the beginning of the end for Japan.

As chairman of the Federation of Economic Organizations, Ishizaka was the spokesman for Japanese industry and commerce. He told me that while many businessmen wanted to trade with Communist China, he foresaw Peking using methods that would be destructive and disruptive to Japanese business. "They will try to take over Japan," he said flatly.

But Japanese have the same arrogant confidence that Germans used to have about the Russians: *We will know how to handle them.* Since the Japanese would approach dealings with the Chinese Reds as part of the normal pursuit of business and diplomacy while the Chinese Communists would approach Japan as a huge pie being baked for the eating, the contradictions would be continuous.

Many Japanese businessmen in talking about China light up their eyes with avaricious anticipation based on memory, not on reality. In the old days, China was a principal market for machinery, textiles and sundry goods, all that junk with which Japan flooded the shops and street stalls of Asian villages. That China is gone. Although autarchy is far from complete, Red China is not spending foreign exchange or even bartering pigs or humans to bring in Japanese bicycles, radios, textiles, sewing machines, and such. Most of those items are made in China now. Japan would seek again, as it had before, a considerable part of its iron-ore needs, and salt and coal from China.

The capriciousness of doing business with Red China has not gone unnoticed in Japan. Peking abruptly broke a trade agreement with Japan in early 1958 because of an incident involving the display of the Nationalist Chinese flag. Aside from that, the Red Chinese failed to fill orders, canceled goods already manufactured according to their specifications, proving themselves as customers to be more trouble than they were worth. Still, the hunger persisted, and the magic words continued to have a seductive lure—trade with Red China.

"If we now have difficulty in showing China that we are not her enemy," a Japanese government official explained to me, "at least we must show the people in Peking that we wish to be friends."

Peking has price tags on that: Japan must abrogate its security treaty with the United States; Japan must abandon its recognition of Nationalist China on Formosa. Neither price is too high for Japan to pay. But not for the present.

Japan counts on the United States moving toward an adjustment with Communist China. Any Japanese prime minister who failed to be one jump ahead of President Kennedy and at least one week ahead of a U. S. rapprochement with Peking would be dead politically, and instantly so. Therefore, Japan delicately but insistently has jogged the U. S. into taking a more favorable and lenient attitude toward Red China, and to advance that cause Prime Minister Ikeda met with President Kennedy in Washington in June, 1961.

But it is a thin and shaky bridge that Japan attempts to travel between Taipei and Peking. Its trade with Nationalist China is worth a hundred million dollars a year; best estimates of Red Chinese trade run about half that amount. So, in the framework of trade, Red China would have to offer more business before it could call itself a substitute for Formosa in the Japanese cash register.

On the broader picture, the Japanese Government has constant nightmares of China having atomic weapons. That is Peking's definite objective. Japan will not have atomic weapons. That is Tokyo's firm desire. When the decade of the sixties comes to an end, if the end is normal, China will have almost 900 million people. Japan's population will have leveled off to about 102 million. As a prerequisite for survival, Japan seeks friendship or tolerance with Red China. This automatically requires a loosening of the military ties with the United States as a prelude to breaking them.

All over Asia, young people speak glowingly of events in Red China. They have heard part of the story, and what they have heard and the visual propaganda floating before their eyes have been enticing.

*"You wonder whether you can count on us for trade, to maintain our economic ties with you even if our military alliance decays? But that is an absurd question."*

It is indeed. The ties that bind the U. S. and Japan are economic, not ideological and military. An age of "the good things of life" has opened for the Japanese people. Although only a small percentage of Japan's 94 million people has been able so far to do more than goggle at them, the vision of sampling them soon has been dancing before the eyes of all. That prospect has been the most powerful and seductive reason why the association between the United States and Japan has been so strong. Few if any Japanese want their country to take any action in any arena that might jeopardize the individual's access to television sets, washing machines, electric rice cookers, modern kitchens, small tractors, a motorcycle or even an automobile. The Ikeda Government has promised to double national income in ten years, and although a promise only recently made, it has already become a calmly accepted and settled expectation of the Japanese public. They never knew that prosperity could be so wonderful or that life could be so beautiful.

If the United States had been able to do what Japan has done in the past few years, we could count ourselves more wonderful than all the people in the world put together. Japan's rate of economic growth has been triple that of the United States. Since the war, Japan's economic expansion has been without parallel in any country in the world: 17 per cent in 1959, about 12 per cent in 1960, an expected 10 per cent in 1961. Prime Minister Ikeda has promised a 9 per cent increase per year through 1964, making the Japanese boom the phenomenon of the world. And all this has come about with prices kept reasonably stable. In 1960, with a gross national product of 40 billion dollars, the per capita income rose to $365, highest in Asia, comparable now to southern Europe.

Of course, the more Japan succeeds with trade in some markets, notably the United States, the more trouble it invites. Its trouble is secondary to its need. Unless Japan succeeds even more in the markets it now has and finds additional markets, the country cannot hope to survive. This compulsion is acute, each day more so than the day before. It is as acute for the Japanese nation as gulping in air is for a man who has tightening hands on his throat. Living with it, gasping for breath really, as 900,000 new jobs must be found each year, has developed in Japanese businessmen and government officials the arrogant attitude that they now own, have a vested right in and are really the possessors of a percentage of the U. S. market for everything from salmon to textiles to bicycles.

More than self-interest engenders this arrogance; Japan has the U. S. by the throat as well. Japan buys more from the United States than any other country does, except Canada. And the U. S. sells more to Japan than it sells to any other country, again except Canada.

Both U. S. senators and union members often forget or more likely never knew that during 1960 Japan bought $1,300,000,000 worth of American goods and the United States bought $1,100,000,000 of Japanese. So Japan does not quake in its kimono and Japanese do not jump off Mt. Fuji when unions in the United States threaten to boycott textiles or rubber shoes or transistors. In the past year the Japanese have brushed aside these threats with the casual comment, "Don't bother us with such nonsense." They now know that President Kennedy has recognized that if U. S. foreign policy is to be made by, for example, the Amalgamated Clothing Workers' Union, then U. S. cotton growers, for example, will be buried under the products of their soil instead of selling cotton at a handsome profit to Japan. In the trade arrangements between the United States and Japan, however few the joys and however lofty the irritations, one fact stands out crystal clear: It is impossible even to pretend that one nation is the prisoner of the other, or that one has superior weapons.

The only hope Japan has of achieving its plans for economic growth lies in the development of overseas trade. The only genuine hope of improving the democratic climate in Japan rests on a base of continued economic growth. Since the Japanese are panting to secure more foreign trade, and the U. S. yearns for more domestic democracy, every effort to expand trade between the United States and Japan, and not erecting barriers against it, would be sound policy.

But if trade is a matter of mutuality, so is reform. Japan lives and breathes trade. Preoccupation with it to the exclusion of other matters in Japan is phenomenal. In that field, though, Japanese immaturity is striking. Short of everything for self-sufficiency, Japan would die as quickly as a fish out of water if trade were to halt. But the Japanese have a constricted understanding and a myopic view of the truism that "trade is a two-way street."

Despite a painful and painfully slow movement toward leniency in trade restrictions, most Japanese business and government leaders feel that Japan should have insurmountably high walls to keep out foreign goods. But all markets in all the world should be wide open to Japanese goods.

For every big businessman in Japan who extols the virtues of open trade, there are five middle businessmen who prefer to ignore that Japan owes more than any other country to foreign connections and skills. Business and industrial and commercial isolation in Japan is strong. Foreigners are often regarded as objects to be tolerated, and if possible, to be discouraged. Through internal persuasion and external pressure, and much more of that is called for, the Japanese might come to shed the notion that Japan does not need Westerners and would be better off without them.

"Have your cake and eat it, too." A Japanese prime minister who failed to expand Japan's markets, or who called for austerity in a country now scrambling for every gadget known to confuse modern man, would be overwhelmed at the polls or stabbed to death. And probably both.

*"You want to know whether you can count on us to be your friends. In this world, who is friend, who is enemy? What do the words mean? For many centuries we have been born and raised with distrust for foreigners, the barbarians,* gaijin, *people from the outside. In a decade and a half you want to erase the belief of centuries and call us by first names, American-style, and shake hands American-style. Have you noticed that fewer Japanese want to shake hands now than*

*did a few years ago? We are able to repulse that custom now.
Well, yes, our economic interests, yes, I suppose our major
political interests, are now similar. Let us say we travel the
same path. We wave to each other in friendliness. What
more need you ask?"*

The date: March, 1961.

The place: Tokyo Kaikan, a showplace restaurant for important banquets, weddings, status affairs.

The Occasion: The America-Japan Society holds a *sayonara*
for Ambassador Douglas MacArthur II.

Gist of Remarks: "Unbreakable ties of friendship between
our two peoples."

American and Japanese heads nodded in vigorous assent,
especially the Japanese heads. These were the presidents of
Japan's mighty corporations, makers of ships, molders of
steel, purveyors of transistors, marketers of gadgets for young
and old, white and yellow, happy and frustrated, sellers to
all, the free and the chained. The shoguns of Mitsui, Mitsu-
bishi, Sumitomo—keystones of the powerful Zaibatsu the
Occupation would break up—were there smiling happily.
They could well afford to. They had outsmarted the Occupation. The cartel arrangement, their lovely Zaibatsu, was
back together again and they were earning more profits than
in the days of Empire.

These were the men, listening now to the U. S. ambassador
with the distinguished name reciting the virtues of Japan,
who had lived for so many years with grandiose schemes for
controlling U. S. industry and operating the industry of all
Asia "after Japan won the war." These were the fabulously
imaginative, enormously competent and fanatically determined men who collaborated unreservedly with militarism to
make a dream come true. Their tragedy, or so it seemed
to them at the time, was that the dream evaporated in a
mushroom cloud.

Their current dream was already rich with reality. And

the prospects for the realization of more luscious dreams of reaping profits from everything from avalanching tourism to compact cars appeared limitless.

The pragmatic men who puffed happily on cigars or fingered cigarettes while MacArthur bid his *sayonaras* were not ideological captives any more than they were in the late thirties. The impulses and rewards that led these tycoons into joyous collaboration with domestic militarists led them to the same association with the U. S. Occupation. The same prospects of rewards would as easily and as smoothly lead them into a similar path with the Communists.

At the same hour the luncheon honoring MacArthur was being held in a sea of platitudes, at the nearby Kudan Kaikan the convention of the Japan Socialist Party was in progress. It was heavily larded with denunciations of "imperialism," meaning always, in the lexicon of the Japan Socialist Party, the United States, and never Communist China or Soviet Russia. Hovering over the Socialist gathering was the image (as well as the portrait) of the recently assassinated party chairman, Inejiro Asanuma, who laid down the rule that "the United States is the common enemy of Japan and China."

These two simultaneous gatherings by apparently political opposites demonstrated that the cement holding Japan to the West was economics not ideology; the tie that bound was opportunism not gratitude.

*"If we felt more secure within ourselves, if we had recovered our sense of honor, we would not have endured your criticism of our domestic behavior when President Eisenhower was forbidden to enter Japan. You will forgive me, perhaps. Does the United States have the right to criticize another for immature democracy? Is that not American arrogance? The free world is in torment and no part is free from it. While your Mr. Kennedy charts a path to his New*

*Frontier, do not count on Oriental serenity in Japan. We are not finished with our brawling."*

Two hours from Tokyo, the driver wheeled the car through a narrow, clay-sided cut in the hill, wide enough for only one car. The road ended in a clump of white birches on a hilltop. Spread below in an elongated bowl of a valley the camp's grounds appeared something like a well-endowed Boy Scout vacation area. There was one long, frame building newly finished, another almost similar building waiting only for the tile roof for completion. Fields of fig trees soon to burst into leaf occupied half the saucer.

This was a privately organized and privately financed camp for the training of rightist action squads. There were dozens of these camps in Japan. This one was the incubation arena of *Hinomaru Seinen Tai* or Circle of the Sun Youth Corps, or National Flag Youth Corps. It was a unit of the Gijin Party, named for Gijin Takahashi who founded it, has supported it financially and one day proposes to use it to gain his ends, which he considers to be in the highest traditions of Japanese patriotism.

At this particular camp, a dozen young men were undergoing a year of training in *kurate* and *kendo,* or Japanese dueling with sticks; they were being taught how to break an adversary's collarbone, to knee him, to throw him over the shoulder and into the ash heap. They were being taught the intricacies of street fighting, the speediest methods of assassination, how to fire a pistol accurately. They were being instructed in the supreme duty of Emperor worship, the more prosaic chores of infiltrating unions and the newer techniques of propaganda.

Gijin Takahashi does not differ markedly from other right-wing ultranationalists in Japan. He and several of his brothers operate a construction company (but he said he had to sell a small hotel he owned to finance his youth project) and they call themselves dedicated anti-Communists and Japanese patriots. Takahashi visited the camp the day I was there.

Without drawing odious comparisons, Takahashi in appearance reminded me of a well-fed, chunky Heinrich Himmler. And, again unrelated to his past or present, I could not shake loose the visual comparison all the time I was with him.

"I hate Communism," he said as we walked around his domain. "I want the United States to fight against Communism hand in hand with Japan."

"Do you suggest that the United States should start a nuclear war against Soviet Russia?"

"No, no, that is not good at all. If a nuclear war starts, there are no rightists, no leftists any more."

"Do you think the Emperor should be restored to his pre-war position?"

"If possible I would like very much to do so. Our effort is to return Japan to the old days. I would not say we should have the same military forces. I am referring more to morality. In the old days we used to say, for example, 'when you walk with your teacher, follow three steps behind him and do not even step on his shadow.' Then, young people paid proper respect to their teacher. Japan is a country of beautiful moral traditions but most of them have been destroyed in the postwar trends. What I am trying to do is to bring this morality back to the youth. We all think that if what we do is for the Emperor then we are glad to die for him."

When we talked about the assassination of Socialist Party chairman, Inejŭro Asanuma, by a seventeen-year-old rightist (in October, 1960) who later killed himself in jail, even my interpreter was awed by the vehemence of Gijin Takahashi's approval of the murder.

"I would not say that I educate the young men here to commit assassinations. No, I would not say that. But if each boy considers a matter carefully and reaches a conclusion that somebody should be killed and he does it, I will approve fully. Such an act is no longer violence but a punishment from heaven, it might be called."

"This is your private army, then, and it is your intention to use this army to fight your battle?"

"More or less, yes. If an enemy is too big and I cannot cope with the enemy myself, I might use the young men I have trained here. I expect we will win the war within Japan. We will bring Japan back to the old days, where the Emperor had absolute power and the morality of the Samurai dominated our lives. We will have the code of Bushido again."

Police authorities, who keep a watch on this and other rightist camps and leaders, estimate there are 100,000 people imbued with the ultranationalistic notions to the point of battling in the streets when the time comes. Most rightists claim that there are as many as 500,000 prepared to man the barricades. Perhaps the numbers game is not worth playing in the brewing battles between right and left in Japan. There are enough on each side to keep Japan in turmoil and to make legislation in the streets.

Leftists in Japan are much stronger, therefore far more dangerous as a menace to the governmental structure, than the rightists, who have a greater capacity for pin-pointed terrorism since the quick dagger is their favored device for eliminating opponents. And there has been no shortage of those in Japan.

About 300,000 students in Japan's universities, half of the total enrollment, are theoretical members of Zengakuren, the Japan Student Self-Government Associations. In practical fact, only about 10 to 20 per cent of those are available for actions of anarchy. Zengakuren is split into two factions, the main stream which is Trotzkyite and dedicated to absolute anarchy; the anti-main stream which is Stalinist, devoted to Khrushchev and under direct control of the Russian Communists. But each faction has its splinter groups as well. The internecine disorder in Zengakuren is of less concern than the devotion of its members to the destruction of parliamentary government.

Zengakuren is militant, thirsting for action, seeks identification with causes; most of its members feel themselves fervent crusaders for peace. All that makes them easy marks for exploitation by the Japan Socialist Party, the General Council of Japan Trade Unions (Sohyo) and the official Communist Party of Japan.

Leftists enjoy infinitely greater acceptability and respectability than rightists. Few intellectuals feel at home in the rightist camp. Hordes of professors, teachers, writers, social workers, newspaper and magazine writers and editors, artists, engineers and science workers can be found on the leftist side of any domestic or international issue.

"If the youth of today," said one Japanese weekly, "are to be the leaders of tomorrow, we are in for a rather sad and violent future." Not many months before he became Ambassador, Professor Reischauer wrote in *The Japan Quarterly:*

The self-righteous fanaticism of certain intellectuals and students during the May and June troubles reminded me most painfully of the attitude of the young officers in the 1930s who "knew" that they were right when they overrode the wishes of the majority, thus destroying democracy and leading Japan into disastrous military adventures.

To me the wonder of it all is not that 1960 produced the worst political crisis since Japan's defeat but that the Japanese held themselves in check so long after regaining their sovereignty and the right to be crazy on their own time. The impact of military defeat on Japan has never been properly assessed, because the impact is far from over. It was not until John Hersey's report appeared several years after Hiroshima that the Japanese paid much attention to the atomic bombing of the city and then only as a device for political opportunism. The more enduring residue of defeat was the total collapse of the old system of values. And the most significant victim was respect for authority in Japan, every kind of Japanese authority from Emperor to parents.

"I do not have to listen to you," a parent told me his child retorted. "We are a democracy and everybody is equal."

And parents hardly have the will and strength to remonstrate. Most adults are bereft of confidence in their own judgment on how to handle minors. Children have been accustomed to say to their elders, more as a weapon of rebellion than a reprimand, "You brought this nation to disaster, so why should we respect your advice or your opinion?" Out of that has come the tendency of many Japanese families to follow a policy of *jiyu honin shugi* which literally means "policy of freedom and letting alone." Unable to understand or deal with his child, the father leaves him or her alone. That policy has widened the gap between children and their elders. It reflects itself in every aspect of Japanese life. There is communication, of course, between the generation of the war and the after-the-war generation. But it is largely unintelligible.

The turbulence facing Japan and the sandpaper being prepared for U. S.-Japan relations stem from the breakdown of ideals, weathered for 2,500 years and then shattered in four. The substitutes have not been adequate—television sets, installment buying, ferro-concrete apartment houses, things on wheels.

*"Compliment us on one thing. We are no longer the avaricious imperialists of former years. You should be delighted with our restraint. We are bursting at the seams, and I am not using an Americanism; we burst but we are restrained."*

Japan has performed the remarkable feat of cutting its birth rate in half and now ranks modestly in the "population explosion" business with Anglo-Saxon countries. But the need for "living space" persists.

Few Japanese dream of the past glories of Empire but ashes of the dream remain. I recall Emperor Hirohito's avid interest in one of his former overseas possessions when he received me in audience in 1951. In response to his question, I began describing conditions in various countries around the world that I had just visited. But it was only when I came to Formosa, once the star sapphire in the Imperial colonial crown, that Emperor Hirohito exhibited his keenest interest. But Japanese territorial expansionism is not an issue or a threat in the decade of the sixties.

Partly out of appetite for a lost Atlantis, partly for its potentials as a political firecracker, Japanese officials and agitators (sometimes they are one and the same) are building a smoldering case out of Okinawa. The 67 Ryukyu islands, of which Okinawa is the largest, stretch between Japan and Formosa. They are administered by the United States under terms of the 1951 peace treaty with Japan. But Japan wields "residual sovereignty," which means in the end Okinawa is to revert to Japanese control, to become again as it was before, one of the prefectures of Japan. But who is to say when the end has been reached? Three possibilities are visible: When the U. S. is forced to abandon its bases in Japan, when the U. S. is pushed out of the Western Pacific, when ICBMs and satellites or disarmament make bases in Okinawa unnecessary.

In the meantime, though, Okinawa remains an unresolved and ready-made issue for Okinawans to protest, and for mainland Japanese to echo, that they are being hammered by U. S. "colonialism." We may expect that each new Japanese prime minister each year will broach to the United States Government the "early return" of Okinawa, the rest of the Ryukyus and the Bonin islands to Japan.

One can cherish and admire the tremendous up-from-the-bootstraps drive of the Japanese, their remarkable disciplines, their pitiful yearning for world respectability and even affection, and still be alert to the Japanese capacity for deception and pursuit of a course contrary to American hopes.

Responsible Japanese leaders would like the United States to believe that the new postwar, modern Japan is up-to-date in ethics, devoted to a democratic concept of government, and can be relied upon as a friend and ally. To visitors, the friendliness of 94 million Japanese people living in a territory the size of California, only 16 per cent of which is arable, appears to be an insurance policy for a happy future between Japanese and Americans. But Japan and the Japanese people have an unforgettable and historic capacity to turn out to be not what they seem to be.

*"We Japanese seem to others to be a disciplined people and it is truly so. It is a special caliber of discipline, producing national restraint and also national frenzy. The course of discipline depends upon leadership and it may also be driven in strange paths by instigation. I offer this brief character analysis of my people because I have wondered—please, I am hesitant, I have never before wondered this aloud to another person—what will happen to Japan and with Japan when Communist China explodes its first atomic device."*

According to the best information available, Communist China's nuclear schedule calls for a detonation in the 1961–62 period.

When that happens the most charitable description of what will occur in Japan can be described as utter panic. The real possibility is that when the Chinese Communist atomic explosion occurs, the shock waves will overturn the existing Japanese Government, probably set fire to the U. S.-Japan Security Treaty and send millions of Japanese diving into neutralism.

It is a foregone conclusion that the moment the Chinese

Red bomb, or whatever it is, goes off, the left-wing newspapers of Japan, which include almost the entire press, will stampede for neutralism. Likewise, the left-wing groups in Japan, from students to Socialists to unionists, will march on the Parliament shouting for peace at any price with Communist China.

That spectacle looms in Japan because the Japanese Government, the Liberal-Democrats, the conservatives, the Socialists, the newspapers, the liberals and the left-wingers are all engaged in a conspiracy of silence about the imminence of Red China entering the atomic club. With Communist China on the threshold of nuclear activity, the subject is never mentioned in public in Japan and so far as can be determined, never breathed in private by officials of the Government.

This horrendous bashfulness is not an internal matter for obvious reasons. It is, however, an aspect of the dream-world quality of Japan's approach to world problems.

Since the future of U. S.-Japan military relations rests upon the reaction in Japan to Red China's detonation of a nuclear device, the most urgent need of U. S. policy in Japan is to prepare the Japanese public for this event.

The task is immensely difficult, since Japanese governments are tragically inept in communicating information to their own people and to the outside world, and the Japanese press is highly resistant to information contrary to her neutralist convictions. But in the multitudinous problems facing President Kennedy and Ambassador Reischauer in achieving an understandable dialogue with the Japanese, none could have greater priority than reassuring words to a Japan which finds an Asian power with atomic weapons.

The first requirement would be for both the United States and Japanese Governments to say openly and often that Communist China is *going* to have nuclear weapons. That, at least, would attract some attention in the Japanese press, command comment and promote public talk about the subject. It would lay far more groundwork for the event than is being laid now.

Another important step would be to locate reasonable and amenable conservatives, liberal democrats, stalwarts of big business and giants of the academic world, and gently "brainwash" them into showing the courage to discuss the coming power of Communist China in the nuclear field and Japan's relation to it.

Such discussions, in public meetings, in newspaper and magazine articles, in television debates, in speeches in the Diet, might even take the direction of showing how sensible it is for Japan to have a Security Treaty with the United States.

Although the conservatives of Japan are remarkably inarticulate, one or two might be found to frame into words the salient point that a nuclear power, the United States, stands ready to protect Japan, a virtually defenseless nation, against nuclear-powered China. (Japanese are not impressed by that word "protect," but then neither is anybody else in the world; the only real protection for any nation is in deterrence and the Japanese have no right to ask for more than that from the United States, which is what they are getting.) For some time in the future, Japan will be only mildly menaced by Red China, if the Japanese keep their head.

There is a long way between a detonation and the manufacture of nuclear weapons and then quite a distance to go before achieving methods for delivering nuclear devices. No Japanese would be able to doubt that the three stages would be traveled by Red China, but the aim of a U. S.-Japan information policy would be to remove the present areas of ignorance and mental unpreparedness, and thus avoid the panic of shock and the stampede of unreadiness.

The massive effort to prepare the Japanese public for the red-letter day that Red China becomes an atomic power will have to be undertaken with the greatest skill, urgency and effectiveness or the left wing will push the panic button in Japan on that day, with consequences and catastrophes of benefit only to Communism.

—CECIL BROWN

CECIL BROWN, based in Tokyo, is Chief Far Eastern Correspondent for NBC News. Arriving in the Far East on this assignment in July, 1958, he returned to an area in which he had won reportorial distinction during the Second World War. After covering the fighting around Singapore he was aboard the British warship *Repulse* when the Japanese sank it. For his coverage of that action he won the Peabody Award and many other major honors. Born in New Brighton, Pa., he was graduated from Ohio State University in 1929. Eight years later, following jobs with several newspapers in this country, he joined the International News Service in Rome. His career as a foreign correspondent was highlighted by adventure and drama: he was expelled from Italy by Mussolini, captured by the Germans in Yugoslavia, bombed by the Japanese and, more recently, headline copy in Japan on proposals to change that country's constitution.

# 9.

## SOUTHEAST ASIA:

## *"The Massive Issue...Red China"*

AMERICA'S confrontation with Red China in Southeast Asia produces the unlikeliest situations. The unexpected is the rule. Only in lotus lands like Cambodia could an American World War II landing craft have served as the stage for a "peaceful co-existence" maneuver by the Peking government.

Pacific war service and the Indo-China fighting had scarred the craft I boarded in December, 1956, at the Royal Pier in the Cambodian capital city of Phnom Penh. She was rusted the ochre brown of Mekong River waters that were silted with soils from Tibet, China, Burma, Laos, Thailand, Cambodia and Vietnam along a 2,800-mile course to the South China Sea.

This American naval relic had nothing in common with the sleek, nuclear-armed vessels I had seen with the U. S. Seventh Fleet. Flying southward from Hong Kong I had watched Navy jet bombers on gray carrier decks, paired muzzles of gun turrets aboard cruisers, and hints of submarines patrolling beyond destroyer screens. This was the mightiest assembly of seaborne firepower in our peacetime history; a twentieth-century "Great Wall," fortified yet elusive off the coasts of Communist and Free Asia to contain Red China's aggressive armies.

Flying toward Phnom Penh across Southeast Asia's paddy lands, I was thinking of the roles sometimes forced upon this proud vanguard of America's military presence in Asia. There had been evacuation of the Tachen Islands, a Nationalist Chinese outpost that was snatched from under our guns in a calculated Peking gamble. There had been the rescue of frightened refugees who were fleeing North Vietnam ahead of the Communists.

I found no guns aboard the landing craft in Phnom Penh. Gay bunting had transformed her into Cambodia's Royal Yacht. Her mission that day was a Sunday afternoon outing on the Mekong River for Chou En-lai, the Foreign Minister of Communist China. Chou, who has since become Communist China's Premier, relied for firepower upon his inexhaustible arsenal of diplomacy. The targets were Cambodia's neutralist Prince Norodom Sihanouk and a group of Western newsmen.

Sweat-stained and apparently unwelcome, we correspondents gathered near the vessel's stern. Chou En-lai suddenly strolled toward us, handsome as always in a gray, high-collared Sun Yat-sen style tunic. His voice was pitched octaves higher than his looks suggested. But his phrases were carefully chosen; they were translated by a suave, Yale-educated interpreter in Brooks Brothers tailoring.

"We must thank you Americans," Chou En-lai said. "After all, our best Communist cadres were educated in America." There should be, he hinted, some intellectual kinship. The Communist government in Peking would like to welcome

American engineers to aid China's industrialization; Peking
would pay for the help.

Chou En-lai turned to me and smiled: "You must not be
angry with your Mr. Dulles for refusing to allow you correspondents to visit my country. He has his reasons."

I was among the twenty-four U. S. newsmen with visas for
Communist China. The State Department, however, had
banned the trip.

"Just remember that we Chinese know our two countries
are presently like this." Chou En-lai moved his hands apart
to dramatize his point. "But slowly, certainly, we will come
together in understanding," he added, interlacing his agile
fingers.

This conversation was a trial balloon. It exemplified that
oscillating diplomacy which Chairman Mao Tse-tung practiced—relaxation after the push, negotiation after the fight.

Should Washington have taken him up? We had been use-
lessly talking with Peking at Warsaw since mid-1954. But it
seemed to me, intimately conversing with Communism in the
heart of Southeast Asia, that Chou's forecast deserved attention. If nothing else, U. S. correspondents had an opportunity
to penetrate Red China's dark isolation. Just how much an
able American newsman could uncover was no secret to
Washington. The State Department reversed its course years
later. Mr. Dulles said that we could enter Red China and
theories were advanced that newsmen could be the vanguard
of broadening cultural contacts. But by that time Peking
had canceled our visas.

American engineers in China would have been a powerful
lever to pry Peking loose from the Soviet industrial machine.
But U. S. diplomatic bureaucracy, mesmerized by the
McCarthy allegations, could not act or could undertake only
the most cautious gestures. Our diplomats on the scene were
hamstrung by Mr. Dulles' "do-it-alonemanship." Unau-
thorized contacts with the Chinese Communists on the South-

east Asian periphery meant career suicide. For American correspondents, defiance of the State Department ban on visits to Red China was rewarded with the suspension of passports and the threat of further punishment.

This fossilization of American diplomatic initiative in the Far East dismayed Asians who recalled the heady days of 1945. In the wake of World War II triumph, the U. S. proudly, but briefly and often naïvely, had been the standard-bearer of revolution in Southeast Asia.

Japan had whetted Asian appetites for independence. Her puppet regimes had preached "Asia for the Asians." Her southward dash to the frontiers of White Australia had ended Oriental kowtowing to the pretensions of racial and technological superiority of Western imperialism. Then Japan's abrupt and total defeat bared the emotional wounds of colonialism that were festered with color consciousness and nationalistic passions.

We were generally popular. The Atlantic and the United Nations Charters, illumined by America's own shining light, dazzled Southeast Asia's enslaved millions with glowing images of the Four Freedoms. Democracy exuded the magic of a made-in-America miracle drug.

Sixteen years later that magic was suspect and the miracle drug was diluted.

Hindsight develops three general periods of about five years each during a decade and a half of transition for American fortunes in Southeast Asia. In the spring of 1961, a completely new period began amid tensions as complex as those of 1945.

There was a confused glamor surrounding the Asian capitals where I watched recovery from the war spill over from colonialism into bids for independence. Bangkok was typical of this laissez-faire political climate in the late 1940's. In a girl-filled bar could be seen a renegade British Army captain staring morosely at his whisky. He was in Bangkok to buy arms for rebel Karen tribesmen fighting a private war in Burma.

A stroll along New Road usually would be interrupted by the appearance of a scrawny, excited Vietnamese, who would giggle with delight as he would confide the details of his latest conversation with the ghost of Benjamin Franklin; Ben, it seemed, urged Vietnam's fanatic Cao Dai religious sect to revolt. Communist Vietnamese agents, whose complexions were sickly yellow from life in the jungle, whispered messages from Ho Chi Minh's secret revolutionary headquarters in northern Vietnam.

Always there were Chinese, some serving ideologies, others pursuing money, sipping sweet coffee in bland anonymity while studying lists of supply sources. One could buy the keys to power in Southeast Asia: pilots to airdrop anything to anyone, anywhere; weapons for guerrilla bands; opium and tawny women to tranquilize or seduce an enemy, and the hatchet men to murder him.

There were men of ideals, also; men afire with passion to see their nations free of the hated colonial taint. By definition, they were opportunists, but America welcomed the strongest among them as they surged toward independent leadership. In keeping faith with its national principles the United States was a major force in the dismantling of the colonial structures. The one inconsistency was the record in Indo-China, where the U. S. had to pay heavily for guilt-by-association with French colonial power that stubbornly but futilely sought to dam the flood of nationalism.

One might defend the American lapse in this instance by holding that the American way could not survive in the harsh climes of Southeast Asia. But Washington, at least, was guilty of failing to blueprint a comprehensive follow-through for all the consequences of this drive toward freedom.

The material conditions of Burma, for instance, from

communications to the coolie rice bowl, were better under British colonialism than they are with independence. The once neat boulevards of Rangoon are splattered with the spittle of betel-nut addicts who espouse democracy but who are unwilling to exercise self-discipline in its service. The Burmese countryside is a no man's land of armed bandits and rebels of many persuasions who leave corpses and devastation as reminders of their presence.

The heavy-handed pressures of Dutch colonial policy that once energized sprawling Indonesia into a semblance of unity were cast off violently by Djakarta's national revolutionaries. What replaced that colonial order was, for want of a better word, anarchy.

The legacy of the first five postwar years, therefore, was a distortion of the soaring American dream. To decry Southeast Asians for failing to realize their own finest aspirations begs the question. By historic design and as a consequence of America's position in world affairs, the U. S. had become the responsible pilot at the controls that had been unwillingly abandoned by our European allies. And it had failed to manipulate them effectively.

One consequence of the absence of stable authority accompanying colonialism's ebb was the Communist capture of China. I was teaching at the time at Tsinghua University in suburban Peking.

Chilling autumn winds from the Gobi desert were tinting the sparse trees in northern China's landscape when Mukden fell in 1948 to Communism. This was the first major Chinese city caught in the final rise of the Red tide. Mao Tse-tung's fabled Eighth Route Army, surviving two decades of harassment by Generalissimo Chiang Kai-shek and war with the Japanese, had expanded into many armies on the impetus of sweeping victories in Manchuria.

Peking, the eloquent cultural symbol of a civilization unbroken from the dawn of Chinese history, was now threatened. Chiang Kai-shek summoned his military commanders to Nanking for angry recriminations. Then he appeared within Peking's ancient walls with his beautiful wife for what was to be their last pilgrimage. From a distance I watched the Generalissimo walking pensively in the manicured gardens of Pei Hai Park; significantly, Peking's politically alert citizens were withholding any applause which, while it would have distracted him, certainly would have cheered him.

Chiang Kai-shek's ablest general, Fu Tso-yi, deployed several splendidly trained units superbly equipped with American weapons for Peking's defense. Along the ridges of the western hills we could glimpse, through field glasses, the vanguard of Mao Tse-tung's legions. They came on silent canvas shoes, cradling battle-worn Japanese rifles, scouting in bands of four or five.

General Fu's Nationalist garrison made a brave show outside Peking's high encircling walls; artillery rumbled onto the Tsinghua University campus. For two sleepless nights and days, the guns bellowed at an enemy still mostly invisible beyond the quiet hills.

Then they came, a squad of Mao Tse-tung troops in fur hats loping through the rice stubble. The Nationalist soldiers fled across the four miles separating them from Peking's walls. In a touching, medieval gesture against the new barbarians, the massive gates to Peking ponderously swung shut.

Mao's peasant legions drew a tightening circle around the city. I heard amazement and doubt that this ragged force, unable to match the U. S.-supplied firepower arrayed for Peking's defense, could challenge General Fu with its arsenal of obsolete weapons.

I had underestimated traditional Chinese deftness with compromise. I had not been initiated in the Mao Tse-tung doctrine of war: "To annihilate the enemy means to disarm him, or to deprive him of his power of resistance, and not to annihilate him completely in the physical sense."

Peking, in fact, was lost over teacups. General Fu surrendered his command, his troops, and his American arsenal to the persuasion that there was no other alternative.

A Communist Chinese platoon leader visited me often at Tsinghua University in those days. His puritanical zeal withstood all anti-Communist argument. He had a Marxist slogan for each of China's massive problems. His devotion to duty was fanatic; his "do-good" dedication was as thick as cement in a nation once gifted with sparkling, if divisive, vibrancy. "Of course we will win all China," he said dogmatically. "Afterwards, we will win all Asia. We are fighting for a cause we know, not blindly against one."

The loss of China dramatized the fact that if the United States was not adequately prepared to fill the power vacuum in Asia, another force was ready to rush into the void. Yet, in 1950, the United States seemed resigned to abandoning self-interest on the Asian mainland.

It was Joseph Stalin who caused a reassessment. Stalin's unbridled ambition stayed the evacuation of major military commitments in the Western Pacific and the forsaking of Chiang Kai-shek's shrunken remnants in exile on Taiwan. Well briefed on the pitiful state of South Korean defenses and primed by hints that this mainland peninsula lay "outside the U. S. defense perimeter," Stalin ordered his North Korean satellite army to march. The hope of the first five postwar years thus faded into a cycle of wars that pitted the United States against Soviet-fueled Communist aggressions.

Battle-proved American generals wept in frustration amid revolutionary warfare in which immediate military victory was not the overriding consideration. Ruthless blackmail in Great Power diplomacy and the ignition of volatile racial and nationalistic passions were weapons as decisive as massed artillery on the battlefield.

General Douglas MacArthur's masterful exploitation of his brilliant Inchon landing, rolling United Nations' columns northward to Red China's Manchurian border, has been subject to endless controversy. An alarmed Southeast Asia saw only American countenancing in Korea of the aggravation of China's known obsession for insulating her borders. It did not see the full diplomatic hedging of the gamble with prior agreement from European allies for all the possible consequences. The United States, benefiting from the strengths as well as the entanglements of its alliances, was not then prepared to "go it alone" against the Sino-Soviet military machine on the mainland of China itself.

My base of operations during the Korean war, between the two Communist occupations of Seoul, was the shell-splattered correspondents' billet. Mess-hall conversation recalled the home-front warriors of World War II who boasted: "One Yank can whip six of those little Nips." But it was an Indian journalist who gave the phrase an Asian twist in 1953. "You chaps should understand now that we Asians are better fighters, man for man, than you are," he said, smugly wagging his head.

In the narrow view of Southeast Asia we lost the Korean war by the very fact that we did not defeat China. The boast that Americans had been "exposed as paper tigers" seems laughable to a nuclear-armed United States. But on Taiwan, I saw the ill-concealed, irrational smiles of some Nationalist Chinese officials when the Red Chinese avalanche smothered outnumbered U. S. Marines in North Korea. From ancient reservoirs of racial chauvinism that motivated Chinese psychology there flowed an irresistible pride for Chinese soldiers fighting as effectively as the Western "devils." Such racial jingoism cannot be dismissed as merely irrelevant. Sensitivity of race and color infects all associations in Asia. The onus belongs on both sides.

As wars rumbled from Korea through the Indo-China states to Malaya's guerrilla conflict, Americans assumed an additional role. There came the first phalanxes of U. S. administrators soon to appear in every Southeast Asian city. Their mission was to succor and encourage impoverished Asian states with Far East versions of aid programs that had been successful in Europe. In the quagmire of Asian misery and corruption, the end result all too often was a squandering of the U. S. taxpayer's money. Wealthy Orientals, with polite but avaricious alacrity, moved out of stately mansions to make room for Iowa farmgirl stenographers assigned by bureaucratic standards to suitable quarters. A single annual rental surpassed a lifetime's cash income for the average Asian who never would enter such a home unless to sack it with a revolutionary mob. The desk-bound American invasion inflated urban living costs. Grumbling about high-living American officialdom began then, and still goes on.

The often thoughtless criticisms in Asia obscure the real worth of this civilian army in its cold war role of besting the Communists on the economic battlefield.

It may be comforting to know that Moscow faces a similar dilemma of giving Russian officialdom status symbols without aggravating Asia's racial sensibilities. We tend to caricature Soviet features as a Slavic blending with the Oriental. But I saw Premier Nikita Khrushchev discomfited when he tried this gambit on a Mandalay audience in 1955. Under the tropical sun a sweaty Khrushchev had the pasty puffiness of a fish's underbelly. The polite brown Burmese audience heard the Soviet Premier's interpreter translate his bellowing: "We are brothers because, like you, I am an Asian." Titters erupted into a roar of disbelieving laughter.

Mao Tse-tung gave Communism its Asian face; Ho Chi Minh of Vietnam added a mask with Southeast Asian features.

From their very identity with Asian aspirations both are more subtly dangerous than Nikita Khrushchev in the struggle for popular allegiance in the new states in Southeast Asia.

Aggression in Korea was part of a larger plan. With it had come the intensifying Communist-directed, nationalist-inspired offensive against France in Indo-China. Jungle guerrillas, from Burma to the Philippines, added their bloodletting to the grand military strategy for expelling the United States and her European allies from the Western Pacific.

The design traced back to Leninist doctrine common to Moscow and Peking. But Red China long before had put into formal phrases what that Communist platoon leader had said to me more simply at Tsinghua University in 1948. Mao Tse-tung wrote:

>...the liberation campaign [in China] cannot be separated from the liberation campaign of the peoples of Southeast Asia. ...the Chinese people will facilitate the struggle of the peoples of Southeast Asia.

Physically frail but durable, Ho Chi Minh carried Communism into Vietnam, to form a Red bridgehead in Southeast Asia for successive crises in Laos and South Vietnam. Ho's strength was his identification with patriotic Vietnamese hunger for independence. I met European diplomats in Southeast Asia who argued vehemently that Ho, in the crucial years of his lifetime struggle, made it clear that he preferred an independent Vietnam free of bondage to subservience to either power bloc. British intelligence agents held that in one period "Uncle Ho" came under considerable suspicion from such zealous Vietnamese cadres as Mao Tse-tung's adept disciple, General Vo Nguyen Giap.

There is a residual anti-Chinese sentiment among many Vietnamese as there is in all the Southeast Asian states. It still has political force. The most dedicated Vietminh soldier has in his racial consciousness the centuries of pillaging by marauding Chinese war lords from the north. Unfortunately, it has been Moscow that has exploited these emotional weapons in back-room contests of personalities whenever Peking had challenged Kremlin authority too far. United States diplomacy, condemning one Communist as very like another, left itself no scope for maneuver in this subtle arena.

Mr. Dulles had considerable justification for blaming the worsening Indo-China war on "the political system of Communist Russia and its Chinese Communist ally." Communism gave Ho Chi Minh a systematic organization he needed, and eventually the material support. United States alarm over French military failures brought us to the brink of intervention. Our generous military support of the French had us competing with Soviet and Red Chinese aid for General Giap's murderous guerrilla units.

The basic American diplomatic posture was a forceful military response to the ruthless cold war which Stalin had launched in the late 1940's. We had been the model for independence by revolution in Southeast Asia; now, in Indo-China, we were pressuring a wobbly colonial power to thwart an independence drive because it served Communist strategy.

In many Asian eyes, Ho Chi Minh still embodies nationalism. The average Asian had not then, and still has not, a fear of Communism great enough to match his hatred of the Western imperialist past. Our Indo-China role splashed part of that hatred over ourselves. If Mr. Dulles was aware of the nationalist impetus sustaining Ho's Vietminh in the Indo-China war, American diplomacy never hinted at trying to turn that force to our advantage.

In Laos in 1961, I remembered the burning villages, the shattered forts and the pathetic refugees of Indo-China in 1954. I remembered also the heavy U. S. armament backing French and anti-Communist Vietnamese units—and the rigid military philosophy encasing them in archaic Beau Geste

forts that dotted the jungles and paddies already lost to
General Giap's lightly equipped but mobile guerrillas. United
States generals in Saigon sputtered with disbelief while brave
French paratroopers leaped into the circle of guns and
Vietminh assault units for the final tragic sacrifice of Dien
Bien Phu.

"Send a relief column," barked one of our better-known
infantry officers.

"Get your strafing fighter planes down to effective altitudes
where American civilian pilots make the airdrops," begged a
U. S. Air Force adviser.

But Dien Bien Phu fell to the military doctrine of Mao
Tse-tung. By then the French in Indo-China were hating our
sideline coaching as much as the deadly gadflies of Ho Chi
Minh. We were watching the second major demonstration of
the Mao doctrine for guerrilla insurgence; all local forces—
political, military, terrain, and popular emotions—were exploited for the final objective.

The second five-year cycle in Asia—1950 to 1955—ended
on a note of retreat and more retreat. Entangled in webs of
conflicting priorities, our necessary European alliances too
often were at odds with Asian emergencies. Once more, we
settled for armistice talks with Communism. Truce in Korea
had proved no prelude to real peace; at Geneva, in 1954,
truncated new nations again appeared: Communist North
Vietnam was divided by an armed border from South Vietnam; Laos and Cambodia lay uneasy in the shadow of Asian
Communist states.

A growing body of Asian opinion credited the expulsion
of French colonialism to Ho Chi Minh; the United States, as
one American diplomat reportedly put it, had been "the
last French colonialists in Indo-China." In this gloomy climate, John Foster Dulles fathered the Southeast Asia Treaty
Organization in a further military effort to seal off Southeast
Asia from new Communist aggressions.

The smear of "colonialism" hampered SEATO in Southeast Asia from its birth in 1955. This served Communist propaganda and swayed some Asian opinion, yet it was unjustified. The Far East interests of France and Britain were dwindling so rapidly that they signed up only with reluctance. Australia and New Zealand, concerned that Red China one day might emulate Japan's southward march, became members. From Asia came the Philippines, jittery because of the Communist-directed Huk guerrillas, and Pakistan, for reasons perhaps known only to Mohammed. Thailand was the single state on the Southeast Asian mainland persuaded to join.

For all the criticism (it was, and is, difficult to find any SEATO admirers in Asia) the alliance, and its much-maligned author, Mr. Dulles, did play a contributing role in the containment of Communism in Southeast Asia.

Certainly, after the Communist conquest of Northern Vietnam, no other Southeast Asian state fell to military aggression in seven years. The American-built military defense perimeter of Asian armies and treaties deserves due credit.

In the third five-year cycle—1955–1960—the Communists sporadically tested Mr. Dulles' cordon, which included such variables as the loosely knit SEATO alliance and the clear defense commitment to Taiwan. Peking rewrote military handbooks with unique artillery challenges to the offshore islands of Quemoy and Matsu, but held the gun range short of provoking the encircling U. S. Seventh Fleet.

The weakness in our defenses since 1955, however, were showing up in the limitations inherent in Mr. Dulles' "massive retaliation" policies symbolized in Southeast Asia by the Seventh Fleet's nuclear shells and bombs. Massive retaliation became a frightful bogey in the moderate, pacifist-tinged climate. The immediate military enemies were Communist-trained foot soldiers prowling the jungles. This was a human-sized threat for which Asian history had answers other than a titanic nuclear melee.

Communist grand strategy for this twilight zone between the two world power blocs long had subtly changed. The political battlefield of coexistence rated as much, if not more, priority than the harassment of subversion, the sniping of guerrillas and the menace of nuclear missiles from beyond the horizon. A suspicious U. S., gun in hand, hesitatingly and, too often, belatedly, scouted this new form of warfare. Economic aid, once the camp follower of our military strategy in Southeast Asia, became respectable and finally queen of the tournament.

But aid is a treacherous ally. I sprawled one day in an oxcart rut to escape the luxurious Mercedes-Benz speeding through Laos' dusty capital of Vientiane. At the wheel was a delighted Lao farm-boy chauffeur whose driving school probably had been the back of an ox; relaxed in the rear seat was an aid-fattened local businessman. An evening in the Lido night club found the pro-American cabinet of Laos weighing affairs of state—an imported Hong Kong beauty on one knee, a dollar-filled wallet seductively open on the other. An exaggeration? Unfortunately, not. Laos was a flagrant example of the greatest spending spree ever known in Southeast Asia.

I watched rusty bicycles pedaled along empty superhighways wandering off into the Vietnamese jungles. An embarrassingly long stretch of a U. S.-financed road in Cambodia crumbled into dust. Rising from the lush Southeast Asian landscape factories appeared where a wheel never turned. Housing modeled after suburban American communities arose among Asia's thatched mud huts, guarded and marked FOR AMERICANS ONLY. Asians sneered at the "new colonialists" and their "extraterritoriality." Governments historically accustomed at least to an agricultural surplus economy urgently found they needed dollars because "the Communists will get us if you don't look out."

For the strong and cunning, Asia always had been a free-booters' paradise; now the mood had the heady champagne aura of the mad twenties in the United States. The U. S. taxpayer underwrote the freewheeling expense accounts.

A Scripps-Howard correspondent in 1959 publicized scandals in the U. S. aid program for South Vietnam. A worried American aid administrator in Saigon sighed with relief when he read the clippings. "Thank heavens, that guy only scratched the surface," he said. In Bangkok, an aid official assigned to Thailand brushed aside my questions about delinquencies with a pious reply. "Look, friend," he said, "either some corruption—or it will be the Commies."

That this brief survey of the difficulties in economic aid administration in Southeast Asia is harsh, and of almost cartoon-strip simplification, is fully realized. The abuses flourish, I believe, because in my travels I met only one U. S. investigator with the specific assignment to check into the numerous and frequently ingenious misappropriations. Much of the aid, also, was involved in situations where the wastes inevitable in military machines were compounded by the fact that these were traditionally corrupt Asian military machines, even if under our guidance.

The true value of American aid for the future must be sought in the new schoolhouses, the roads that are built well, the lifesaving medicines, the emergency food shipments, the beginnings of industry, and the limitless American generosity of motive behind this unprecedented largesse to benefit and give hope to distant and unknown peoples. For aid must continue. Its worth in the Southeast Asia struggle is attested by the Communist effort to match it.

Soviet Russia and Red China learned from our mistakes. Instead of the equivalent of outright cash gifts, difficult for the donor to control, Moscow and Peking chose long-term credit redeemable in Communist-made goods. Where we concentrated on people's welfare with such "invisible" projects as back-country malarial control, the Reds offered crowd-pleasing extravaganzas like football stadiums, hotels, or a single towering factory.

The American way, in my view, is much to be preferred, and ultimately, in the almost timeless pace of Asia, will prove the more convincing. But in outspending the Communist bloc by considerable amounts, too often have we parodied a worn cliché: "Ruble wise versus dollar foolish."

The specter of the Ugly American, however, looms larger in Washington than it ever has in the Far East. "Fictionalized half-truths obscuring the facts," grumbled one Filipino official about that controversial book.

A Vietnamese diplomat, Tran Van Dinh, glowing with excitement over the stimulating experience of his first visit to the United States, told me: "Now I understand the American situation. You see, in my country government service is an honorable career. But your government does not necessarily attract the very best personnel available. Private industry appears to capture the finest graduates from your universities . . . and quite often, it seems, those who do not succeed in your free-enterprise capitalism only then turn to the security of government service."

Tran paused to arrange his English words from thoughts initially framed in Vietnamese. Then he continued: "I never knew the American mind until I had such happy conversations with your people in their native homes. But although they appraise international affairs with great intelligence, none of those I met wanted to work for the government. Your people look upon government service as a kind of demotion in American society."

This Asian capsule judgment of relative American social values, while having a certain validity, still falls short. One meets in Southeast Asia American government officers of the finest caliber (but not yet enough) who restore pride in our over-all record, whatever the splotches of the past. If there is a lesson still to be learned, it is that the Administration must pay full heed to their intimate knowledge of Asian nuances before formulating hard policies indebted to domestic political compromise.

The challenges of the 1960's are as diverse as Mao Tse-tung, Nikita Khrushchev, and the histories and maverick interests of Southeast Asian states. Central to our diplomacy is the unanswered question of what to do about China; with Taiwan, it is "two Chinas." The embers of brush-fire wars smolder or flare in the jungle fungi of Laos, Vietnam, Burma, and Indonesia. Increasingly, Southeast Asian leaders, especially those outside our chain of military treaties, are attracted to non-aligned neutrality as an escape from the potential hazards of cold war participation.

The U. S. Consul-General in Hong Kong (now Ambassador to Iran), Mr. Julius Holmes, once reminded me of a perspective on immediate crises that is more applicable to Asia than anywhere else in the world: ". . . history is solving many of them for us." I thought of his remark when I last met China's Chou En-lai at a press conference in remote Katmandu. China holds the long view, although quick to grab at opportunities.

Mr. Holmes was not discussing Taiwan at the time, but his remark emphasized certain inflexible realities about that island redoubt. Taiwan is part of China. Our military commitment to the Nationalist Government inevitably must interfere in a civil war. Yet there are two Chinas just as there are two Koreas and two Vietnams. Whether it is a Peking plaint or a Western suggestion, prattle about creating "two Chinas" is meaningless. The diplomacy of the major powers in the fifties has made the existence of two Chinas a fact.

It is just as meaningless to view Taiwan as a Western Pacific Gibraltar in long-term military strategy. Compromise or an internal uprising could change the local political cli-

mate, even if the Republic of China government remains in
the United Nations. Direct aggression across the Formosa
Strait is unlikely while the U. S. Seventh Fleet stands by.
The only certainty seems to be that Communist fury will
continue to menace the offhore islands, Quemoy and Matsu;
we must weather it out, adjusting local diplomacy to enlightened self-interest.

Crises such as Laos and South Vietnam in 1961 are instances
of U. S. policy in Southeast Asia creaking too stiffly in local
breezes. The overriding direction obviously must be toward
a stable, essentially anti-Communist cordon around Red
China until Peking's aggressions are emasculated.

Vientiane had the electric intensity of a tropical storm
that August day in 1960 when self-dramatizing Captain Kong
Le used his U. S.-equipped paratroopers to jerk a sluggish,
venal government from power. With "gee-whiz" boyishness
he delighted the have-not lesser citizenry with the mere suggestion that corruption could end, interfering foreigners go
home and Laotians luxuriate in neutrality. Kong Le was
prescribing a magic potion to cure the ills of that abused
jungle people.

Seen in proper context he was a confused, semiliterate,
ambitious young man with that rare power that sways multi-
tudes; he had the stuff that makes revolutionaries and ignites
revolutions. Heedlessly, and needlessly, we lost the opportunity to use him for wiping out many of Laos' real sick-
nesses. The Communists did use him, and too many others
just like him. The U. S. belatedly veered from the position
that "neutralism is Communism" to a commitment to fight
for a militarily non-aligned Laos. Communism, successively
more Asian in the axis running from Moscow through Peking
to neighboring Hanoi, used neutrality as the formula for
battening down Laotian discontent. Then it attempted a
complete subversion of that strategic little Southeast Asian
kingdom.

The South Vietnam crisis is less obscure but eventually more critical to our position in Asia. Communism here ripped off the mask of neutrality and fought behind a "national liberation front"—in fact, a civil war. Behind this dialectical disguise the North Vietnamese invaders have dribbled down the Ho Chi Minh trail through Laos into South Vietnam. They claim a "grass roots" legitimacy for toppling the Ngo Dinh Diem government; their methods are pillage, blackmail, and murder. This, the Communist cadres say blandly, represents the true aspirations of the people.

A growing number of Vietnamese patriots in 1961 were agitating for their Government to reply bloodily in kind to North Vietnam. One U. S. official in Saigon, however, was more cautious in prescribing for Communism some of its own medicine: "Armed infiltration into a police state can end only in disaster."

He may or may not be right; the anti-Communist Southeast Asian countries we arm and support never yet have retaliated in such a manner.

Yet why should a relatively prosperous state like South Vietnam supinely continue on the defensive against the impoverished, aggressively hostile Communism to the north? Whatever Ho Chi Minh might have wished in the past, North Vietnam has become the hostage of a fanatic minority ruthlessly degrading the most fundamental human aspirations of the majority and actively striving to expand its tyranny, so far with impunity, beyond its borders.

North Vietnam under Communism, of course, is but a transistorized example of the massive issue facing us in Southeast Asia—Red China. I peeked into this Communist Bastille in the spring of 1958. A voyage up the winding Whangpoo River to Shanghai afforded a composite picture of Mao's New China in the first period of the commune's "great leap forward." Modern factories spewed smoke across the ancient

alluvial mud. Warcraft slipped down the ways of modest
shipyards. Richly green rice fields beyond the industrialized
river banks turned blue with the coveralled ranks of laboring
peasants. Everywhere there was the militant blare of loud-
speakers swamping thought with stultifying odes to the virtues
of "Father Mao."

The German skipper on the tramp passenger-freighter
scanned the bustling panorama. "Most efficient port in the
world, Shanghai," he said. "Nobody steals a thing."

A colleague duplicated this jaunt to Shanghai in the spring
of 1961. He told me of a China stumbling in mid-leap. The
factories no longer resembled human hives. Half-finished
vessels corroded in idle shipyards. Ragged peasants listlessly
squatted in paddies which had failed to feed them and Communist industrial and military ambition. Only the loud-
speakers clamored on in uninterrupted paeans to Communism.

A Swedish freighter captain returned stiff-faced from business in Shanghai. "The old corruption is back," he said.
"Bribery everywhere. And it goes surprisingly high up the
scale of officialdom."

Marxist-Leninism, rewritten by Mao Tse-tung, is failing
where nobler dynasties also had failed to master China's awe-
some burdens. The supersalesmanship abroad of Chou En-lai
is part of a power-mad Communist momentum still bombard-
ing the United States with vituperation. Ironically, in 1961, it
was ships heavy with grain from Canada and Australia that
were the Chinese people's hope for surviving the year. Axis
partner Russia expressed concern; but any help from Moscow
meant another heavy bill for payment.

Seven hundred million of some of the most gifted people
on earth are struggling for survival inside the politically
diseased shell of an otherwise great power. To the north
are still relatively empty pasture lands in the Soviet Union's
shadow; to the south are underpopulated Southeast Asian food

surplus regions unattainable because Peking aggression had forced the U. S. to give the rightful inhabitants barbed-wire protection.

The U. S. is striving for alternatives to this Asian range war, seeking to draw Peking into civilized conferences where the guns might be on the table, but not treacherously underneath.

It is already evident, Communism notwithstanding, that China must seek free world co-operation or perish. There will be a billion Chinese by 1975, a voracious maw swallowing nearly all the world can produce.

We are offering China peaceful solutions. The choice between famine, war or mutual aid ultimately is up to the Chinese people.

—JAMES ROBINSON

JAMES ROBINSON, Hong Kong Correspondent for NBC News, covers all of Southeast Asia. One of the few Western newsmen in the Orient who is thoroughly trained in Asian affairs, he studied and taught at Tsinghua and Yenching universities in Peiping before the Communists took command of the China mainland. Later, he worked in Japan and Thailand before joining the NBC News staff in 1952 to help report the end of the Korean war. Almost half his life has been spent in the Orient as a student, teacher, newsman and member of the U. S. armed forces. Born in Minneapolis, he was educated at Washington State College before going to China. Fluent in Chinese, he has covered stories in every major part of Asia. He is married to Barbara Soong, a member of the well-known Soong family of China.

# 10.

## LATIN AMERICA:
### *"Presidents and Dictators"*

O NE sunny day in San José, Costa Rica, I stopped to watch a group of ten-year-old boys playing in and around lampposts, cars, trees and adults. Using toy revolvers and rigid index fingers, they were playing what seemed to be a Latin-American version of cowboys and Indians.

The Indians were being killed off at an unconscionable rate. There came the last burst of "Bang, bang, you're dead." The cowboys had won. I asked the youngsters if they were really playing cowboys and Indians.

"No, señor," the leader replied. "We are playing presidents and dictators."

Presidents and dictators are more a part of recent Latin-American history than are cowboys and Indians in the United States. During the lifetime of these boys, five Latin-American dictators have been deposed. Juan D. Perón fled

Argentina one step ahead of the armed forces in 1955. Marcos Pérez Jiménez was forced to leave Venezuela. Manuel A. Odría quit Peru before he was ejected. General Gustavo Rojas Pinilla was relieved of power in Colombia. And on New Year's Day, 1959, Cuba's dictator, Fulgencio Batista, piled himself, his close friends, his relatives and his gold onto a plane in Havana's Camp Columbia and flew off to beg political asylum from the dean of all Latin-American dictators, Generalissimo Rafael L. Trujillo of the Dominican Republic.

During the lifetime of these boys, two Latin-American dictators were assassinated. In September, 1956, General Anastasio Somoza was cut down by an assassin's bullets while attending an election campaign dance in the Nicaraguan city of León. Eight days after he had been wounded, General Somoza died in the U. S. Army hospital in the Panama Canal Zone where he had been flown to see if an American team of surgeons sent to Panama by President Eisenhower could save his life. Somoza had ruled Nicaragua since 1935.

On the night of May 30, 1961, thirty-one years of the Trujillo dictatorship of the Dominican Republic ended when enemies machine-gunned the sixty-nine-year-old Generalissimo. Trujillo was on his way to one of his many ranches to visit his mistress of the moment. The Dominican Government claimed that the assassination was the work of an army general who had a personal grudge against the dictator. Trujillo's son took over the reins of government, promising to hold them less tightly than had his father. Few observers were ready to take young Trujillo at his word.

In August, 1954, Getulio Dornelles Vargas shot himself a few hours after yielding to military pressure to resign as president. Vargas, seventy-one years old, has been a dictator in Brazil for almost a third of his lifetime.

These dictators, in their violent deaths or in their hasty exoduses, left their countries in a financial and political mess.

They managed to cart away (or had already banked away) millions of dollars, leaving the financial cupboards bare—not so much because of what they stole, but from the way they ran the economy of their countries while they were in power.

Perón and his wife, Eva, set an unparalleled example of rule by whim and force, and sometimes farce. He left behind, as a monument to their cupidity, an empty treasury and a loyal following.

For ten years Perón ruled Argentina by "justicialism," his manufactured word for his political credo. As Perón himself was to describe it, it was Fascism purged of the errors of Mussolini. But his hold over Argentina came from his definition of Perónism. "Perónismo" recognized only one class of men—those who worked.

Trade unions flourished as never before or since in Latin America. Workers had only to hint that they would like added benefits be they money, social security, summer vacations, housing, or what have you, and they got them. Some of these benefits were long overdue, but when first given they were rewards for political support and absolute obedience.

The first years under Perón were flush years. The treasury had a surplus of foreign exchange earned from selling the Allies wheat and meat during World War II. That was soon used up and inflation hit.

Perón ran for a second term, conveniently forgetting that he had promised not to. Eva Perón almost ran as vice-president on her husband's ticket until the army persuaded Perón to have her strike that role from her growing repertoire.

By July of 1952 mutterings against Perón were growing louder. A few brave unions even tried illegal strikes. Inflation grew worse. Eva Perón died of cancer.

Perón accused the Catholic Church of plotting against him and ordered the arrest of priests and the deportation of two bishops. Perónista bully boys burned and sacked some churches.

The army had had enough. But it took two tries to get Perón out. One, in June of 1955, failed to dislodge him, but three months later better planning and co-ordination accomplished the objective.

Perón established a dictatorship with his own particular flair. The others—Pérez Jiménez, Rojas Pinilla, Odría and Batista—were essentially old-fashioned strongmen. All ruled primarily with an iron hand wrapped in a deceitful glove.

The fifties were a decade of the dictator's demise in Latin America because countries were ripe for change. But why had the dictators come to power? In a few cases, they represented the forces of stability against violent revolution. It was easy for a dictator to see himself as the continuing savior, and therefore ordained to perpetuate his power to liberate the people.

Millions of illiterate, undernourished, unschooled, underpaid, exploited Latin Americans saw the rich get richer and the poor get poorer. They had no way to go but up. The right to vote meant less to them than food and a chance to educate their children so that the next generation would not go through the same threadbare existence.

The demagogues had an advantage unavailable to democratic leaders: they could promise improvement and, sometimes, immediate prosperity. It made no difference that the wheels of social and economic justice could not turn that fast. The demagogues said wheels could be made to turn, and their assurances found ready favor among the majority of Latin Americans who saw themselves bound to serfdom and the land.

Sixty to seventy per cent of the people in Latin America led marginal lives. They ate and wore what they grew, and they bartered for what few necessities they could not produce. The tin and cardboard slums of cities like Bogota, Lima, and Rio de Janeiro were a result of living on land that did not produce a living. Hundreds of thousands of peasants came to the big cities looking for a better life. They gravitated toward the shanty slums; illiterate, superstitious and gullible, their hatred of the Government and the "rich man" mounted steadily.

The core of the problem was land and the way it was used. Less than two per cent of the population of Latin America owned more than half the productive agricultural land. Wealthy landowners resisted any attempt to make an equitable distribution of this land to turn some of it into food-crop acreage or to make it feed people instead of the bank accounts of the aristocracy.

The landowning aristocracy had for decades, even centuries, paid little attention to anything except making money, lending it at usurious rates, amassing more land and wealth and power. Owning real estate was the ultimate status symbol of most of Latin America, with no regard for any of the human values.

A few years ago it was not uncommon to see ads in newspapers offering real estate for sale, and the clincher in the ad was "plus 200 peasants." Peasants, tenant farmers, serfs, call them what you will, were so in debt to the *patron* they could be bought and sold like cattle.

But the day is coming when the landed, wealthy aristocracy will have to move from the pleasant, lucrative but untenable "status quo." They will have to start paying taxes; a duty that they have thus far managed to avoid. They will have to agree that huge tracts of their land must be reapportioned.

I was talking about this problem with one of Brazil's fashionable aristocrats while she sipped her tea. Flashing glittery diamond and emerald rings at me, she insisted that the rich of Brazil well understood that social and economic reforms must come. She illustrated her grasp of the problem with the case of so and so.

"He is a multimillionaire, but he puts his money in circulation. Just the other day," she explained triumphantly, "he sent a plane all the way to France to bring back fresh truffles for a banquet in Rio."

To make doubly sure that I realized and understood her concern with the problem of redistributing wealth and opportunity she offered another illustration. "The lady who won the prize for the best costume in Rio's last carnival paid sixty thousand dollars for it," she said. "Just think of all the people who got work, sewing on those semiprecious stones."

There were other reasons why Latin-American dictators came to power.

South America has the fastest growing population in the world. Whatever social progress leaders may bring to their people, their work makes the labor of Sisyphus seem like a limbering-up exercise. The population increase (a difficult figure to give precisely since some countries keep such inadequate records) has been at least 2.6 per cent a year. Some ecologists consider it closer to 3 per cent a year.

Figuring the present population of Latin America at 195 to 200 million persons, the population should double by 1980. More than 400 million persons in Latin America will far outnumber the expected population for the United States and Canada combined.

Obviously, one way to plan for the needs of the coming generation of Latin Americans would be to see to it that there were fewer of them. Slowing down the population growth is talked about often but, as couples all over the world have known for centuries, talking about not having babies is not a very effective contraceptive.

Birth control in Catholic South and Central America is not advocated. Infant mortality is more than 110 per thousand in Latin America, compared to 30 per thousand in the United States. The average U. S. citizen can expect to live to be 70. In some Central-American countries, life expectancy is 36 years; the average for all Latin-American countries is 45.

United States and UN programs to fight infant mortality, disease and malnutrition have already increased the life expectancy of the Latin-American citizen—and will continue to do so. But once he is alive, and lives longer, the South-American citizen must be re-oriented to the land so that he can raise the kind of crops and flocks which are needed to keep the agricultural economy in some sort of balance. Less than one-twentieth of Latin-American land is productive, whereas in the United States nearly one-fourth of the land area is utilized.

It does no good to get someone to work presently nonarable land if there is no way to get his produce to market. Roads and railroads are imperative, and this takes money.

Honduras, for example, has sixty miles of paved road. It has a few hundred miles of all-weather roads. All-weather roads meant, as nearly as I could judge, that they were as bad during the rainy season as they were during the hot, dry, dusty ones.

Lands themselves need fertilizer, irrigation. They need the men, women, and children to farm the unused acres, and the farmers need hoes, plows, spades and seeds. All this takes money and planning. A few countries have some planners; none has enough money.

The Latin oligarchies had their reasons for wanting to retain the status quo. In most countries they aligned themselves with the military to make sure that their wants and wishes would be protected. For decades, particularly in the smaller countries, Colonel "so and so" and his regiment were up for sale. The highest bidder in money, or the promise of a soft job in the next regime, got the most regiments to overthrow a government which might be getting out of line.

Standing armies could be a stabilizing force in a country, as they are in Argentina, because they are by nature conservative. Or they could lead the way in revolutions from either the left or the right. Most rulers, be they democrat or dictator, are highly sensitive and responsive to army pressures, because the army is the place that the next ruler is apt to be found in Latin countries.

Bolivia, a land-locked, mountainous mining country, with an economy no longer viable with the expiration of its tin mines, got rid of its regular army in the revolution of 1952. Tired of the game of musical military chairs played by the regular officers, the new revolutionary government decided to arm civilians who would protect the fatherland, and to disarm the army.

Walter Guevera, an ex-minister of the interior, once told me that this assured civilian rule of a country. Guns in the hands of the populace had been tried in Switzerland and had always worked. He forgot to add that Bolivia was not Switzerland and that Bolivians were not Swiss.

In Chile, most military and civilian leaders have paid lip service to disarmament proposals made by President Jorge Allessandri, but they have done little or nothing about them in terms of paying for plows instead of guns, or books instead of destroyers.

To the impoverished Latin, this splurge for surplus arms is an appalling waste of the little money which his country has to spend. He sees the power of military cliques as an unnecessary reminder of the era of gunboat or gunpoint diplomacy, or as the sword of conservatism hanging over the throat of any liberal movements within the country. In most Latin countries, the army usually has been used against its own people rather than to make war on a neighbor.

These things are changing, but not quickly enough to assure the average man that military rule would be good enough for him or his country. It was against a background of this kind that right-wing dictators came to power in Latin America. Too many remain in power.

General Alfredo Stroessner and his army run Paraguay the way they want it run. Generalissimo Rafael Leonidas Trujillo Molina, during thirty years in power, operated the Dominican Republic as if it were his private finca.

On the other half of the island of Santo Domingo, President François Duvalier with his secret police and his rubber-stamp parliament rules the impoverished, overpopulated Haiti. In Nicaragua, Luis Somoza, who inherited the reins of government from his father, is trying—with what seems to be all deliberate slowness—to allow his opposition a weak and regulated political voice in that country.

Then there is Fidel Castro, a new kind of Latin despot—a dictator of the left. Although Latin America made giant strides toward representative democracy while toppling the dictators of the right during the fifties, Castro's headlong dash to the left cut directly across the problems facing the hemisphere in the sixties.

How this decade will turn out in Latin America depends first on the twenty Latin American nations and what their governments will do about necessary reforms; second, on the United States and how much we are willing to spend and how much trouble we are willing to take to understand Latin America and keep evolution from becoming violent revolution; third, on how successful the USSR and Red China, and their ardent disciples in Latin America, will be in convincing the people that needed changes can only be brought about by revolution.

Castro has dramatized the urgency of Latin American problems. The Batista regime he supplanted was dictatorial, brutal, and outrageously corrupt. It eventually rotted from within and collapsed when its demoralized army, tired of fighting an endless civil war, gave up. This inner collapse produced Batista's defeat, not Castro's victory. While army morale wavered, Cuba's middle class never wavered in its fight against the outrages and abuses of the Batista regime. Castro later rewarded the middle class for its decisive part in the fight by destroying it, just as he had destroyed the very wealthy.

Castro has declared his government "Socialist," which in Cuba means Communist. His chief lieutenant, the professional Argentine revolutionist Ernesto "Che" Guevara, is an admitted Marxist. Regardless of labels or party affiliation, the fact is that Castro and his cohorts removed Cuba (just ninety miles off the Florida coast) from United States influence and brought it into the Soviet orbit within a matter of months. That was quite a feat, no matter what kind of a card Castro carries.

This feat and its consequences make one of the most fascinating stories of the sixties. Communist domination of satellites in Europe was perhaps understandable in terms of geography and even philosophy. But Communist domination of Cuba, heretofore linked emotionally, economically, and physically to the United States, was to say the least incredible.

Conditions existing in Cuba—poverty, misery, exploitation, lack of housing, schooling and hospitals, and pity—are more than mirrored in the rest of Central and South America. If Castro could happen to Cuba, he or someone like him could certainly arise in other countries south of the border.

Castro and his Communist mentors have been shipping pistols and pesos to underground groups all over Latin America. But they did not have to. This is a decade of discontent. The average Latin knows that there is a better way of life than the one he knows, and he feels that the time has come to do something about it.

Is the only solution, the only avenue for these inevitable changes, a Communist revolution, armed and supplied from Russia through Cuba? Or can we and the governments of Latin America engineer the kind of social and economic revolution which will keep these other countries out of the Soviet orbit?

In his first year of power Castro built ten thousand family dwellings. The money came from the government-operated national lottery, and the proceeds went into a building program instead of politicians' pockets.

He ordered landlords to cut rents; 50 per cent for rents under one hundred dollars a month, a 40 per-cent cut for the one-hundred to two-hundred-dollar-a-month bracket. Since there were more tenants than landlords, it was a popular move.

While he still had some money to do it, Castro built new roads, repaired hundreds of miles of beatup roads, built new sidewalks, schools, airports, parks, zoos, museums, motels, and public beaches. During his first year—1959—he finished and equipped ten hospitals left partially constructed by the Batista regime.

Castro has made millions of Cubans feel that they have a part in running his government. He did it by invoking what he has called "people's democracy." That is, when Castro and his colleagues decided what they wanted to do—rip up a treaty, denounce the United States, the OAS, or what have you—they convened a general assembly to vote "yes."

Cubans are trucked, walked, marched, and railroaded into Havana. They come to praise Castro and to vote; "vote" being the loose term which Castro uses to denote "approve." At one rally hundreds of thousands of *guajiros, campesinos,* and *milicianos* were asked, "Shall we denounce the Mutual Defense Pact?" Although most of them had never heard of the Pact, they raised their hands and shouted "Cuba sí, Yanquis no!" Motion carried.

One uniformed *miliciano* told me that he got a kick out of being asked to participate in a massed parliament of the people. He knew enough of democratic procedures to make the crack: "When I was asked to vote, I stuffed the ballot box. I raised both hands!"

The politically aware know that a unanimous vote of approval at a hysterical mass rally is so far from a working democracy that it is both tragic and comic. But the great majority does not recognize the drama, and even if the peasants were aware, they would still feel that they were at least being consulted. They never had been before.

The first 26th of July celebration which Castro called in 1959 touched off an all-out campaign to get a turnout in Havana's Plaza Civica.

TV and radio stations ran round-the-clock marathon interviews with *guajiros* from the countryside. Fast-talking announcers queried the coutry folk on their reactions to the big city. One gnarled old man surprised them. When asked how he was enjoying himself and if he had ever been to Havana before, he said, "Yes."

"When was that?"

"Batista brought us all into town a few years ago for a rally like this."

Most television stations switched to other types of programing immediately.

One of Castro's most forceful and underrated maneuvers almost overnight gave him the support of 40 to 60 per cent of Cuba's population. For many years Cuban Negroes had been discriminated against in clubs, restaurants and hotels. Officially Cuba, even before Castro, had been desegregated. In practice, it was not. Now, although the luxury hotels are empty of the American visitors who made tourism Cuba's third largest industry (sugar and tobacco are numbers one and two), they have become available, as is every other pleasure dome, to Cuba's Negro population.

Garish night clubs with lavish shows are still open for a trickle of customers, mostly Cuban. The little white balls of the roulette tables still swirl and click into place, but they swirl and click for Cuban pesos and not for the American dollar. The lovely swimming pools and cabañas of the glamorous hotels are no longer populated with shapely, bronzed blondes from Yankeeland, but with all colors and shades of Cubans and their blond friends from Communist Europe. For the Cuban Negro, Fidel Castro has been the great emancipator, and they are grateful to him for making them first-class citizens.

While Castro was doing these positive things, he was even more positively swinging Cuba into the Communist camp. He has completely tied the economy of Cuba to the Soviet bloc. He has purchased small arms, tanks, artillery, and aircraft from Czechoslovakia or the Soviet Union. He has ten times the amount of military equipment Cuba had under any other dictator. He has armed every citizen who wanted to be, and many more who did not, with Czech automatic weapons while creating a civilian militia which has taken the place of the rebel army as "protector of the fatherland." He grabbed without compensation more than a billion and a half dollars' worth of American investment and property in Cuba. He has taken Cuban businesses, homes, cars and personal bank accounts. The Agrarian and Urban Reform laws and wide ranging nationalization have given the Cuban Government practically every money-producing business in Cuba. Castro has control of every public information medium.

Castro has maneuvered all professional associations and labor unions under government control. Universities have lost their autonomy. Leftist student unions decide which professors are "qualified" to teach and which students are "qualified" to be students. In short, Castro has made Cuba a Soviet-dominated, totalitarian police state. How?

For one thing, Castro has been able to capitalize on his original popularity and his continuing ability to convince his audience that black is white, gray, and red.

In April, 1960, I had my last long sit-down interview with

Fidel Castro. (I have talked to him since then, but more casually.) We talked at some length about the French munitions ship *El Coubre,* which had just blown up in Havana Harbor. Castro, immediately following the incident, had made a speech in which he said the United States did not want Cuba to have arms to defend the revolution, so it followed that the U. S. Government had been behind the sabotage.

During our three hours he made it quite clear that he had been misinterpreted, misquoted, by his own government-controlled press. He claimed he never said, nor had he meant to imply, that the U. S. Government had anything to do with the disaster. There were people in the United States, said Castro, particularly in the Pentagon, who were not unhappy about the incident. But "any other interpretation of my remarks is inaccurate."

Last Spring, on the first anniversary of the *El Coubre* explosion, Castro unveiled a monument dedicated to the martyrs of imperialism and reminded his audience that the United States had perpetrated that savage massacre, and he had told them so the day after it happened.

Documenting or delineating Castro's inconsistencies will be a full-time job for some future historian. But Castro does have the ability, which all demagogues seem to have or acquire, to sell his emotional and irrational claptrap by sheer force of personality. He is the Messiah. He is omnipotent. The most popular portrait of Castro in Cuba is one which has the faintest of halos over his untrimmed hair. The likeness to pictures of Christ is not accidental.

Nor was it accidental that a nativity scene outside the government television studios in Havana during the 1960 Christmas holidays portrayed Fidel Castro, "Che" Guevara, and Juan Almeida, Negro chief of the Cuban army, as the three wise men.

Children, even childlike adults, thrive on hero worship

and Castro is astute in using this to his advantage. An elementary schoolteacher quit in disgust after being told, and monitored to see that she followed instructions, that any child who gave a good recitation should be rewarded with the phrase, "Fidel would be proud of you." A pupil who did not recite well, or misbehaved would be punished with "Fidel will not allow boys who do not study (or who pull little girls' pigtails—or whatever) to join the militia to help kill Yankee invaders." According to the teacher, the children loved it!

A surgeon now working in the anti-Castro underground told me that he and his wife had decided they were not going to become involved in politics. They were going to do whatever they felt they should, and keep their minds on their work (she, too, was a doctor), leaving the pros and cons of Castro to others. They did get involved after one dinner table conversation. They were discussing Castro and what they felt was his sell-out to the Communists. Their ten-year-old son said, "You'd better stop talking like that or I'll report you to the police."

"Where did you get this idea?" asked his father.

"That's what our teachers tell us we must do when we hear counterrevolutionary talk."

At that moment the doctor and his wife became involved.

Castro put most of his rebel army in the field, literally in the fields. From his first month in power, Castro ordered his army into the country to work on building projects and land reform.

It is not difficult to imagine the early enthusiasm and the dedication of young Castro officers to the task of creating a better life for the Cuban *campesinos*. In Oriente Province, a young lieutenant, pointing out land newly planted with beans and tomatoes, explained what he felt he and his soldiers were accomplishing:

"These people have for generations been tied to the sugar crop and its bittersweet harvest. When the sugar cane was ready to be cut and ground, they had jobs. When the crop was in, they had no work, but life and debts went on. Debts carried over to the next crop—sometimes life did not—but crops never kept pace with debts for most workers. Now we're planting food. The people are working all year long and they are not in debt to company stores."

The young lieutenant, dedicated to and proud of what he was doing, missed the political overtones of the Castro agrarian reform program. He was not really interested. He was only interested in his own little territory where he was doing something with almost nothing, and rightfully proud of his achievements. My wife and I talked to this young Cuban more than a year ago. He may still be working in the fields of Oriente Province. Or he may be in prison for failing to meet his production norm, or to "educate" the *campesinos* in his district properly.

I met one such "failure" during a seventy-two-hour enforced visit to a Castro jail. Officially, I was never told why I was ordered to sit and sleep for three days and three nights on a creaky cot in a pantry hallway of a rococo mansion converted into army intelligence headquarters.

One of my fellow inmates, who shared the pantry with three other Cuban political prisoners and myself, knew why he was being held. And why he had been there for three months. His crime against the revolution was that he had, as a Captain in the Rebel army, been put in charge of a "people's store" in one of the provinces. The "people's store" had failed to make money, a failure which any first-year economist could have predicted after reading a mimeographed syllabus. But he had also advanced some unsolicited criticism of the way INRA (National Institute of Agrarian Reform) ran the co-operatives and "people's stores."

After three months in jail, he was still surprisingly free of bitterness and surprisingly free with criticism of Castro's current policies. He was proud of the part he, as a military man, had played in trying to rebuild and reshape Cuba.

During my departing handshakes he asked if I would leave behind my shaving cream and a copy of C. Wright Mills' book *Listen Yankee*. The emotional and nonobjective defense of Cuba's revolution by Professor Mills will probably elicit some rude comments and guffaws from my former jailmates. The shaving cream may prove more useful.

The ill-fated attempt to overthrow Castro in April, 1961, proved that the strength of his police state and the loyalty of his militia had been seriously underestimated. The landing attempt was a bumbling disaster. CIA agents, referred to as "Brinksman's Brother's Boys" by some Latin Americans, took complete control of the planning. Beset by political and personal rivalries, Cuban exile leaders were pushed into the background to wait until a beachhead had been established. It never was.

Castro's militia and secret police moved fast, rounding up thousands of Cubans who had been even remotely suspected of disagreeing with Castro's police state. Except for a few men hiding in the Escambray Mountains of Central Cuba, the anti-Castro underground movement on the island was decimated.

In the past few years, the Central Intelligence Agency has been mistakenly allowed to become a policy-making organization.

In the case of the Cuban exiles, the CIA's decision to back Antonio "Tony" Varona came months before the April invasion attempt. This decision kept other organizations with better underground connections from getting the supplies they needed. By deciding to back Varona, the CIA, in effect, decided who the future leader of Cuba should be. That, surely, was a policy decision which should have been left to men politically more adept than on-the-spot agents.

There are indications that the Kennedy Administration

will take steps to curtail or supervise the freewheeling Central Intelligence Agency. It will be high time.

Latin-American reaction to the attempt to topple Castro was swift and predictable. Communist organizations hurried out demonstrators in almost every Latin-American country. It was not just the Communists and the Castristas who were angered at the ill-disguised U. S. involvement in the attempt to unseat Castro. Many pro-Americans, particularly in Guatemala and Nicaragua, were furious that their governments had allowed their countries to be used for training areas and jump-off points. They saw no reason, and said so, why their governments should violate the credo of nonintervention. "Let the United States make a fool of itself in the eyes of Latin Americans," one Guatemalan told me. "But leave us out of it."

Guatemalan President Ydigoras stuck to his official fictional story that "no foreign troops" were training in his country even after captured rebels in Cuba named names, places and dates.

That was by no means the biggest mistake Ydigoras made. When pro-Castro groups held nightly demonstrations denouncing the invasion of Cuba, Ydigoras' government unofficially organized anti-Castro demonstrations.

One night the two groups marched toward each other. Plain-clothes men in the crowd opened fire with pistols, killed a student and a worker in the Castro group and a Honduran who was watching the fracas from a hotel balcony. Ydigoras gave the Castro crowd two martyrs.

Other Latin-American countries were more careful in their riot control. But no amount of police or government planning will be able to dissuade Latin Americans from believing that U. S. involvement in Cuba was just another of Uncle Sam's attempts to dictate policies south of the border.

Many Latin Americans remain unconvinced that a Communist state 90 miles from Key West is a threat to U. S.

security. They are even less convinced, through ignorance, naïveté or persuasion, that Castro and Communism are a threat to their particular countries. Obviously, some leaders are aware of the dangers, but they will have an increasingly difficult time keeping resentment, distrust, and hate of the United States under control.

As one pro-American Guatemalan put it, "We know Castro must go. We know that the U. S. will have to help. But the United States must be prepared for Latin Americans to resent and distrust the intervention."

A revolution of the left is not exactly a new phenomenon in Latin America. In Mexico, the only Latin nation sharing a common border with the United States, revolutionaries swung to the left in pre-World War II days. Exploiting latent anti-Americanism and anti-clericalism, they put the Good Neighbor policy to a severe test and sorely strained Mexican-American relations by nationalizing the United States oil companies.

But there was no militant Soviet bloc to step in to capture the Mexican revolution; the outbreak of the war submerged local problems. Nor were Mexico's revolutionaries so radical as the Cubans. Moderation eventually prevailed.

Despite the close friendship between Mexico and the United States, the Mexicans have staunchly refused to condemn Castro. They have firmly asserted the rights of national sovereignty and self-determination as well as the almost sacred policy of non-intervention. The Mexicans perhaps felt that they had earned the right to respect revolutionary regimes.

Still Fidel Castro may serve a useful purpose in the history of the hemisphere. He was the "Sputnik" of Latin America.

Castro's career was launched with a roar of approval from most of the world. The path he followed led right into the Soviet orbit. North Americans should now be aware that there is another half of the hemisphere, a Latin America which could go the way of Castro's Cuba.

Fidel Castro, as did the Sputnik, jolted the United States into realizing that there was a price to be paid for our years of complacency. Castro has proven dramatically that all is not well in our part of the world, and that it is time to do something about it.

Generally, the farther away that one gets from Cuba, the weaker is the fanatical support for Castro and his policies among the Latin left. But most governments still figure that it is the better part of political savvy not to condemn Castro officially.

In fact, during the recent ill-fated invasion of Cuba and subsequent discussion in the United Nations, while the United States pointedly abstained from a pious vote on non-intervention, Latin-American countries joined in the eighty-six-nation vote to deplore intervention. The question of intervention in the internal affairs of any country continues to be an extremely touchy point in Latin America. Guatemala, in the rather "iffy" position of being the only country recently to benefit from the direct intervention of the United States in the overturning of a Communist government, has gone on record as saying that the United States ought to intervene officially in Cuba to get rid of Castro.

Eight countries have broken diplomatic relations with the Castro regime at this writing: Haiti, the Dominican Republic, Guatemala, Peru, Nicaragua, El Salvador, Honduras and, of course, the United States.

Other countries have remained cool, but correct. President Betancourt of Venezuela has had ample proof that Castro agents and Venezuelan Communists had been plotting his downfall, but he preferred to act as if his real enemy were Trujillo of the Dominican Republic.

Brazil's new president, Janio Quadros, is publicly a warm supporter of Castro. (Though there are Brazilians who insist that Quadros is simply trying to take the steam out of Brazilian leftists. I suspect this is supporter sophistry.)

Quadros took office on January 31, 1961. During his first three months in office he refused to be interviewed by any newsmen, foreign or domestic, with one exception: Jorge Masetti, the Argentine director of Castro's propaganda wire *Prensa Latina*. (He has since resigned.) Masetti, a former member of Perón's propaganda machinery, brought greetings from Castro and Che Guevara and a frogskin brief case. He took back to Cuba "the full support of Quadros for the Cuban Revolution," if one is to believe the printed Masetti version of the interview.

On April 14, in his first news conference after assuming office, Quadros said publicly that Brazil "supports and defends the right of self-determination" in Cuba and favored "any effort" to heal the breach between Havana and Washington. That was before the exile invasion of Cuba on April 17. Quadros called for "comprehension and tolerance" for the regime of Fidel Castro. He considered Castro "imbued with idealism and firmly disposed to assure the independence of his country, to create a more dignified life for its citizens," while admitting that the Cuban leaders had indeed "committed errors and occasional excesses."

There are several reasons why some Latin-American governments are leery of criticizing Castro and his methods in public. First, the Fidelistas in their own countries are strong and powerful.

The Prime Minister of Peru, Pedro Beltran, broke relations with Havana after seeing ample evidence that the Cuban embassy in Lima was getting direct financial support from the Communists and using it to plan the overthrow of the Peruvian Government. The expected riots and demonstrations did not materialize after Beltran expelled the Cubans. Without the financial and spiritual support of the

Cuban embassy, the Fidelistas were reduced to an impotent minority.

Panama began confiscating crateloads of propaganda shipped to the Cuban embassy for distribution to schools and supporters. The Cuban consul in Colón was politely asked to pack his bags and get out.

The harder Castro's embassy worked in Panama, the more active anti-Castro elements became. The United States is a prime target in Panama for everyone's ire. The American-owned and -operated Panama Canal is there for everyone to see and brood about.

The secondary target is the businessman, Panamanian or North American—anyone with money and property. The more propaganda poured out of the embassy, the more property owners countered by forming anti-Communist, anti-Castro organizations with their own pamphlet campaigns.

Governments which have taken a strong stand against Castro have not toppled. But things differ from country to country, and some still excuse themselves on the ground that they do not dare appear unfriendly to a brother Latin state, even though it is led by Castro.

A virulent resentment remains in most of Latin America over "big stick" interference in internal affairs, and many who would like to see Castro fall are afraid that if they condone "interference" in Cuba, any one of the other nations could be next. The example of Guatemala still rankles throughout the continent.

Castro's antics fail to worry some Latin leaders for another reason. They do not see the twofold menace of Castro/Communism affecting their own countries. They feel that the Communist threat is an invention of the United States to rationalize Castro's seizure of American property in Cuba. Not all who hold this view are Communists or Fidelistas —they call themselves nationalists. It is difficult to convince such nationalists that if they continue to bury their heads in the sand, they are going to get kicked in the pants. It is an ungainly posture, but many Latins prefer it that way.

One such leader who for a long time turned a blind eye toward the danger of Fidelism was President José Ramon Villeda Morales of Honduras. Villeda Morales is an amiable man, interested in advancing his backward country and even more interested in staying in power. To do that, boxed in by leftists and Communists in his own Liberal Party, he had to compromise and to close his eyes to the very active Cuban embassy in Honduras which handed out an estimated $35,000 a month to newspapers and students.

"Castro," he once told me, "has no influence in Latin America except a psychological influence. All we need to do is surround the Castro and Communist movements with enough indifference and they will fall." Yet at that very same moment a sign emblazoned across the university gate, one block from the heavily guarded palace, proclaimed WIN WITH CASTRO. By April 24, Villeda Morales—over strident student protest—joined the list of countries breaking relations with Cuba.

While leaders discuss Castro on the level of political sophistication, the peoples of Latin America also discuss him. One discussion I had was with a man whose tattered clothes covered a undernourished body, a tattered hat shading his weather-beaten face. This man was a peasant in Nicaragua who earned seven cents a day for his sunup to sundown labor in the fields. We smoked a cigarette together, a luxury for him, and talked about Castro.

"Castro has done things for the Cuban worker," he told me. "They have their own homes now, I hear. They own their own land and their own tractors. The rich don't spend all their money on automobiles. They don't have any money. It's been divided among the workers, I hear. Their children are all going to school. I have seven children—living—and they have not seen a school. No doubt about it, Fidel has done things for Cuba. We need a Fidel here."

But Castro's way is not the only way. Leaders in Latin America, hampered by sluggish economies and mushrooming social ills, are trying to cope with their problems in other ways.

Argentina's President Arturo Frondizi boldly announced a stabilization program in December, 1958. It was austerity and all that went with it: tightened belts for Argentines who had lived too well, too long; price and wage controls; a new oil program which allowed American companies to drill for Argentine oil. This gave nationalists and Communists a chance to scream about "imperialist exploitation" without considering the fact that Argentina might become an oil exporting country rather than a country importing a million dollars of oil a day. The average Argentine does not know this, or if he does know it he does not care. It is too easy to scream about a foreign profit-making venture stealing the money which should rightfully be going into Argentine pockets.

It has taken all Frondizi's political adroitness to weather the attack from workers and unions and to keep the army from moving in on him with accusations of having too many Perónistas in his government. When Frondizi announced his stabilization program, betting in Buenos Aires was heavy that it could not work. So far, the critics have been confounded.

Other Latin leaders have shown an equal amount of political courage. Prime Minister Pedro Beltran of Peru, President Betancourt of Venezuela, President Quadros of Brazil, are all taking unpopular but necessary steps to replenish their economic cupboards.

Brazil, being the biggest country, has the biggest problems and the greatest potential.

I have often wondered if somewhere in Rio de Janeiro there is not a school for taxi drivers. Not one that teaches them how to drive, but as I imagine this school, one that specializes in economics, geography, philosophy and psychology. Once a week there must be a guest lecturer—a politician by training, a painter of rosy futures and a promiser of everything. For Rio taxi drivers are strongly imbued with the pioneer spirit of Brazil. Many have lectured me on the same general premise: "You come from the United States. In ten years Brazil will be more important than the United States. We will be richer and happier. We are the people and the country of the future. Brazil is the awakening giant."

I hear the lecture, I overtip, and welcome this exciting prospect of the future. It may well be right.

The area of Brazil is almost half that of all South America; it is big enough to put all of the continental United States within its borders. Its potential resources, mineral deposits, hydroelectric power, unexploited agricultural and forest regions are so vast that estimates range from the fabulous to the fantastic.

Yet in his inaugural address, President Quadros said that the financial picture of Brazil today was "terrible." It may be worse than that. Former President Juscelino Kubitschek and his economic advisors concentrated on two goals—progress and the new capital of Brasilia. Both were accomplished and Brazil has yet to pay for either one.

The official Brazilian foreign exchange deficit for 1960 was 337 million dollars, nearly twice the 1959 deficit. During the first year of the Quadros Administration, interest on a 3.8-billion-dollar foreign debt will come to around 600 million dollars. Senhor Quadros has already moved to make fiscal and administrative reforms, and those moves have earned him an inevitable decline in personal popularity.

He cut the federal budget about 30 per cent without referring to congress (which Quadros does not control). He slashed the government payroll, eliminating all employees appointed after September 1 (one month before elections), and banned any government appointments for at least one year.

Quadros ordered federal employees to work a seven-hour day—from 8:30 in the morning until 11, and 2 in the afternoon until 6. Cries of outrage and indignation could be heard from public officials from Rio to Brasilia and a mutter of "It's about time" from non-government job holders.

Federal employees used to start work at 11 A.M. and worked straight through until 5 P.M. Many stretched the starting hour to noon, just in time for a two-hour lunch. Some, who had long practice in the art of not working very hard, showed up after lunch to put in a few hours before quitting time. And there were those who showed up only on payday, to collect their paychecks.

While the previous government work schedule was in force, employees could and did hold two jobs. They had to, to make financial ends meet a little short of disaster. The Quadros Administration feels that with government officials expected to work a seven-hour day, many will quit the public payroll. It may cut down on official overhead, but it will not do much to help the already serious unemployment situation.

Quadros has his work cut out for him, but even his enemies agree that if anyone can set Brazil's house in order, Quadros is the one. "That Janio Quadros is the one to wield his political symbol—a broom."

He has already caused considerable consternation at home and abroad by ordering his United Nations delegation to vote for the inclusion of an agenda item on the admission of Red China. This does not, as foreign office officials point out, mean that Brazil will vote for admission of Red China into the United Nations. Quadros merely thinks that the matter should be aired. Brazil's foreign minister, Alfonso Arinos, has said that these maneuvers were the result of a realistic view of world affairs.

There may be another reason for Quadros' emphasis on foreign fields during his first few months in office. The five-year administration of President Kubitschek will always be remembered in Brazil as one of progress, despite the nearly catastrophic inflation which accompanied it. So if Quadros is to make his mark, it will have to be in the realm of foreign affairs. Whatever he does internally is sure to be necessary, and just as sure to be unpleasant and unpopular.

But in foreign affairs, he has a chance. First, he must prove that his foreign policy is neither directed by nor controlled from Washington. Second, he must establish himself as a spokesman on the world stage. He cannot join the big four or five; his voice would be lost. But he may have an influential word to say among the Neutralists—Nehru, Nasser, Tito, Sukarno and the others.

Quadros is determined to make Brasilia, the world's newest and most modern capital, the capital in fact as well as theory. He spends most of his time there, and he is going to see to it that the government is run from there. He may not have agreed with the theory, nor the money spent on this awe-inspiring city on the plateau, but he is going to make sure that it is used.

Just how much money Kubitschek spent on Brasilia is impossible to tell. Some say five hundred million dollars and others put it closer to a billion. But whatever it cost, it has been worth it in psychic income for Brazil. She has gained worldwide renown for the beauties of Brasilia. The city, built in five years, has sent architects, city planners, travel writers and tourists off into paeans of praise about Brazil. Its citizens are proud to be Brazilians.

Perhaps it will be best to judge Brazil's progress over an entire decade: five years with Kubitschek and the five years to come with Quadros. Those who have faith in Quadros and the Brazilian people believe that these ten years will be the ten to go down in history as the Decade of Brazil.

Despite the fact that too many Latin-American generals still dominate the political situation, things are getting better. And often overlooked is the more enlightened role of armies in Latin-American politics; had it not been for some of these same armies, some of the now deposed dictators would still be in power. The armed forces threw them out. We cannot have it both ways. Either military men do take some professional interest in preventing leaders from assuming total power, or they do not.

It would be better from the U. S. point of view, if the armed forces of all Latin countries were as apolitical as British and U. S. armed forces are. But we are not likely to see that in our generation.

In several countries—Brazil, Chile, Argentina, and Honduras—the armed forces may well be the steadying conservative influence which will keep leftist minorities from getting into power. And Uncle Sam's real or imagined meddling might result in disastrous decisions on the part of the local military.

However, U. S. military services could stipulate that a much larger part of the Military Assistance Program should be channeled to provide, both at U. S. facilities and those of the Latin country, training in the basic technical skills sorely needed for the internal development of that country.

Thanks to the initiative and foresight of some U. S. military men who have been assigned to Latin-American posts, steps have been taken in this direction. For example, based upon the strong recommendation of the Chief of Naval Mission to Ecuador in 1954, the Ecuadorian Government built a service school for its navy. The U. S. Military Assistance Program helped to train instructors and to provide equipment for this school which prepared both military and a limited number of civilian personnel in essential technical skills. There are other U. S. naval and army officers trying similarly excellent programs in other Latin posts.

Private investment in Latin America runs to about a half-billion dollars a year. Latin America could use much more than that. The problem of getting private investors to put their dollars in Latin America will always be difficult so long as governments have a way of nationalizing companies if they happen to be doing well.

Obviously, American companies are in business to make money, a point seemingly lost on Latin-American critics of Yankee money. They seem to feel that American companies should be dedicated to altruistic endeavors.

If Latin-American nations would give some protection to foreign investments and if Latin businessmen could be persuaded to re-invest their profits, prosperity, while not just around the corner, would be less than light years away. But that would be expecting the millennium.

Meanwhile there are other bright and hopeful signs in Latin America. There are men and women, a good many of them, who are democratic, forceful, and dedicated to making a free society work in their countries. There are men and women who are speaking out against demagoguery and tyranny of both the right and the left. There are men and women who, intellectually unable to take the easy way out, defend the United States even in anti-American meetings.

Ricardo Castro Beeche, editor of San José, Costa Rica's, *La Nacion,* and a likely candidate for president before long, countered the recurrent sneer at Yankee imperialism this way:

Yankee imperialism means a country that has gone to two world wars with enormous sacrifice of lives and money which has not taken a single inch of land from any of the defeated countries.

It means a nation which devoted hundreds of millions of dollars for the reconstruction of defeated countries after the war—the very countries whose people were victims of their own dictatorial governments.

Yankee imperialism means a country which has spent millions of dollars in technical assistance and food over all these years to save many peoples of the world from hunger and misery. Yankee imperialism says a man has the right to happiness through a worthy life.

And there are other men actively engaged in pro-democratic pursuits, such as the School for Democracy. It used to be a combination restaurant-night club. Present occupants have painted the place and fixed it up so there is now a school in this reconverted roadhouse, a school for democracy. Students range from a Guatemalan farmer with a sixth grade education to a man who at one time held a responsible position in his government. All twenty-three students from ten different Latin American countries, representing sixteen different political parties, want to have more of a democratic say in their home governments.

They are getting a tough, three-month indoctrination course in democracy: what it is, how it works, why many times it does not work, and what they are up against fighting the graduates of Moscow training schools.

This school's official name is the Institute of Political Education, paid for and sponsored by sixteen democratic political parties in Latin America and one U. S. organization, the Institute of International Labor Research. It is an outgrowth of an idea a former Costa Rican president, José "Pepe" Figueres, had years ago and is located near San José.

The students are enthusiastic. I watched the simple, informal graduation ceremonies where speakers and students smoked and listened to long speeches. Sometimes they did not listen. Diplomas were handed out without any particular fuss.

But the men, the graduates, know that diplomas and graduation speeches are not going to do them any good. The only thing that can help them is their desire to make democracy work when they go back home. Many of them could not go back home to countries ruled by dictators. When, or if, they do, they will be fighting against tyranny, apathy, corruption, and the trained and disciplined Communists.

Perhaps five years from now we shall know how successful Costa Rica's Institute of Political Education has been.

Relatively few North Americans have had any interest in Central and South Americans during the last two decades. Whether this is right or wrong, good or bad, smart or stupid, is beside the point. We took Latin America, its allegiance, its unquestioning loyalty, for granted.

We took its needs, its revolutions, its political and physical catastrophes—if we noticed at all—as just one of the things happening to a family unfortunate enough to have been born on the other side of the tracks. In this case, south of the border.

Our governments pinned medals on the expansive and over-decorated chests of dictators. We sent money and arms to those we could trust to say all the right words about the dangers of Communism. Since opposition to dictators in the eyes of dictators is always "Communist inspired," we opposed opposition. We opposed, or certainly did not encourage, land and tax reforms because these, we were told by dictators and the oligarchies, smacked of Communism. We let some North American big businesses which had large investments in Latin countries have their say about who should rule those countries, and how.

If we listened at all, we underestimated the grievances of our Latin neighbors. The late John Foster Dulles made a trip to Caracas in 1954 to address the Inter-American Conference. He made a stirring speech about fighting Communism, made little or no attempt to listen to Latin leaders on their problems, and when the anti-Communist resolution was passed, Mr. Dulles flew off somewhere else.

Christian Herter at later conferences in Santiago and San José stayed through the long and often reduntant speeches of foreign minister colleagues. He invited each one in for a private chat, and Latin-American officials were surprised and pleased. They hoped it might presage a change in the whole North American attitude, a transition from the era of unconcern and neglect.

Governments and ruling classes of Latin America have made mistakes of commission and omission. They should not forget that fact in the years to come. However, it is time to stop dwelling on mistakes of the past. It is time for the U. S. and Latin-American Governments to work to see that these are not repeated.

—WILSON HALL

WILSON HALL is NBC News Rio de Janeiro Correspondent. Prior assignments have taken him to all parts of Latin America and for a time during the first two years of Fidel Castro's assumption of power in Cuba, he was head of the Havana office. No American broadcast newsman has had as close a view of Castro in action. A native of Champaign, Illinois, he attended the University of Illinois and the Yale School of Drama with an interlude of Army service in Germany. His theatrical aspirations were interrupted by a call back to service for the Korean war. As a public information officer, he paved the way for a career as a broadcast newsman. He joined NBC News in 1953, reported briefly from Korea and then opened an NBC News bureau in Cairo. His reporting of the Latin-American scene began in 1959. Joining him on his foreign assignments has been his wife, Lee Hall, also a correspondent for NBC News.

# 11.

## WASHINGTON:

## *"No Reason for Despair"*

THE correspondents who have contributed to this book
are, individually, delightful fellows. Collectively, they
will drive you to drink. It is not necessary for me to labor the
point. You have read their chapters. If you are cheered by
their cumulative effect, then somewhere along the line, there
has been a failure of what the sociologists are fond of calling
"communication."

It is a novel experience for us to be depressing between
hard covers. Usually, we gather at the end of each year when
NBC News brings home its foreign correspondents who sit
down with one or two from Washington. These correspondents then present their views on an annual program which is
a discussion of the past year and a projection of the year
ahead. Though we do this immediately after Christmas, there
is usually little cheer.

During the last week in December, 1960, James Robinson

and Cecil Brown said we were in trouble in Laos. They were right. John Rich said we were going to have a crisis over Berlin. Edwin Newman told us that President Kennedy would find in French President de Gaulle an ally who would pose as many problems as an adversary. Mr. Kennedy eventually had to journey to Paris to find out whose side General de Gaulle was really on. Welles Hangen and Irving R. Levine, both of whom had been assigned to the Congo, disagreed about the role of the United Nations there, but agreed that unless we changed our policies in Africa, there would one day be a white man's burden too heavy to bear. Joseph C. Harsch was concerned whether Britain would find her proper place in the pattern of an emerging West European unity. Few problems now give the British greater cause for concern. Wilson Hall said that whether we liked it or not, Castroism was popular in Latin America. He was right. John Chancellor was bothered by two things: would the Soviets find him a decent apartment for his family; and would they be able to control the Chinese Communists? The Soviets found Chancellor his apartment. They are still working on the other matter.

These are all sensitive men; and as so often happens when sensitive men live abroad for long periods of time and are depressed by what they have seen, heard and reported, they return to their own country filled with the hope that somehow it will find a way to confront, with courage and wisdom, the problems that beset the particular area of the world they are covering.

During the week we spent together in 1960, they developed a flattering yet disconcerting habit of turning to me to ask: "What will Kennedy do?" My answer did not satisfy them, for I had to say that I did not know. I was not even sure that the President-elect knew, himself. I could only tell them that Mr. Kennedy had to have time to review United States policy around the world. They argued there was not that much time. I said that while this might be so, the new President simply needed time to set his own house in order. It was not his fault that his policies had not been completely formulated. It was the fault of the American political system.

John F. Kennedy spent all of 1960—and most of the preceding three years—in an effort to seize the Presidential nomination from a party that was not sure it wanted him to have it. Then, for three months in the fall of 1960, he campaigned for the Presidency and won it from an electorate that was about evenly divided about the desirability of having him sit in the White House.

He knew during all this time that there were many problems waiting for him. He came into the White House with a better understanding of the office than any President since Woodrow Wilson. He had been briefed very carefully, both by his own advisors and by President Eisenhower and his officials. Being an intelligent man who reads widely, there was much he already knew. What he knew did not satisfy him. He wanted a change in our policies. But it was one thing to have criticized those in office for what they had and had not done. It was something else to know exactly what he would do once he was President.

During the two and a half months between the election and the inauguration, Mr. Kennedy knew three things: He had to form a cabinet and an administration; good men were hard to find; and Nikita Khrushchev wanted to meet him at the earliest possible opportunity. He formed his cabinet and his administration. He managed to find good men. He made it clear to Mr. Khrushchev that he would have to wait. The President-elect needed time to see what had to be done.

It did not take long for President Kennedy to learn that time was not his handmaiden. He told Congress in his State of the Union message that time was not on our side. The problems closed in on him—Cuba, Laos, an atomic test ban treaty and Berlin. He was right. Time would not serve him. He served it instead. Yet, he was doing well. His popularity soared higher perhaps than that of any other American President during his first months in office. Our prestige around the world was rising. Then came Cuba.

The President was badly advised on Cuba, though this fact, as he said later, did not relieve him of the ultimate responsibility for the fiasco. The Central Intelligence Agency told him the natives were restless. They may have been, but only up to a point. His Joint Chiefs of Staff, especially his Chief of Naval Operations, advised him that a rebel landing could be effected in the Bay of Pigs.

Mr. Kennedy was once described to me by a close political associate as a man with the "most politically sensitive viscera" of our time. He meant by this that the President had an uncanny way of feeling whether a decision was right or wrong. The President, of course, should have known better about Cuba. Here was a man who had won the nomination and the Presidency by throwing away the rule book. He had ignored the experts. He had done it his way, and his way was right. Yet, when the time came for a decision on Cuba, he trusted the judgment of others more than he trusted his own judgment. It was an excess of modesty committed at an expense of shame. The talented newcomers he had brought with him to Washington were no less at fault. They, too, had been, as one of them told me later, "snowed" by the experts.

It takes a lot of courage to stand up to the experts. Winston Churchill is the only Western statesman to have done it in this century. It was surprising that President Kennedy, a close student of history and an admirer of Churchill, should have allowed himself to be so led by the experts. They told him that we had to move against Castro before he became too powerful. They told him that Cuban pilots would soon be returning from training in Czechoslovakia, ready to fly MIG jets over the Caribbean. He was assured that an invasion force

of Cuban exiles could topple the Castro regime, that if he did
not put them to use, these exiles who had started training under the Eisenhower Administration would soon become dis-
enchanted and start to drift away from their training camps.

There were important individuals within the Administration who opposed this adventure. But they were beaten almost from the start, beaten because they were unwilling or
unable to contest with vigor the opinions of the Washington
branch of the American establishment.

We have heard for several years now about the British
establishment. Because Britain is a more or less homoge-
neous country, it is easier to pin down with accuracy those
individuals who make up the establishment. If you took the
time, you could almost work out the power structure of
Britain so that it would resemble the structure of an atom.

It is not that simple in the United States. In Washington itself, however, the difficulties lessen. In the case of Cuba, you
had three vital elements of the American Establishment at
work. They were: the Central Intelligence Agency, the Joint
Chiefs of Staff and, to a lesser degree, the State Department.
The thing to remember about all these institutions is that
even though the faces in them change from administration
to administration, their policies remain almost unchanged.
They avoid originality as if it were a medieval plague. Yet
they have gone on, year after year, influencing and, in some
cases, dominating our national policies without ever being
seriously challenged from a *policy* point of view.

President Kennedy was aware of all this when he took
office. He had been advised by Professor Richard Neustadt of
Columbia University to create a staff of advisors around him
who would not tell him "this is the right course of action,"
but would present to him *all* the courses of action, then let
him choose the best one under the circumstances. This suited
the President's temperament. It was so ordered.

In the case of Cuba, it did not work out that way. The able

and intelligent men he had selected were apparently unwilling to argue with passion against the course of action that was advocated by the C.I.A., supported by the Joint Chiefs of Staff, and acquiesced in by the State Department. It takes some courage to be a nay sayer to the President of the United States. Yet the irony was that the men who should have said no were the very individuals who for some years past had been attacking, publicly and privately, just this sort of thing in the Eisenhower Administration. So the invasion proceeded according to confusion and failed miserably.

It was a disaster, not simply because of the lives that were lost, not because it damaged our reputation too severely in Latin America (there is not a political leader in office in Latin America who would not like to see Castro dead), but primarily because it damaged our steadily rising prestige in all parts of the non-Communist world.

There was one important person in Washington who argued vigorously against the Cuban invasion—Senator J. William Fulbright, Chairman of the Senate Foreign Relations Committee. In a memorandum submitted to the President before the invasion, Senator Fulbright argued against it and pointed out the dangerous position we would find ourselves in even if the invasion proved successful. He told the President that while Cuba might be "a thorn in our side, it was not a dagger at our heart." His advice was not heeded.

It may have been the fact that his advice was ignored over Cuba that led Mr. Fulbright to say publicly a little while later that he was opposed to American military intervention to save Laos. It is impossible to exaggerate the effect this had on the crucial negotiations then going on with a view to arranging Laotian cease-fire talks. We must not blame the Soviets for taking seriously the words of the Chairman of the Senate Foreign Relations Committee. If he says on a Sunday that he is opposed to intervening militarily in Laos, and on Monday the Senate majority whip, Hubert H. Humphrey, says the same thing in front of the White House, are the Soviets to be blamed for not taking President Kennedy's implied threat of intervention too seriously?

I think it is possible to say that until these statements were made, the Soviets did not know for sure whether or not we would commit military forces in Laos. President Kennedy had given the nation a chalk talk on television on the importance of Laos. Vice-President Johnson had said we would not allow the Asian kingdom to be "gobbled up" by the Communists. It can even be argued that despite the way the Cuban invasion was bungled, it might have given Mr. Khrushchev pause and made him think that this fellow in the White House really meant business. Even if he did botch up the Cuban affair—Mr. Khrushchev has had his share of blunders—he did try to put a stop to what he considered to be a threat to the national interest of the United States. Perhaps he would also intervene in Laos.

There was no such doubt after the Fulbright and Humphrey statements. I remember leading off my evening radio report that Monday night of the Humphrey statement by saying flatly that the Administration had decided not to intervene in Laos. But the Security Council continued to meet. The White House issued heated denials at the time. Still it was true that we had no intention of going into Laos in the spring of 1961 after top Senate leaders said they were opposed to military intervention there.

The President's decision on Laos was right at that time. Laos was a mess handed him by the Eisenhower Administration. There was little he could do to save it. He could have tried to minimize its importance from the start, but this would not have been in keeping with a charming ritual that has developed over the years in Washington which demands that political leaders say that we will garrison the world.

Yet after the decision had been made and the Laotian

peace talks in Geneva seemed to indicate we were being had by the Communists, the President began to worry about the effects of this decision elsewhere. If we had said we would do something to save Laos and had not, would our word have any meaning elsewhere, say in Berlin? Would the Soviets take our word seriously in a place like Berlin where our national interest was vitally involved? Was there not a danger now that Mr. Khrushchev might miscalculate with terrifying consequences?

It was for this reason primarily that the President decided he had better have a talk with Mr. Khrushchev. He had put him off at an earlier time; then, when Soviet Foreign Minister Gromyko came to the White House in early April, the idea was revived. Nothing much was done about it, however, until the end of April, when it became clear that Mr. Khrushchev was again interested in meeting the President. Finally, in the second week in May, the story broke prematurely—the President was to meet Mr. Khrushchev in Vienna following his talks with French President de Gaulle in Paris at the end of May.

At first, it was thought that the announcement of the Kennedy-Khrushchev talks would take some of the bloom off the President's visit to Paris. It probably did, initially. Mr. Kennedy had decided about ten days after he took office that he was going to see General de Gaulle. If the Atlantic Alliance was to be revitalized, this would have to be done. Normally, Western leaders come to Washington. But de Gaulle was no normal leader. Besides, he had been to the United States the year before and he had enough trouble at home and in Algeria not to ask him to repeat the journey.

Fortunately, the decision to see Premier Khrushchev did not ultimately lessen the impact of the President's decision to go to see President de Gaulle. Mr. Kennedy went to Paris armed with the most important and popular export since

Coca-Cola replaced Pernod in Parisian sidewalk cafés—his wife, Jacqueline. It is difficult to assess properly the impact that Mrs. Kennedy had on France—and unfortunately, this is not the place to do it. Suffice to say she did not hurt the President's cause in Western Europe, and certainly she helped his relations with General de Gaulle. At one luncheon, the French President almost completely ignored the woman on his left and talked in animated fashion throughout the luncheon with Mrs. Kennedy. Since General de Gaulle usually speaks to no one below the rank of President and God, Mrs. Kennedy's achievement was a formidable one.

The President's trip to Paris was a perfect example of the possibilities and the limitations of personal diplomacy. Not since Britain's Edward VII journeyed to Paris in the first decade of this century to raise his country's prestige in France has a state visit had such a fortuitous result. Edward conquered with sheer graciousness. It was much the same with the Kennedys, but they had something else working for them as well.

Whether they liked it or not, the Kennedys, by the time of their Paris visit, had become international status symbols, possessed of the attributes most individuals would like to find in themselves—wealth, beauty, position, intelligence and what the auditors of society like to call good breeding. Visiting a continent nearly bereft of royalty, it was to be expected that the Kennedys' every movement and utterance would receive wide coverage. That is exactly what happened. But this personal popularity, while gratifying, did little to change the realities of power politics.

It was said by his advisors beforehand that President Kennedy was not going to Paris seeking agreement with General de Gaulle on all questions. As Edwin Newman pointed out in his chapter, there were certain demands that de Gaulle had made which would be difficult to satisfy. The President instead tried to establish a mood of confidence between himself and General de Gaulle. This did not mean that questions of substance were avoided. It meant simply that Mr. Kennedy did not seek to exacerbate the already troubled relations between the United States and France by arguing at length about matters which could not be settled at the time or at any time in the foreseeable future. He went so far as to minimize the use of certain words like *NATO, the United Nations* and *atomic weapons* which have a tendency to produce a certain predictable and unpleasant response on the part of President de Gaulle. He tried to use synonyms instead. It was almost as if he were following an injunction laid down by Winston Churchill in a wartime memorandum: "Do not argue the difficulties. The difficulties will argue for themselves."

Berlin dominated the discussions. President de Gaulle and West Germany's Konrad Adenauer had been concerned about Britain's tendency to equivocate over Western rights in Berlin. Similar doubts had been generated in their minds by certain things President Eisenhower had said in the closing years of his Administration. Assurance was sought from President Kennedy that our position on Berlin would be a firm one. This assurance was given, yet there was not complete identity of views.

President de Gaulle, and we may assume Chancellor Adenauer as well, wanted a firm Western position spelled out to deter the Soviet Union from changing the Berlin *status quo* in any way. Mr. Kennedy, however, who on most positions is a careful man of the middle ground, would like to see the exact nature of Soviet action before spelling out our response. It is certain that he would not commit this nation to the use of armed forces solely over who controlled the access routes to West Berlin as long as those routes remained opened and unfettered to Allied traffic. Both he and President de Gaulle agreed, however, that the Allies should plan for any eventuality.

If few substantive problems were settled by Presidents Kennedy and de Gaulle, at least one thing emerged from their talks. It was clear that for the first time President de Gaulle felt some regard for an American President. He has had none for any of the others he has had to deal with since he first became a national leader during the early days of World War II. Apparently, he was impressed with Mr. Kennedy's willingness to look realistically at grave issues, and even though agreement could not be reached on many of them, President de Gaulle was at least impressed by Mr. Kennedy's ability to recognize that they existed. This is not my assumption. It received verification at the end of the Paris talks when responsible French reporters, obviously briefed by the Quai d'Orsay, sought out their American counterparts to report the good impression President Kennedy had made on President de Gaulle. For this reason alone, Paris was useful.

Then there was Vienna and Khrushchev. President Kennedy returned from his two days of talks with Premier Khrushchev a troubled man. It was one thing to have had an intellectual conception of the Soviet leader. It was quite something else to meet with him, talk to him and find intransigence on every single issue discussed with him. Nothing was settled at Vienna. Nothing was meant to be settled there. The meeting was not a success; neither was it a failure. It was simply a meeting designed to enable the leaders of the two most powerful nations on earth to take the measure of each other.

In a sense, it fulfilled the Churchillian conception of what a Summit meeting should be. There has been a great deal of confusion since Mr. Churchill made his now famous speech in the House of Commons on May 11, 1953, calling for a meeting at the Summit. The Churchill idea of a Summit meeting was for the leaders of the United States and the Soviet Union—and since he was then Prime Minister, the leaders of Britain and France, as well—to meet in as much privacy as possible with no fixed agenda and with few advisors present.

None of the Churchillian conditions for a Summit meeting had been truly met until President Kennedy met Premier Khrushchev in Vienna. Most of the time, they were alone with their translators. Neither man gave an advantage. Neither man received one. It was a mutual exchange of views stated, we have been told, with courtesy and without abuse. The President apparently searched for some area of agreement with Mr. Khrushchev on certain outstanding issues and found none. He left Vienna with more to preoccupy him than his aching back.

In his report to the American people upon his return from Vienna, Mr. Kennedy said, "The most somber talks were on the subject of Berlin and Germany." He is not a man given to overstatement. For this reason, the word *somber* had a chilling effect. My colleague John Chancellor has mentioned the arrogance displayed by the Soviet Premier in Vienna. The description is apt. A man does not behave like Mr. Khrushchev does unless he is certain that power, time and history are all on his side.

We have now been alerted by Premier Khrushchev to expect a crisis over Berlin by the end of 1961. He told President Kennedy in Vienna that West Berlin was a bone stuck in the Soviet throat and that it had to be removed. The proper response, of course, was that it was not up to us to remove the bone. That was Mr. Khrushchev's task, not ours. This fact should be remembered in all these discussions.

There is only a West Berlin problem in the sense that Mr. Khrushchev wants a change there in the *status quo*. There is, however, an East German problem because the leaders of that Soviet satellite have told Mr. Khrushchev that a free West Berlin provides the opening through which the most useful people in East Germany are drained off daily to the West. Some people have argued that we live in a different world from the one in which the arrangements of Berlin were drawn up and that we must take into account the change that has taken place in the world balance of power. There is some persuasiveness in such an argument, but not enough. We can also sympathize, but not unduly, with Mr. Khrushchev's fears that unless a German peace treaty were signed, the borders of East and West Germany would not be stabilized and a *revanchist* West Germany, led perhaps by the present Defense Minister, Franz Josef Strauss, would upset the present demarcation lines in Central Europe by the force of arms, probably atomic. But this begs the central question which still remains: Do we have a right to remain in West Berlin? Whatever Mr. Khrushchev may say, dressed in his World War II uniform, we are not in Berlin by sufferance. We are there by right.

The problem, then, in Central Europe is not primarily West Berlin. It is East Germany. We should not allow Soviet propaganda to obscure this fact. If this is the bone that sticks, we really should not be asked by Mr. Khrushchev to remove it. He has never been so obliging to us. Of course, geography is on his side. But Mr. Khrushchev should be asked whether or not he is ready to go to war to change the *status quo* in Central Europe. It is a question best put to Mr. Khrushchev through private diplomatic channels, for on questions like this one, it is foolish to back your adversary into a corner from which he must emerge in a bellicose manner to save nothing more important than his prestige and honor.

President Kennedy must also put a question to the American people and we must be ready to answer it: Are we ready to fight, if necessary, to maintain our rights in West Berlin? If the Soviets say there is no room for a decision except on their terms, we must be ready to move to the next phase of the dispute.

The next phase is whether or not the East Germans, assuming they have signed a peace treaty with the Soviets, will try to prevent us from exercising our rights in West Berlin and our obligations to its people. We should make it quite clear to Mr. Khrushchev that this could mean a war. This is a fear that he, as well as ourselves, must live with, and a possible course of action he must explain and justify to the Soviet people.

Senate Majority Leader Mike Mansfield said shortly after the Vienna meeting that we should consider making all of Berlin a free city. This proposal, made on the floor of the Senate, could hardly have come at a worse time. The Soviets were well on their way to believing that we were seeking any way out of a crisis over Berlin. Senator Mansfield's speech was well-intentioned, but it was unfortunate, nonetheless. If this sort of a debate has to go on over Berlin, it would be best done privately. I know this flies in the face of what we have been told about the necessity for public discussion in a democracy. Unfortunately, the good that might flow from such a discussion would be overweighed by the Soviets' mistaking it for disunity and lack of resolution.

I do not mean to suggest that President Kennedy should sound a jingoist note over Berlin, though there certainly was enough of that sentiment current in the country during the period following the Vienna meeting. He should explore all possible ways to maintain what he considers to be our rights in Berlin without resorting to force of arms. It is necessary, I think, to insist to Chancellor Adenauer that West Germany be prepared to accept the present demarcation lines between the two Germanys. Everyone else does. The United States, Britain and France accept it privately, but do not say so publicly. The Soviets accept it and welcome it privately, and say so publicly. It would not be wise to take the lead in offering Mr. Khrushchev public or even private acceptance of the present demarcation line in Germany for the time being. It should be discussed perhaps privately with Mr. Khrushchev, but it should not be offered as a concession to allow us to maintain the rights we think are ours in West Berlin. Mr. Khrushchev would regard such a premature offer as a sign of weakness. This and any other proposals we may have to make should come later rather than sooner. First, Mr. Khrushchev must be convinced that we mean what we say about staying in Berlin. For only then will he consider seriously any proposal that we make. Our offers of negotiations are likely to be treated with contempt if Mr. Khrushchev feels that they are being made to avoid a test of will between the United States and its Allies, and the Soviet Union. George F. Kennan, in his book *Russia and the West Under Stalin,* writes:

In thirty years' experience with Soviet official literature, I cannot recall an instance of a non-Communist government being credited with a single generous or worthy impulse. All actions of such governments favorable to Soviet interests or even responsive to Soviet desiderata are invariably attributed to motives less than creditable: as a bowing to necessity, a belated yielding to the demands of outraged opinion, or the accidental subsidiary of some sinister ulterior motive.

There is no need for panic over Berlin. It is not only unbecoming a great people, it is also unnecessary. We should never forget that Berlin is a useful tool for Mr. Khrushchev. He turns on a crisis there whenever it suits his purposes. Since 1958, he has been alternately turning it on and off. Unfortunately, the attitude that every turn-off produces in the West has been rather like the emotion displayed by Winston Smith in George Orwell's *1984*. After being tortured and degraded by the secret police, Smith is sitting in a grimy sidewalk café. He looks up at a picture of Big Brother and is grateful to him for having ended the torture. We should not be too disposed to be unduly grateful to Mr. Khrushchev for ending, every now and then, the torture he began. If we must have our Pavlovian responses, we ought to save them for more rewarding stimulations than those provided by him.

There is really no limit to the surprises that Mr. Khrushchev has in store for us. President Kennedy has learned that life with Mr. Khrushchev is never dull, there is always the unexpected. We went into the Geneva atomic test ban talks, when they resumed in the winter of 1960, hopeful of the possibility of agreement. But the Soviets made it clear almost immediately they no longer had any interest in reaching agreement on an atomic test ban treaty. They seemed not only anxious to test their own nuclear devices, but they also appeared unable to guarantee that Red China would abide by any treaty signed by the United States, Britain and the Soviet Union. Even in the unlikely event that President de Gaulle had bound France to such an agreement, the Soviets still would not have been able to deliver the Red Chinese.

Thus the Russians introduced the "troika" principle into the atomic test ban talks. All international control bodies, they insisted, had to represent the true balance of power in the world—the West, the Soviet Union and the neutrals, each with the power of veto. There are no neutral men, Mr. Khrushchev told Walter Lippmann, and this belief was raised in dramatic form first at the United Nations in September, 1960, when he demanded that the UN Secretary General be replaced by a three-man directorate, then later at the atomic test ban talks. But its larger implication is, I believe, in the struggle that we are waging with the Communists in what Sir Oliver Franks has called the southern half of the globe.

President Kennedy noted in the Vienna talks how Mr. Khrushchev kept returning again and again to the subject of the underdeveloped and uncommitted nations. There is no question in anyone's mind about Mr. Kennedy's having more interest in the battle to be waged over these nations than his predecessors had. He was oriented that way when he came to the White House, by temperament and by his Congressional experience. His Secretary of State, Dean Rusk, in his former position as head of the Rockefeller Foundation, had as much to do with the leaders of these emerging nations as probably any other American. His Ambassador to the United Nations, Adlai Stevenson, had traveled widely in these nations, knew and was respected by their leaders.

The countries of the southern half of the globe needed help. But by the time the Administration's foreign aid bill was before Congress in the summer of 1961, there was widespread disenchantment with the entire concept of foreign aid. It manifested itself in the Congressional hearings. Congressmen were reflecting a neo-isolationism on the part of the American people, a reluctance to be taxed for the support of countries like Laos and Korea where billions of dollars in foreign aid had not produced the results they had been told that it would. There was, however, something even more fundamental behind Congressional resistance. Many members of Congress—a great many of them supporters of foreign aid—simply did not trust the people who were administering the programs around the world.

Congress is not a willful body. Its members are, for the most part, responsible individuals. The White House knew the mood of Congress. Hubert Humphrey, Senate majority whip, warned Lawrence F. O'Brien, the President's Congressional liaison assistant, that the Administration was not sending up qualified people to testify on behalf of foreign aid. Already aware of Congress' mood, the White House had looked over the list of people administering foreign aid and, in many cases, especially those in charge of our overseas missions, it had found them second rate. But it is not easy to attract individuals to work in this field. The financial rewards are not that great. The pitfalls are numerous. The White House found it was even difficult to persuade outstanding American citizens to serve on the President's Committee for

International Development. All this indicated that the entire concept of foreign aid had lost the attraction it had when we started the Marshall Plan.

This was a pity. After years of proliferation of authority in the foreign-aid field, the President decided to centralize foreign-aid functions in one agency. The Administration came up with a long-term approach to foreign aid that, despite certain shortcomings, was the best thing seen around Washington in years. It asked for authority to put foreign projects on a long-term financing basis without forcing the Administration to return every year to Congress for appropriations. Foreign governments could plan their projects secure in the knowledge that the capital would be forthcoming until the completion of what they had started.

It also called for political, economic and social changes to be made in the recipient nations. Nowhere did this have greater application than in Latin America. The President's plan for Latin America, the Alliance for Progress, was predicated on the necessity for these changes to be made. We do not have to go to Asia to find misery, and poverty, and vast inequities between the very rich and the very poor. It was all very near us in the Southern half of the hemisphere.

When Adlai Stevenson returned in June, 1961, from his fact-finding tour of Latin America, he told the President that conditions, if anything, were worse than they had been when he was there the year before. He found that many ordinary Latin Americans did not share our awareness that Fidel Castro had allowed Communism to betray the earlier aims of the Cuban revolution. They only knew, or thought they knew, that Castroism was aimed at eliminating the factors that were making for a dangerous situation all over Latin America: "an explosive birth rate, low productivity, a social system of feudalism and social injustice, the misuse of resources, falling prices of exports, and at the same time, an increasing demand for social services." The United States, he said, could help these nations in many ways, but we could not do the job for them. "All we can do," said Mr. Stevenson, using the President's words from his Alliance for Progress speech, "is to help them help themselves."

This is the key to our aid program in Latin America and our programs elsewhere. We must insist that changes be made before our help is given. There will always be nations rushing to us crying, "If you don't help us, then we'll have to turn to the Communists for help." It would be a useful experience if in one or two cases we replied, "Go ahead." Since the changes will have to be made sooner or later, it would probably be most helpful if, in a polite but unmistakably firm way, our attitude on giving foreign aid was "no tickee, no washee." Either the changes are made or no foreign aid. This has never been tried on a really widespread scale. It might work. It certainly would go a long way toward convincing a doubting Congress that foreign aid had some value, especially in the minds of the real supporters of the program, for it is in their minds that the efficacy of foreign aid is most seriously in doubt. Another useful exercise would be for us to take the advice of my colleague Welles Hangen, who warned that there is a danger that our expectations of progress in underdeveloped countries rise so much faster than those of the people involved that we tend to become discouraged. The job, he noted, takes generations. If we were more modest about the possibilities of what foreign aid can and cannot do, we might not be disillusioned so often. But this is a task for the President. Only he can explain it to the American people.

He might also explain to a large number of well-meaning but soft-headed people that while economic aid is a vital part of our foreign policy, we also must aid uncommitted countries militarily to resist Communist subversion, especially the so-called wars of national liberation. Because military aid has often been given just to keep a ruler's army happy, this does not mean that we should give up the idea entirely. It is foolish to believe that Communists move into positions of power in primitive society simply because there is widespread discontent. This helps their cause, but guns and Soviet airlifts also help. We should not be starry-eyed. Eliminating economic and social discontent is important, but we must also aid independently minded nations to crush terrorist movements within their borders. This is predicated on the assumption that they have the will to maintain their independence. In the case of Laos, this assumption was not entirely valid.

The last six months of 1961 may one day be recorded by historians as a time of testing for President Kennedy. They will be seen as the time when he had to decide whether or not the United States could resume nuclear testing without losing much of the prestige it gained in the world by its behavior at the Geneva talks; when he had to prepare the United States for a test of will with the Soviet Union over Berlin; when he had to throw his enormous authority behind the kind of foreign-aid program that he thought was long overdue, and, above all, the time when he had to take the lead in revitalizing the Atlantic Alliance, restoring to it a sense of mission and destiny.

The President will also have to defend the United Nations from Soviet attack. Mr. Khrushchev has made it clear that it is open season on the UN and all its parts. He wants it moved to Vienna. He wants a three-man directorate to replace a single individual as Secretary General. He wants the Communist bloc to be given a greater share of the administrative positions in the world organization. Whether he wanted it or not, there would be other nations, many of them non-Communist, who would press for the admission of Red China to the United Nations.

The problems are enormous and seemingly everlasting. Yet we do ourselves a disservice if we allow despair to overcome us. We have our problems. But Mr. Khrushchev has his own. He is not a superman. He puts his pants on just like the rest of us, one leg at a time. The Red Chinese are constantly on his back, demanding more from him, demanding because they need all the help they can get. They have had another crop failure. Mr. Khrushchev has had his own problems with agriculture and they will continue. It will not satisfy the Soviet people to be told by him that he has eaten horse meat and though he thinks it is a bit too fatty, they would find it perfectly adequate. East Germany is being drained of its most qualified people and its Communist leaders are making demands that Mr. Khrushchev might find are too risky to satisfy.

Secretary of State Dean Rusk has said, "Power gravitates to those who are willing to make decisions and live with them." That is the key to the test through which President Kennedy is now leading the American people. In his campaign for the Presidency there was never any attempt to take the easy way out. All the decisions he made were difficult, many were daring. He met the question of his religion head-on and turned it to his advantage. He told a people who for eight years had been told something else that our power was waning, that our prestige was on the decline. It was not easy for a sanguine people to accept, but Mr. Kennedy's boldness won him the Presidency.

After six months of rather close observation of the President and the people around him, I see no reason for despair. We are ably governed. The opposition is responsible. We have freed ourselves from the crippling effect of earlier national demagoguery. The people have given every indication they are willing to be led. Mr. Kennedy has had the time to examine our position in the world and to see where it is he wants to take us. He is the President. He has the information, the power and the authority to tell us what we must do.

Whatever we are about to become as a people will flow from whatever it is that John Fitzgerald Kennedy asks us to do.

—SANDER VANOCUR

SANDER VANOCUR is a White House Correspondent for NBC News. He was one of the first newsmen assigned to cover John Fitzgerald Kennedy when the Massachusetts Senator began campaigning for the Democratic nomination for the Presidency. Following the campaign trail through the primaries to the convention and the election, he was then named White House Correspondent to cover the Kennedy Administration. Born in Cleveland, he was graduated from Northwestern University in 1950 and attended the London School of Economics. After a two-year hitch with the U. S. Army in Austria and Germany, he joined the staff of the *Manchester Guardian*. He returned to the United States in 1955 to join the staff of *The New York Times* and two years later became a member of the NBC News organization. He was first assigned to Washington as a general reporter and then as roving Midwest Correspondent based in Chicago. He returned to Washington for his present assignment following the 1960 elections.

11/8/61

43445

D
844
N29

NATIONAL BROADCASTING COMPANY, INC.
MEMO TO JFK FOR NBC NEWS.

## DATE DUE